America Rides the Liners

America
Rides the Liners

by

ADDIE CLARK HARDING

as told by

Garnett Laidlaw Eskew

ILLUSTRATED BY

CONSTANCE ENSLOW

Coward-McCann, Inc.

New York

MANUFACTURED IN THE UNITED STATES OF AMERICA

VAN REES PRESS • NEW YORK

TO THE MEMORY OF MY MOTHER

Maud McCain Harding

WHO WAS MY FELLOW PASSENGER
ON MANY AN OCEAN VOYAGE

Foreword

AMERICAN books on ships and shipping are always happy events. A modern book on ocean travel is particularly welcome, for it is the phase of shipping that holds the greatest appeal for most people. As a matter of fact, a sea voyage is undoubtedly a cherished goal of thousands of families in the nation.

Miss Harding's book *America Rides the Liners,* which should whet that enthusiasm for sea travel, includes in addition an interesting compendium of American maritime history, traditions, and lore of the sea. It should help focus attention on the desirability of additional passenger liners under the United States flag and help keep up the demand for accommodations on such vessels.

The authors, in producing this book, give further meaning to the current slogan "American Ships Serve You!"

CLARENCE G. MORSE
Chairman, Federal Maritime Board
Maritime Administrator, United
States Department of Commerce

Acknowledgments

IN the writing of this book, the authors have received information and assistance from many quarters. They acknowledge with thanks their indebtedness to:

First of all, Miss Helen McNulta, daughter of a former Port of New York official, who brought to the research, editorial assistance and typing, an untiring enthusiasm and a proven ability.

Mr. Gershom Bradford, of the Duxbury Bradfords. He comes of a family of New England shipmen and himself served as executive officer on the USS *Newport* with Captains Felix Reisenberg and Reginald Fay, and shared with us his memories of the sea.

Mr. John Lockhead, librarian at the Mariner's Museum, Newport News, Virginia, and his staff, for friendly and enthusiastic assistance in the matter of making information sources available for research.

Messrs. Frank Braynard and Brad Mitchell of the Merchant Marine Institute, always eager and willing to look up, dig out and transmit needed information.

Congressman Herbert Bonner of North Carolina, Chairman of the House Merchant Marine Committee, who listened to the reading of five chapters, gave several excellent suggestions and encouraged us with his approval.

Mr. Ralph C. Cropley, assistant curator of the Seamen's Church Institute, New York City, for detailed information on famous ships culled from the fine Cropley Collection in the Smithsonian Institution, Washington, D. C.

Dr. Robert S. Multhaugh, of the Smithsonian Institution,

Acknowledgments

who was of great assistance in our culling of the Cropley papers.

General John M. Franklin, President of the United States Lines Company, America's leading steamship operator, for encouragement and assistance in several ways.

Mr. Steve Manning of the Maritime Administration, and Messrs. G. E. Smith, Washington Cunard representative, Walter Jones of the United States Lines, Fred Sands of the Grace Line, Allison Graham of the American Export Lines, James C. Findlay of Furness-Withey, Ltd.—all for friendly advice and information.

A. C. H.

G. L. E.

Contents

Contents

America Rides the Liners

1922

1. Ships in My Life

I'VE always loved ships. It's a love that's come both through heredity and actual experience. Some far distant ancestor of mine—so the Harding genealogical records maintain, though without actual proof—was a Norse navigator. It may be true, and I hope it is.

I like to picture that ancient viking, old Olaf Hardynge, standing in the prow of his long-oared boat, his eyes straining through the mist to discern some distant landfall. Each time I'm on a ship approaching some port of call, I feel an extra peculiar kinship with Olaf; and I stand at the forward rail, my eyes alight with a Christopher-Columbus glow of discovery, as we glide into port.

Then, when months go by between ocean voyages, I feel my lawless seafaring forbear prodding me with seductive words: "Addie, the sea is calling you again!"

"Aw, shut up Olaf!" I tell him. "Leave me alone!" And I try to turn my mind to other things. But it's no good. Though I live in landlocked Chicago, my mind immediately goes back to the sea; and once again, in fancy, I seem to feel the heave of a liner's deck beneath my feet. The wet wind, as of old, whips my raincoat about me and takes the curl out of my hair. The fragrance of the salt ocean—pungent, alluring, inspiring—stings my nostrils. In my heart I know I'll not be satisfied until I'm once again aboard ship and heading for distant parts.

I made my first trip in 1922 . . . I wonder where the old *Cameronia* is now? She was an Anchor Line ship, built in 1920. The first time I saw her at her pier at the foot of Twenty-Third Street in New York City, her single black funnel topping the pier-shed, I thought she was surely the largest ship that ever floated. When I went aboard and stood in the stern and looked forward, her bow seemed a mile away. She was about half the length of the *United States* and the Cunard *Queens,* and, I recall, was among the first of the ships to demonstrate that "student third class" (along with first and cabin) would be a popular way to go to Europe.

In the years since that first ocean trip, twenty-four different ships have taken me to all quarters of the globe. Each of these voyages was a pleasure trip. Each and every one of the ships has left me memories—happy memories.

What did John Masefield say about the ships he knew and loved?

> "Yet though their splendor may have ceased to be,
> Each played its sovereign part in making me;

4

Ships in My Life

Now I return my thanks with heart and lips
For the great queenliness of all those ships." [1]

Like the poet laureate of England, I am making my acknowl-
edgment and returning my thanks in this book for the beauty
and grandeur of ships. Not only for the ships I know and love
but for all those other ships—the whole mighty American
merchant marine, from the earliest caravel of the first English
colonists down to our latest *grande dame* of the Atlantic, the
sleek *United States,* superlative example of American shipbuilding. The American merchant marine has been made up
of all kinds of ships: sloops; schooners; brigs; barks; packets;
clippers; early side-paddler and combination sail-steam vessels;
coal burners; oil burners; toiling, valiant cargo carriers; slender and majestic liners; light-footed river steamers, graceful
and airy as a summer hotel; officious but indispensable tugboats. . . . One and all, they make up the American fleet, past
and present; one and all they had a part in writing the epic of
America. I love every one of them. And other ships of other
flags, too—as they also had a part in writing the American
story.

Like people to whom you are attracted, ships have a way of
involving your affections. Hours of association with a ship serve
but to deepen that attachment. Spend days aboard an ocean
liner, following with her the blue, mysterious sea lanes. Walk
her decks, drinking in the remembered loveliness of sunrise
and sunset. Stand at a point amidships, look forward and watch,
exhilarated, the slow, inexorable rise and dip of her shapely
prow as she rides the heaving ground-swells. While aboard
ship, you find that even rough weather has its compensations.
It proves to you the sturdiness of your ship's "timber," gives
you an added feeling of confidence in her.

At her sumptuous board you eat gargantuan meals. You

[1] John Masefield, "Ships," in *Poems* (New York, The Macmillan Company, 1953),
p. 200.

listen to her orchestra play on deck in the moonlight; dance in her ballroom; retire at night, weary but happy, to such a sleep as only the sea in its great swaying restfulness can afford you.

While you're aboard, the sky, the sun, moon, and stars become your intimate companions. From the deck they seem close by, more friendly than ever they were on land. Meantime, the sea itself reveals to you hitherto unsuspected facets of beauty and interest. The strange sights and sounds and movements of life aboard ship become, within a couple of days, familiar and close to your heart. You feel yourself, in spirit, a part of the ship's company. . . .

When you leave a ship on which you have thus traveled, you part from her as though from someone you have learned to love and respect. If you are anything like me, you can never again think of that ship as other than a beloved personality.

We hear a great deal these days about overseas air travel. So much so that some of us are likely to lose sight of the continuing volume of travel by sea. Glance at the record. Last year (1955) more than a million American travelers rode steamships to and from foreign lands. That was a larger number than in 1954, the year preceding; the 1954 figure was in turn ahead of that of 1953. All this indicates that this nation still realizes the advantages and unflagging dependability of travel by ocean ship when compared to other forms of overseas travel.

Granted, air travel is faster. Planes get you there in jig-time. For an emergency crossing, when your sole objective is to demonstrate the shortest and quickest distance between two given points, air travel is perfectly swell! Also, it's getting to be safer than it used to be. But when you go by air, you see nothing interesting en route. You completely lose sight of the sea and earth, rise far above the clouds. Only through occasional cloud rifts are you able to catch a glimpse of the earth or sea far below you.

Going abroad by air, your vacation does not actually begin until you've been put down at your destination. Going by sea, on the other hand, your fun starts the moment you cross the gangplank and go aboard. Steamship companies—at any rate all those operating the luxury liners, the "prestige" type ships —go to great lengths to provide an elaborate type of living which leaves the nation's best hotels behind. Hilarious entertainment and amusements of many kinds make your liner trip a continuing holiday, from departure to landing. Many ship travelers desire these added features for the greater enjoyment of their trip. But for those of us who love a ship for the ship's sake, the sea for the sea's sake—we find plenty to occupy our waking hours in the very fact of being aboard.

The great sonneteer David Morton—Kentucky-born but living on the New England Coast these many years—believes in the immortality of ships. One of his haunting poems remains with me.

"There is a memory stays upon old ships,
    A weightless cargo in the musty hold,—
Of bright lagoons and prow-caressing lips,
    Of stormy midnights,—and a tale untold. . . .

"Ah, never think that ships forget a shore,
    Or bitter seas, or winds that made them wise;
There is a dream upon them, evermore;—
    And there be some who say that sunk ships rise
To seek familiar harbours in the night,
    Blowing in mists, their spectral sails like light." [2]

If David is correct about this (and I like to think he is), what a huge fleet of spectral ships must frequent some of the old docks at our ports! New York, Boston, Philadelphia, New Orleans, Norfolk, Charleston, San Francisco—each of our great seaboard cities had its wharfs where, time out of mind, ships have been coming to tie up. They carried in passengers and cargoes of the period of which they were a part and departed

[2] David Morton, *Ships in Harbour* (New York, G. P. Putnam's Sons, 1921), p. 18.

with other passengers, other cargoes. Seaports once great but no longer active—Salem, Newburyport, Mystic, Duxbury, Bath in New England, and Port Royal, South Carolina—would have their ghost ships, too. And the inland cities—Pittsburgh, Cincinnati, Louisville, Memphis—all once great centers of river shipping and shipbuilding.

What does the author of the *Pageant of the Packets* have to say about dead and gone river boats?

> "Yet here on sombre nights I think there floats
> A ghostly company of lovely boats—
> Dark shapes against a dark like amethyst,
> Dim misty hulls, yet whiter than the mist;
> And moving on these channels without sound
> Great wheels ply endlessly around, around,
> And neither waves nor ripples rise and die
> To show the mystery of their passing by?" [3]

American maritime history is older than America itself. Merchant ships planted our earliest colonies—whether for religious or commercial reasons, it matters not. Merchant ships, returning from the mother countries, sustained and fostered the struggling colonies until they were able in a measure to do for themselves. The colonists brought with them the shipbuilding know-how of the land from whence they came.

Since those days of the nation's childhood and youth, shipbuilding has continued, in a greater or lesser volume, to the present.

We who love ships like to hark back in fancy to the days when America led the maritime world. We shall speak of that colorful epoch further along in this book. We lost that leadership, though we are once again near the top of the list of maritime nations.

But there has never been a time, regardless of the size of the

[3] Garnett Laidlaw Eskew, *Pageant of the Packets* (New York, Henry Holt & Co., 1929).

American merchant fleet, when the *quality* of our ships needed to take a back seat for any nation. Today that is more true than ever before.

These fine ships that I have been traveling on during the last thirty years—as, indeed, all modern ocean liners—embody the top expression of a shipbuilder's art. It is a highly specialized art, slowly acquired—an articulated craftsmanship which has been learned, step by step, through the centuries since man first decided he must get to the other side of some body of water and took steps to accomplish his objective.

The sea is a hard but wise old teacher. Mastering her lessons has resulted in better and ever better craft—ships stronger, safer, swifter, more beautiful, and more luxurious than those which have gone before.

As I said a moment ago, for Americans, shipbuilding began when we did. Every generation since has added something that has resulted in finer ships.

To find the first chapter of that story—and it's a lively yarn, seasoned with salt, with adventure, with romance, with history —one must go back a long, long way.

2. Here's the Way It Began

IN CHICAGO, when I was a little girl in the fifth grade, I learned a lot about how our country was colonized. The names of some of the ships, and the dates they brought over the settlers, have remained in my mind ever since.

The Englishmen came to Virginia in 1607.... Three ships come sailing out of the Atlantic mists into Chesapeake Bay— the *Goodspeed*, the *Discovery*, the *Susan Constant*. I could visualize them easily: dumpy little high-riding galleons or caravels; short of keel, with towering quarter-decks and poop decks; colored sails flapping in the early fall winds; stubby little bowsprits sticking out in front like saucy outthrust

10

tongues. See them there, rocking easily over the choppy waves of Hampton Roads to disappear in the mists of the wide James River and come to rest at what we now know as Jamestown Island, thirty miles upstream. . . .

The Pilgrims, 1620. . . . I never needed imagination to picture the *Mayflower*. I'd seen her portrayed by artists, again and again (though they probably had no more definite or exact knowledge of her than I). She couldn't have been far different from the ships that brought the Virginia settlers. So she comes to rest off the stern and rockbound coast, within sight of shore.

The Dutch settlers came in 1625, in the wake of Henry Hudson's *Half-Moon*, to found New Amsterdam. What kind of a ship was the *Half-Moon*? That was easy!

They were singing a song when I was a child about "Baby's boat's the silvery moon." I could shut my eyes and see Hudson's boat—truly a half-moon with sails, something like the crescent shown in the ads for Cascarets I have seen in old magazines—bobbing along through the Narrows and into the Hudson to set ashore her load of Dutchmen, who began at once to bargain with beads for the possession of New York real estate.

Those were the five ships which brought the settlers of the first permanent colonies. One and all they were European craft. Each and every one sailed away again, leaving the colonists to get along the best way they could.

What my school histories did not tell me was that there were other and earlier colonies before those mentioned above. But the earlier ones didn't last. Many of us know of Sir Walter Raleigh's "lost colony" on Roanoke Island, off the Carolina coast, as the story has been dramatically presented in recent years by Paul Green. But did you ever hear of George Popham and his brave but temporary colony established on the harsh shores of Maine? Popham came in the same year that Jamestown was founded—1607, thirteen years before the Pilgrims. He was a nephew of Sir John Popham, who with other British financiers backed a number of colonizing expeditions. George

11

Popham is important to our story. Why? Because he and his settlers built the first American ship of which we have any real knowledge. The first ship built within what is now the United States—the precursor of this nation's present-day merchant marine.

We know a little about this ship. She was named *Virginia* (like the colony to the south) in honor of England's unmarried Queen Elizabeth. The *Virginia* was—to use Popham's words— "a faire pinnace." She had two masts. She was sixty feet in length and her beam measured seventeen feet. We know little more, save that she was a seaworthy craft. She took the survivors of Popham's unsuccessful colony back home to England; that was the purpose for which she was built.

But George Popham himself did not leave with her. He died during the construction of the *Virginia* on the bleak Maine shore.

I like to imagine the building of this first little American ship on that desolate shore. It was right there on the Kennebec estuary that the hardy sailors and craftsmen—for Popham brought along artisans as well as sailors—cut down the tall white pines from the primeval forest, staked out the tiny "ship-yard" only a few feet from the shore. There was the cheerful ring of axes in the chill air, the *swish-swish* of saws cutting through heavy logs! The sweet smell of sawdust and shavings as curved timbers and planking took shape under the action of adz, broadax, and drawknife!

Heavy hammers drove home the long hand-wrought iron spikes and the "trunnels" (tree nails, long oaken pegs said to hold timbers more tightly together even than spikes). Two masts were fashioned from a couple of tall, straight pines.

How did they launch her, one wonders? Did they have horses to help them? They must have brought along plenty of lines and cordage, and sails too! They certainly had no way of making their own sails.

12

Then at last, her towering masts cloudy with sail, she moved out into the estuary and on to sea amidst the cheers of the departing colonists aboard her—going home after an unsuccessful venture, but nevertheless going home!

Sometimes on my way to England, after our ship has passed Nantucket Light and is heading northeastward along the jagged New England coastline toward the turning point beyond the 50th meridian, I have imagined I could see the wraith of the *Virginia,* America's first ship, skimming along with us in the far mist. . . .

Seven years went by. Then Dutch trader Adrian Block put into New Amsterdam to do a little business in furs with the Indians. Right there hard luck hit him squarely between the eyes. His vessel caught fire as she lay in North River and burned to the water's edge. But Block had men and money; the nearby forests had timber. So—down at the foot of what is today Broad Street in the heart of New York's present financial district, the stolid Adrian set to work with his crew to build himself a new ship. She was a tiny vessel. Block spoke of her as a "yacht." He named her the *Onrust.* She was only forty-four feet long and of sixteen tons burthen. Aboard her Block and his men—if they carried any cargo, it must have been a very small one—returned to Holland.

She was America's second ship.

Both these vessels, the *Virginia* and the *Onrust,* native to America though they were, were merely "escape" ships. They provided their owners and crews with the means of getting away from the shores of the New World, although the *Virginia* is said to have returned several times to trade with the American colonies.

Hardly had the early colonies been planted than the need arose for ships. Down in Virginia they required oared barges and ketches and pinnaces to navigate Chesapeake Bay and her tributaries. Such craft enabled the bushy-bearded Captain

13

John Smith and his followers to explore the Virginia rivers—the James, the York, the Rappahannock, the Potomac—and the upper reaches of the bay.

Up in Massachusetts the Pilgrims and the Bay Colony had wisely brought along some ship's carpenters—artisans trained in constructing seaworthy craft. As additional shiploads of colonists came over to swell the New England settlements, more shipbuilders came along too. They began turning out "good and strong shallops," a big lighter or two, and several "catches."

"What we need," said Massachusetts' Governor Winthrop at Boston in 1631, "is a full-rigged ship."

So he sent his carpenters into the woods to bring out locust timbers, the strongest material for stems, keels, and ribs. From these he built a trig little sloop of sixty tons near the mouth of the Mystic River—*The Blessing of the Bay*. In her construction he combined commercial utility with potential defense. He built her with gun ports and other warlike features so that she could, if the need arose, lay aside her peacetime role as merchant ship and fight.

The Blessing of the Bay foreshadowed today's maritime co-operative arrangement. Most privately owned merchant vessels are now built so that, during a national emergency, they can quickly be converted for U.S. defense use. In return for this, the government subsidizes a part of the cost of building the ship.

Before long Winthrop's *Blessing* was busy coasting around between Plymouth and the Bay colonies carrying passengers, cargo, and news. To Boston she brought the intelligence that Plymouth carpenters were busy building fishing smacks and larger vessels for the fishing trade, to augment the income from the meager crops yielded by their thin, stony soil.

As time passed, shipbuilding in New England flourished. Sometime prior to 1641 the Salem settlement sent out its first

14

ship—the forerunner of the future great shipbuilding activity of that town. She was named the *Desire*—a sail ship named *Desire!* Turning her snub nose southward down the coast, she passed the Virginia capes; braved the rough seas off Hatteras; skirted down the Spanish coast of Florida; crossed the Caribbean and put into Havana, Cuba—the first ship from the colonies to the West Indies. Back to Salem she brought cheerful news. The West Indies were ready to trade sugar, molasses, and fruits for what the New England settlers had to offer—lumber, salt cod, vegetables, etc.

This was news of vast importance to the English colonies because war had broken out in the homeland. Great Britain's trade with her colonies was completely blocked. Hence this trade with the West Indies provided both a new market and a source of supply. *Desire* of Salem pioneered the way. More ships were needed—quickly!

"Stern necessity," wrote Governor Winthrop, "sets us on work to provide more shipping of our own." Real full-scale shipyards mushroomed at Salem, at Boston, at Dorchester. In one year Boston alone built and launched three ships; Salem and Dorchester, one each. All went at once into the West Indies trade, stopping at the Chesapeake Bay colonies for cargoes of tobacco.

Towering above the shipbuilding industry of early Salem looms the forceful figure of a stern-faced man in clerical dress— Reverend Hugh Peters, minister and shipbuilder. When not concerned with the spiritual welfare of his flock, Peters spent his time at the dock-side yards. Though he was a graduate of Trinity College, Oxford, and a renowned preacher, Reverend Hugh also possessed a generous share of business acumen. He must have had some capital, too. A friend of Governor Winthrop, Peters took his suggestion when the governor vigorously urged Massachusetts folk to engage in the fishing industry. Soon a big ship of 300 tons, the biggest yet seen at Salem, began to take shape on the ways under Peters' supervision. Launched in 1641, she became the great sea trader of her time.

What became of Reverend Peters? The call of an exacting conscience took him back to his native England to fight with Cromwell. Not long afterward came the Restoration and Peters paid on the scaffold for his pains. But his ideas lived on in Salem.

"Stirred by his example," announced Governor Winthrop shortly thereafter, "Boston has set upon the building of yet another large ship. Besides many Boates, Shallops, Hows, Lighters, Pinnaces, we are in a way of building shippes of 100, 200, 300, 400 tunne. Five of them are already at sea. Many more in hand at present, we being much incouraged herein by reason of the plenty and excellence of our timber for that purpose, and seeing that all the materials will be had here in a short time."

The good Governor briefly summed up the elements necessary to a shipbuilding center: stands of fine timber close at hand; nearness to the coast so that other supplies could easily be brought in and ships launched conveniently; a vigorous, well-muscled class of workmen. New England had already started America on the way to becoming a maritime nation.

America then, of course, consisted only of the colonies strung along the Atlantic seacoast. Aside from a few muddy woodland paths and roads known appropriately as "traces" (because, most likely, there was barely a trace of them left in the off-season), the colonies kept in touch with one another by ship. American ships—homemade, products mainly of New England, New York, and the new ports of Philadelphia and Baltimore— plied regularly between the various colonies, carrying passengers and news. At the turn of the century, shipbuilding had assumed the proportions of a major American industry.

Massachusetts' Royal Governor Bellamont announced with pride in 1698: "I believe I may venture to say that there are more good vessels belonging to the town of Boston than to all Scotland and Ireland."

During this same general period came the first evidence of the mother country's early jealousy of her colonial children—an animosity which would, nearly a century later, blossom into a war for American independence:

"Of all the American plantations [colonies], His Majesty has none so apt for the building of ships as New England," writes an official of the great East India Company, "nor none comparably so qualified for the breeding of seamen not only by reason of the natural industry of the people, but principally because of the cod and mackerel fisheries. And in my opinion there is nothing more dangerous to any mother kingdom than the increase of shipping in her colonies."

The East India gentleman was commenting more truthfully than he knew. The jealousy indicated in his communication materialized into the restrictive regulations which eventually sparked the American Revolution. And in that conflict this same port of Salem was to send out fleets of trim and sturdy ships which would sweep from the seas many a rich argosy of Royal George!

The eighteenth century saw an increase in the shipping industry. Fishing craft predominated, but there were also brigs, sloops, and schooners. The schooner is claimed to be the first real American contribution to shipbuilding. Before 1713, ships had all been square-rigged. A schooner is a ship rigged with fore-and-aft sails which "lie closer to the wind" than square sails. The schooner can thus be navigated more easily, and with a smaller crew. Captain Andrew Robinson of Gloucester, Massachusetts, built the first schooner in 1713. So successful was she that before long some American shipyards were specializing in that one type.

I've read somewhere that the first schooner was a two-master. But I've heard my grandfather tell of five-, six-, and seven-masted schooners plying in and out of the Chesapeake Bay as late as the 1890's. . . .

Up until 1713, America had built 1,300 ships at its various shipyards. The vast majority of these were owned in Boston; but America's reputation for good ships was getting around, for 239 were built for foreign owners!

3. *America's First "Merchant Navy"*

E NGLAND has the largest Navy in the world," George
Washington told the Continental Congress on the eve of
the War for Independence, adding, "we have no Navy. Start
at once to build fighting ships and recruit sailors to man them."

George was right! The British Army held Boston; British
men-of-war cruised off the coast—an effective blockade. The
colonies had not even one naval ship or one enlisted sailor.
But the colonies *did* have by then a merchant fleet of 2,311
privately owned ocean-going ships of various types, many of
them built and owned in New England ports; others at New
York, Philadelphia, then the capital city; still others at Baltimore. In the seaboard towns were thousands of competent sea-

men, ship's carpenters, sailmakers, and ropemakers. To John Adams of Massachusetts, later our second President, went a great task: Create from this raw material a navy to lick the living daylights out of Great Britain's ships.

Before the Declaration of Independence was signed, there occurred the first sea fight—between an American ship and a couple of British war vessels. Probably you never heard of it. School history books overlook it. But the results gave a terrific shot in the arm to the half-fearful yet determined Americans and strengthened them in their effort to resist the great sea prowess of their mother country.

This first American sea fight in the War for Independence was not a long-drawn-out affair. It was unscheduled, unpremeditated. Several British sloops under the command of a gaily uniformed young British midshipman ran into the harbor of Machias, Maine, one day in May, 1775.

"We want lumber. We've come to get it for His Majesty's use!"

So announced the petty officer who came ashore in the ship's boat at the little seaside town, not too far from where Popham had built his first ship. He did not get his lumber.

For a redheaded young Scotch-Irishman happened to be in port with his lumber schooner. This young skipper's name was O'Brien. He was making money out of the lumber industry, and he had grown to hate the British. His crew were husky young fellows who feared no man—and each carried a musket.

Whang! one of the Britisher's swivel guns barked viciously, and a three-pound shot flew over the harbor.

"Surrender, damn you!"

It wasn't the British officer who yelled that demand. It was O'Brien. And as he spoke his men ran up the sails of his lumber schooner. Feverishly they stacked planks against the ship's side —an effective armor. Then they headed under full canvas straight for the British warships. Dodging cannon balls, they came up within musket range. Then O'Brien's men began, carefully and systematically, picking off the British seamen on the enemy sloops. Down went the bossy young midshipman; his bright uniform proved a marvelous target. Down went Royal Marines and British tars. While a British solid shot occasionally hit O'Brien's ship, American muskets in the hands of men trained to hit a partridge on the wing reduced the British crew to a point where it was evidently unhealthy to remain longer in those parts.

Before the anxious townsmen gathered on the wharf, the British craft turned and ran for it! O'Brien's ship came back to the wharf amid the cheers of the populace. America's first sea fight was victoriously over. An American merchant ship had vanquished two British men-of-war.

Meanwhile, John Adams and his Marine Committee struggled in the early stages of creating a navy. General Washington came up to Cambridge, Massachusetts, to take command of the Continental Army. He found the city beleaguered by General Gage's armies. Off the coast, British ships maintained the blockade. In town, supplies of all kinds had run low—guns especially. Gunpowder? It just *wasn't*. More than ever the new commander realized the need for American ships to act quickly.

"It is not in the pages of history to furnish a case like ours," wrote Washington to the Continental Congress. "To maintain a post within musket range of the enemy, for six months, altogether without powder, is probably more than was ever attempted."

Without waiting for results from Adams, Washington took emergency action. First, he wangled from the Governor of Rhode Island a single merchant ship. Slipping past the blockaders, down she went to Bermuda for a load of gunpowder. From other seacoast communities the General demanded and assembled a little fleet of six American merchant ships. These he commissioned under letters of marque and sent them out as privateers to prey on Great Britain's merchant shipping.

Under these letters of marque, the captain and members of the crew of each ship could be assured of a part of the prize money from captured cargoes—except for the vital munitions of war which the Government needed.

The time would come—during our War of the States—when the United States would declare privateering unlawful, equivalent to piracy. But during the early days of our nation's fight for independence, our budding national conscience was far more amenable. Besides, privateering was too good a weapon to ignore. So the colonists used it to the fullest. What these first American privateers accomplished forms a colorful chapter in the American epic: merchant ships pinch-hitting for an American Navy.

Out of those early days the first American merchant navy emerges, in the New England mists, a hard-bitten sea captain by the name of John Manley. Manley was a Marblehead fisherman. He had been bred in the hard school of Grand Banks fishing. He had also served as a boatswain's mate on one of King George's ships, and he had no love for England. He was an able schooner captain and ran a taut ship. To General Washington, he seemed the best officer available to command the first fleet of six little privateers, all schooners, which issued forth to engage the enemy late in 1775.

Manley. . . . We see him now, standing at the bow of his little "flagship," clad in a makeshift commodore's uniform. Legs planted firmly on the heaving deck as the wind whips his bell-bottom trousers around his legs; his long glass at his weather eye, sweeping the horizon.

His ships go pounding down the New England coast, and for days they encounter no enemy craft. Then, off the New Jersey coast, "Sail ho!" shouts the lookout.

"Where away?" Manley's hoarse voice demands.

Off the port bow, he is told; and soon the lookout makes out that the strange sail is a fat British supply ship. Fine! She's loaded to the gunwales with rich stores for the King's Navy.

But His Majesty's ships never get them; John Manley sees to that.

Signals flash back and forth. The schooners—each of them mounts only six little guns—clear for action. We have no other details of that fight. But we know that Manley captured the Britisher—a full-rigged ship named *Nancy,* and bore her, a rich prize, into the nearest American port.

The *Nancy* is important in America's ship history because she was the first enemy vessel ever captured by the new nation. Not only that, she's important because she had on board a piece of heavy brass artillery—the first big cannon America possessed. It helped to defend Boston valiantly.

But Manley had just started. Obstinate sea raider that he was, he'd discovered that his little ships could be a big help to General Washington. So up and down the coast he ranged, from Maine to Florida, preying right royally on British sea commerce.

In the course of a few months he captured thirteen more enemy craft of various sizes, each with valuable supplies; and John Manley, privateer, suddenly found himself a hero. The swift and sure way he had of slipping up with his little ships and destroying or capturing large enemy vessels became a legend among seamen in those parts.

They have their place in our history—this mosquito fleet of sea raiders. They bridged a gap in time—a period in which Washington, with the munitions and guns thus furnished him, could bluff his way through the hard winter of 1775-1776 and save Boston the following spring.

Privateers, indeed, had as great, if not a greater, part in winning the victory as the Navy ships. These letters-of-marque vessels were also vital in another way. After the war was done, they formed the nucleus of our merchant fleet, and a first-rate nucleus too. Built primarily for speed, for a quick strike and getaway, they were big vessels for their day. They spread a lot of sail. In their hull design they foreshadowed the world-famous clipper ships which, more than half a century later, were to place this nation in the forefront of world maritime powers.

We shall see in succeeding chapters how the clippers developed and the influence they had on the commerce of the seas. How they were built, how they sailed and raced under command of shipmasters who were spiritual descendants of the fierce seamen of Elizabethan England, makes an often-told but still inspiring chapter of the story of American shipping.

Privateering continued and became very popular. The wild free life, no less than the certainty of a share in the captured loot, drew many a sturdy lad to fight with Washington's raiders. During the struggle, the old town of Salem alone sent out 178 such vessels. Many of them were newly built, most had been converted from recent merchant service in the West Indies and the Mediterranean trade.

Merchant Ships into Navy Fighters

Washington well knew, however, that privateers could achieve only a limited result. Destroying and capturing commerce was fine; but a fleet of real navy ships was essential— fighting ships that could meet, battle, and conquer the great men-of-war which England would send against her erstwhile colonies. That was the sort of navy that John Adams and his Maritime Committee were then struggling to create. They decided they would call it—when they got it—the "Navy of the United Colonies."

In Philadelphia Congress had authorized the creation of such a navy. The only trouble was, there wasn't any money to implement that authorization.

Adams and his associates, however, walked down to the Philadelphia waterfront. (Philadelphia had become a busy and important seaport.) There they looked over the ships at the docks or at anchor nearby. One especially caught their eyes.

She was the *Black Prince,* a merchantman engaged in the tea trade with the Orient. Adams, says the record, immediately took possession of her. How? Don't ask me! All I know is that he had Congress back of him. He was to get ships to fight for the colonies. He wasted no time in doing so. The *Black Prince* was one of a fleet of seven merchant vessels similarly appropriated.

Now to arm, equip, and man them! From parks and dusty arsenals came forth a few old cannon which had served in the French and Indian War. Wayside forges and smoky foundries cast a few more cannon.

Adams changed the names of his ships. The *Black Prince* became the *Alfred.* In a matter of weeks she was ready for service, having been altered considerably in her superstructure. In fact, she had been largely rebuilt, her sides strengthened with heavy timbers, her deck arrangements altered to make her suitable for fighting rather than carrying cargo. We'll see, a little further along what *Alfred,* with her 32 guns, and her six consorts were like in the new guise of fighting ships. The consorts were: the *Columbus,* with 28 guns; the *Andrea Doria* and *Cabot*—14 and 12 guns respectively; the *Providence,* with 12 guns; and three little ketches—*Hornet, Wasp,* and *Fly*—each with five guns.

Late in 1775 this fleet sailed down Delaware Bay and into the stormy Atlantic to challenge the royal ships of England. It was the forbear of our present vast U.S. Navy.

There was a young naval lieutenant in the fleet named Jones. On board the *Alfred,* he unfurled the first American flag flown aboard a fighting ship. "I hoisted with my own hands the flag of freedom the first time it was displayed on board the *Alfred,*" wrote Lieutenant Jones afterwards. His other names were John Paul.

In those days there were three general classes of fighting ships—the sloop-of-war, the frigate, the ship-of-the-line. All were square-riggers. All had three masts—foremast, mainmast, and mizzenmast. The top deck was called the spar deck; the aftersection was the quarter-deck, where the commissioned officers were housed. The enlisted men had quarters forward. Generally a gangway led from forecastle to quarter-deck. A sloop—sometimes she was called a corvette—usually carried 20 guns; a frigate, 28 to 44 guns; a ship-of-the-line (we'd call her a battlewagon today), from 72 to 120 guns.

The little merchant ships of the first navy were of all three classes, similar to but smaller than their prototypes. They carried few guns, and they had not been built originally for fighting service. But nevertheless they gave an excellent account of themselves and served throughout a large part of the War for Independence.

Our earliest merchant marine thus supplied the first ships of the United States Navy. The merchant-shipping industry likewise furnished the first naval commanders, among them Esek Hopkins of Rhode Island and John Barry of Massachusetts.

SALEM

4. Seeking Far Ports
and New Markets

WE HAVE England to thank for America's early maritime prestige in world markets. Not that England held any good will—heaven knows!—toward her erstwhile colonies. No more than we held for her. Those were not times for good will. The bitterness of our recent struggle for independence had left scars that still remained unhealed. Because of her jealousy —and very well-founded jealousy too!—of America's growing sea might, England passed restrictive legislation regarding its foreign trade.

As a single illustration, there was that act of 1783. Under it, Parliament ruled that all trade with her West Indies colonies must be carried on in English ships owned by Englishmen and manned by English sailors. With one blow this act cut off from American merchants and mariners their richest foreign trade. We have seen how New England sent her ships down to trade with the islands to the south before the middle of the seventeenth century. By the time America became independent that trade had mounted to millions of dollars annually. Not only

27

New England's ships, but those of other ports—New York, Philadelphia, Baltimore, Charleston—likewise found their way south, bringing back the sugar and molasses and dried fruits the islands had to offer.

As we look back at it, it does seem that England was in a sense biting off the nose to spite the face. For much as the new United States suffered from the loss of the British West Indian trade, the islands themselves suffered a great deal more. Here is a tragic example of it.

Because American ships could no longer bring in the needed foodstuffs—doubly needed because of recent hurricanes in those parts—thousands of slaves working the West Indian plantations died. The plantations' owners suffered fearful losses from ruined homes and unworked acres.

Most likely American shippers didn't recognize this restriction of trade as a blessing in disguise. But that is exactly what it turned out to be. Why? Because the sheer necessity of finding new markets for their products and cargoes for their ships led American merchants and shippers to turn their attention to the Orient—the Near East, China, India, and the far East Indies.

All the original American states faced the ocean. Many of them came out of the war with fleets of ships—some, of course, with more than others. These ships were the privateers which throughout the struggle had played havoc with British shipping and, some folks say, did more to bring victory than the American Navy. Now they crowded the docks, big, fast ships—schooners, brigs and barks—too large for mere inter-colony coastwise trade. They lay at their berths, sails furled, hulls rotting and empty, their crews idle. It was estimated that more than $50,000,000 was thus tied up in stalled shipping.

As a corollary to this situation, the once flourishing ship-building industry also suffered: Great Britain now refused to buy new ships from American builders. In the colonial days, as already indicated, British patronage had meant much to

American shipyards. It was cheaper to build a ship in America than anywhere else in the world. A fine, sturdy brig or schooner constructed of white oak and white pine cost only about $24 a ton. Built of live oak, she'd cost $38 a ton. But that oak ship in England or on the Continent would cost $60 a ton. Very naturally then, England, and some other nations too, had been buying American ships. It was good business. The fact that about one-third of all Great Britain's ships were American built and flew the British flag had added fuel to Britain's resentment. If there was one thing that British shipbuilders disliked more than any other, it was to see British ships being built on the Hudson, the Merrimack, the Mystic, rather than on the Mersey, the Clyde, and Tees.

Along about this time the new republic was beginning to have trouble with those pestiferous freebooters of Algiers—the Barbary Pirates. These sinister gentry went about wrecking and capturing our ships, killing or imprisoning our seamen for ransom. Whereupon John Bull, well satisfied to see American shipping retarded, sat back and grinned. The time would come, however, and very soon, when England herself would begin impressing American sailors on American ships. Meanwhile, old Ben Franklin summed up the situation in regard to the pirates and England: "If there were no Algiers," said Ben dryly, "it would pay England to build one."

Meanwhile the export-and-import merchants and shipowners of New England trained their long-range vision overseas to newer, more distant markets. The *Empress of China* of New York led the way. Under Captain Green, she carried a cargo of American products to China; 14 months and 23 days later she put into New York again with a valuable cargo of imports and a fine profit for her owners.

The name of Elias Haskett Derby of Salem now appears in the picture. Merchant prince, importer-exporter, millionaire, he began by sending out his packet *Grand Turk* to India, to the island of Mauritius (a favorite stopping place for seamen in those days), and to China. The *Grand Turk* went for tea. She brought back a splendid load of bohea, hysong, and other varieties, thus proving it could be done. Before long, tea was coming all the way around the Cape of Good Hope in American ships, thus putting a sharp dent in the monopoly of England's great East India Company.

Other merchants observed Derby, followed suit, and once again the demand for ships mounted. All ships in those days carried both freight and passengers. Not for many years—indeed, not until after our War of the States—would there be ships designated exclusively as passenger ships; others, as cargo vessels.

Comparatively speaking, there was little travel overseas in those days. Primarily ships were—as a matter of course—built to carry cargo. Most of them had accommodations for passengers, of greater or less comfort. If you were making a trip abroad, you traveled not only at the mercy of wind and wave, but at the demands of the ship for delivering and picking up cargo. Cargo came first; passengers, second.

Following in the wake of the *Grand Turk* came the *Hercules* and the *Omphale*—carrying American products for Far Eastern markets. Both proved admirable East Indiamen in the tea trade. Before five years had passed the trade had developed along fairly well-defined lines. Not all the ships were large craft. Many were little vessels which bravely ventured out on the long sea trek and bravely came back—sometimes.

Who can forget the epic of the little river sloop appropriately named *Experiment* (Captain Stuart Dean)? She was built up at Albany, New York, and was busy carrying bricks out of Haverstraw on the Hudson's west shore. But when Captain Dean heard of the *Empress of China's* voyage, what must he do but swear to take the *Experiment* over the same perilous route! Apparently he knew the hazards facing him. The *Experiment* was willing to brave the typhoons of the oriental seas no less than the bloody pirate galleys which cruised about seeking whom they might destroy: the ship was a little gamecock. In addition to her cargo she carried six small eight-pounder brass guns to fight off any would-be attacker, and every man and boy aboard carried pistol and cutlass and knew how to use them.

Not only did the *Experiment's* experiment prove successful (she took out a cargo, sold it profitably, returned with another), but Captain Dean brought her gaily back into the dock at Albany, pennants proudly waving, boatswain's whistle piping loudly, and swearing that not one of his crew, man or boy, had been seasick.

I mentioned Elias Haskett Derby a few pages before. They used to call him "King" Derby, and he seems to have well merited the title. His portrait shows him a man of open face, proud, ever supercilious manner, with a long nose, admirably suited for looking down. But he must have known how to treat his customers, for he was considered the wealthiest man in the United States during Salem's heyday as a great center of world shipping.

"I'll give a Spanish gold dollar to any lad who will bring me news of an incoming ship," Derby told the Salem boys, and many of them are said to have done quite a good business in spotting, since Salem was a busy port then and nary a day went by when one or more ships did not poke her long masts up over the horizon.

Then there were the Crowninshields, father, brother, and son. Their long wharfs and fat warehouses occupied a sizable slice of Salem's waterfront. There was generally one or more of the Crowninshield ships tied up in the harbor, loading or unloading. Pepper, tea, coffee, spices—the whole of that colorful port must have been redolent of the many-scented cargoes the ships brought from the spicy Orient.

Inside those warehouses were ivory and gold from the African coasts; silks from China; and the more commonplace commodities—sisal and iron picked up from way ports. Merchants and individuals traveled to these wharf warehouses to buy and to barter with the Crowninshields. As they stood outside the warehouse, the bright sun danced over Salem's blue waterfront. The salt wind bore the lure of distant lands; and right there, not fifty feet away, lay the tall sailing ships which had brought these costly items—the *Fame,* the *America,* the *Fearless,* and others.

Allan Nevins, in his book *Sail On!,* emphasizes that the slave trade was an important element of New England's shipping industry. Elias Haskett Derby, however, Salem's greatest merchant, is said to have been "far enough ahead of his time to see the iniquity of the slave trade" and hence would not permit his ships to carry such human cargoes.

Derby seems to have been ahead of his time in another way too: He realized that if he was to get the most out of his shipping trade with the Orient, he must be well informed on the subject. So he sent his son to London and Paris to study the how-and-why of the Far East trade. The information thus gained gave him an advantage over other contemporary merchant-mariners, and undoubtedly accounted in no small degree for his vast success.

By 1789—shortly after the Constitution was ratified uniting the hitherto very divergent states—there were fifteen American ships in the trade with Canton, China. Four of these ships were Derby's.

Sometimes a big merchantman would pull out from a New York or a New England port with a variegated cargo consisting of goods of several merchants or firms. Such shipments were called "ventures," since the ship's captain was in most cases to sell the goods for the most he could get for them. For example, the manifest of the *Astra,* under Captain James McGee, reads in part (each item being from a different merchant):

32

10 bags of snuff

1 phaeton and harness complete, with saddles, briddles, etc.

20 boxes containing merchandise to the value of $15,000

10 casks of ginseng [root of a tree growing wild in America and much in demand by Chinese sufferers from various ailments]

A box of 21 pieces of silver plate

598 firkins of butter [one wonders how they kept it fresh] and unrecorded quantities of beer, fish, wines, flour [in barrels] and rum.

The profits on such a shipment were big—make no mistake about it. A captain who brought back a return of cent per cent was thought to have done only fairly well. Triple, quadruple on your money was no unusual return.

In those days Whampoa (harbor of Canton, China), greatest port of the Orient, was gay with the ships of all nations. In and out among the ships slipped the richly caparisoned barges and junks of the Chinese merchants, bartering and trading. And the flag of the new American republic flew conspicuously among the others.

As mentioned earlier, our first ship to venture so far afield as the Orient, bent upon trade, was the *Empress of China,* in 1783. That, mark you, was before the Constitution had been adopted and the states of the nation were yet struggling along as best they could, each looking after its own interests and arguing with its neighbors. But even then there must have been a sort of realization of the united interests of the states— an interest for which the Congress, meeting at Philadelphia, was responsible. Witness the "sea letter" sent to Captain Green of the *Empress* at his request and signed by the President and secretary of Congress. It was a sort of authorization for an American ship to trade in foreign lands and is one of the strangest documents I have ever seen, though I am told the excess verbiage was a fair example of many other such official documents of that era. Apparently Congress wanted to make

33

certain there was no misunderstanding as to whom the letter was addressed.

> Most serene, most puissant, puissant, high illustrious noble, honorable, venerable, wise—presidents, kings, republics, princes, dukes, earls, barons, burgomasters, councillors; as also judges, officers, justiciaries and regents of all the good cities and places, whether ecclectical or secular, who shall see these patents or hear them read.
>
> We the United States in Congress assembled, make known that John Green, captain of the shipp called Empress of China is a citizen of the United States of America and that the ship which he commands belongs to citizens of the United States of America, and as we wish to see the said John Green prosper in his lawful affairs, our prayer to all the above mentioned and to each of them separately, where the said John Green shall arrive with his vessel and cargo, that they may please to receive him with goodness and treat him in becoming manner, permitting him upon the usual tolls in passing and repassing, to pass, navigate and frequent the ports, passes and territories to the end that he may transact his business where and in what manner he shall judge proper, whereof we shall be willingly indebted.

Sid Wright

5. Sid Wright and Little
Manhattan Island

THE second war with Great Britain—1812—fell like a
blight on an America just hitting her stride as a young
sea-minded nation. Between the end of the Revolution and
the outbreak of the second conflict, many things had happened
to set the trend of America's growth and progress. At first
there had been a difficult period. The Constitution had not
been adopted. The Continental Congress governed states un-
able as yet to see eye-to-eye on how to co-operate with each
other to make a real nation—a nation that was able, among
other things, to protect American ships on the high seas. Then
at long last the nation accepted the Constitution. A period of
sudden prosperity followed and the United States began, like
a young colt, to stretch itself as it felt its oats.

As yet a mere string of coastal commonwealths—though

Congress was talking of opening the new territory beyond the Alleghenies—America still faced the sea. She felt her destiny lay mainly in maritime activities. Build ships! Export the surplus which the nation had to sell! Import such products as citizens of the new country needed. These are what would engage the attention of the United States above all else.

As we have seen, both in colonial times and later, American ships had won world-wide respect because of their high seaworthiness; American shipmasters and seamen, because of their high ability in their chosen fields of endeavor.

As we read of America's early sea captains, they seem figures out of mythology, legendary in their disdain for the sea dangers which terrorized ordinary mortals. In 1789 there was, for example, Captain Amasa Delano of the bark *Massachusetts,* largest ship of her period. Captain Delano feared neither sea serpent nor gale, water spout, iceberg, nor pirate. And although Nell Pitcher, soothsayer of the town of Lynn, had prophesied his ship would be lost with all on board, the Captain laughed it off and set about recruiting himself a crew. The *Massachusetts* was a tightly rigged ship meant for sea trade, and he'd take her out in spite of the devil.

But when the crew heard of Nell's pronouncement, they one and all deserted, leaving the captain, profane but still determined, glowering down from his forecastle. Soon he had recruited a second crew. It, too, proved cowardly. The third crew, however, stuck to the job. The *Massachusetts* sailed with a cargo of American products to sell or barter in far-off China.

But the *Massachusetts* had within her the seeds of her own dissolution. Nell Pitcher may or may not have known it, but the ship was built of unseasoned green timber. She'd been put together in a hurry. All shipyards, during this period prior to the War of 1812, had more orders for ships than they could fill, so naturally some ships were rushed to completion. By the time the *Massachusetts* reached Canton her decks were rotting.

Captain Delano did not hesitate. There in the harbor of

Canton, he sold his cargo. Then he sold his ship, too, to the Danes for $65,000. Very likely—shrewd Yankee trader that he was—he considered it a good deal. Being a wise traveling salesman was only one of an American shipmaster's jobs in those times. In addition he had to navigate; be an autocrat with his crew; a diplomat in dealing with foreigners whom he met; a naval officer when it came to fighting pirates or, as the year 1812 approached, resisting impressment.

Impressment was a term one heard often in American seaports in those times. We'll have more to say about it further along. . . .

How did Captain Amasa and his crew get home? The record merely says they "came back as best they could with Commodore McClure."

Meanwhile, Congress, realizing the value of foreign trade, was doing its best to promote interest in ships and shipping, in importing and exporting. It gave American shipowners a 10 per cent leeway in the payment of duties on cargoes. The comfortable profits to be had in the business straightway brought more men and capital into the shipping industries. A geographic change in industrial emphasis became apparent during this era. Though Boston, Salem (and nearby Duxbury), and other New England ports continued to build and launch ships, New York City soon forged ahead of all her neighbors as the great shipbuilding center. In time she would likewise supplant Boston as the nation's chief seaport.

A VANISHED ISLAND

Someday when you are in New York, walk down to the shore of the East River near the end of East Broadway. You'll find yourself just opposite Brooklyn Navy Yard. Though there is not the slightest visible evidence of it, you will be standing on land which once was a separate little island of about a dozen square blocks. It went by the ambitious though imitative name of Manhattan Island. This small separated unit of the larger island was the seat and center of New York's early ship-building industry.

In those days, if you had asked a sea captain where his ship was built and he answered, "Manhattan Island," he would not have been referring to Manhattan Island as a whole, but only to this small area on the East River, once separated from the parent island by a sluggish ditch now long since filled in. There, all day long, one heard the clank of hammers driving home iron spikes and wooden trunnels, and the clatter of carpentry. Those frequent loud splashings you heard were the hulls of new ships sliding stern first down the ways to the river, adding new tonnage to America's merchant marine.

On the island were located the shipyards of Noah & Adam Brown; of Smith & Dimon; of Westervelt & Roosevelt. The Cheesemans had their yard there also. So did Thomas Webb, the Beekmans, Franklyn & Atley, and the Rutgers boys. And in any one of them you would often have heard the name, even in the days before 1812, of a certain young aspiring ship architect and foreman by the name of Sidney Wright.

Born in 1790 on fashionable Fulton Street, Sid Wright was the scion of a family of wealthy Quakers. What he apparently loved more than anything else was ships. What he hated was going to school. Thus one finds him, while still in his early teens, hard at work in the shipyard of the Browns, learning at firsthand how a ship was designed and built. Before he had turned twenty-one, he was building ships of his own design. He won a reputation for planning dependable and shapely craft. Not only that—he knew how to translate those designs into actual ships.

Many a New York boy of Sid Wright's time must have looked on him with envious eyes: a boy hardly older than they themselves who, nevertheless, had risen high in America's most romantic and remunerative industry! Bossing large gangs of workmen, superinteding the construction of one great ship after another as it took shape on the Browns's ways. Yes, he was a man to attract attention. There's nothing to indicate that he suffered in the least from lack of lady friends, although he never married.

Sid's family was important in shipping circles. His uncle and a number of other associates were talking, even during these first years of the century, of establishing a new and totally different packet service to Europe. That, however, remained some years in the future. Meanwhile international matters claimed the attention and services of all.

America by 1812 was once again calling her sons to the colors. Reason—that irritating matter of impressment. What did it mean? Simply that Great Britain's ships were sailing the open seas, highhandedly stopping American ships and lifting American crew members to augment their own quotas. One or two instances of it might have gone by without too much attention. But by 1812 it had happened again and again. Congress decided something had to be done about it.

If you had asked a Britisher how-come his Government presumed to do this, he'd have told you with great plausibility: "Well you see, old chap, it's this way. These lads we take from your ships are really His Majesty's subjects. They were born before your country established its independence and whilst yet under His Majesty's rule. His Majesty, you know, has a right to 'em!"

Cockeyed and specious argument! But Great Britain had managed to convince herself of its logic, and so acted upon it. Thus, during James Madison's Administration, the United States found herself once more in arms against the same mother country from whom, in the course of human events, she had separated herself some thirty-seven years earlier.

Yes, the cause of the war of 1812 was a Maritime matter. The war itself turned out to be largely a naval war. One of the greatest of the naval battles of that conflict, as you recall, was that fought by Oliver Hazard Perry on his *Niagara* (flagship) and her consorts on Lake Erie. . . .

I used to wonder about that battle when I was a schoolgirl in Chicago. Our histories told us how, during one month, trees which had contained nesting birds on the lake shore had been made into the ships which made it possible for Perry to fight and win his battle. The history said Perry built the ships. But shipbuilding is a very specialized craft. How could Perry, I wondered (himself a naval officer, not a shipbuilder) and his men (for the most part unlettered seamen) have built those ships in such jig time?

To that I found the answer only when I'd begun to read America's maritime story. Who built most of Perry's ships for him? Nobody in the world but this same Sidney Wright, builder of American packets on little Manhattan Island in the then young and growing city of New York! It came about this way.

The war found the Federal Government short of both ships and money. They applied to Adam and Noah Brown. Not only did the Browns agree to build the ships, they also agreed to lend the Government money—some $250,000—into the bargain. Quickly they sent Sid Wright with a force of workmen out to Erie, Pennsylvania, to build the ships. The men with the shipbuilding know-how rode on horseback across the wintry, untracked wastes of Jersey and Pennsylvania. Sid had a score of workmen with him on his long 500-mile trek. Other builders came along later, after Sid and his men had set up a makeshift yard on the lake shore and were snaking out the logs.

Thus, within a matter of weeks, Perry got the ships which enabled him to win that don't-give-up-the-ship battle which has added luster to the name of the naval officers who fought it. Wright's accomplishment forms an important though forgotten chapter of our maritime story. Believe me, it was no holiday job. Not only did Wright build adequate ships with inadequate tools and with equipment which a lesser man could not have used, but he also overcame an additional obstacle. A wicked sand bar lies just off the harbor at Erie. After launching, he had to get his ships over that bar and into the deep water beyond. Improviser that he was, Wright designed a pair of makeshift pontoons and, one after another, lifted his ships over the bar, into deep water, and on to victory.

Incidentally, one other of Sidney Wright's accomplishments is often forgotten. On Robert Fulton's design, he built the *Demologos* ("Voice of the People"), America's first steam warship. An outlandish affair she was. In a fighting way she had just about everything. She was 165 feet long—a giant for those times—and had a fifty-foot beam. She had an "enclosed paddle wheel" which worked under her hull in a trough to protect her means of propulsion from enemy gunfire. Her armament? She carried forty-four big guns, some of them hundred-pounders. But that wasn't all: she had, linked up with her machinery, a complicated but workable gear which kept 300 big pikes and cutlasses thrusting in and out from her sides and effectively repelled enemy boarders. Somebody called her a "mechanical porcupine," and I think that name must have been very apt.

Demologos was built during the War of 1812, of course. The British claimed that as a defensive measure she could shoot a stream of 110 gallons of boiling water a minute at venturesome enemy seamen. But I haven't been able to verify that.

On her trial runs *Demologos* performed all right. But Admiral David Porter and other Navy bigwigs did not approve of her: steam was a new and untried agent in fighting ships. Then Fulton died. The war with England ended. *Demologos* was renamed *Fulton* in honor of her late designer, and the Navy promptly tied her up in New York Navy Yard and allowed her to collect barnacles.

Sidney Wright died in 1822, at the early age of thirty-two, having built more ships in so short a life span than probably any other single American before or since. He died of smallpox. Somewhere in New York City he lies in an unmarked grave.

The late President Franklin D. Roosevelt evinced great interest in him and his accomplishments. A Liberty cargo ship built during World War II bore the name *Sidney Wright,* and seamen used to call her "F.D.R.'s pet." My friend Captain Ralph Cropley, Curator of the Museum at Seamen's Church Institute, New York City, tells me there is a family connection between the Wrights, the Roosevelts, and the Cropleys.

6. The Black Ball Sets the Pattern

Cleared: Ship James Monroe, Capt. Owens.
Liverpool Packet. Black Ball Line.

SO RAN a notice in the New York *Commercial Advertiser* on a January day in 1818. Its readers' attention may have been arrested by the word *packet*. This was the first time an American newspaper had had occasion to apply it to a transatlantic vessel.

Your dictionary says that a *packet* is a ship or boat plying regularly in a given trade or route, on a regular schedule. And the little advertisement also carried the information that the *James Monroe* was a vessel in the Black Ball Line. That, too, probably caused some excitement—certainly in shipping circles. For the *James Monroe* was doubly a pioneer. She was the first packet in the all-important North Atlantic trade; more

43

than that, she was the first Atlantic *liner*, in a real sense of the word.

American ships in those days were for the most part individually owned and operated by their masters, who sailed them at will. Or, if a wealthy merchant did happen to own several ships, he sailed them as and when he chose. There were no greater individualists in the world than the old sea captains and shipowners. They did as they pleased. There was a saying among them: "What's the use of being shipmaster if you can't tell people to go to hell?"

Many a packet advertising for passengers and cargo for an announced sailing date would delay departure until, in the captain's opinion, he had enough cargo and a large enough passenger list to make his trip worth while—sometimes weeks or months. As for his passengers, who had expected to sail on a certain date, "Let 'em wait!" the captain would growl.

But the *Monroe,* first ship of her kind, belonged to a "line," or fleet, of ships. As a packet she would sail regularly on a given date. This was what appealed most to prospective passengers who read the advertisements. Travel to Europe at once took on a new allure.

Today when you plan a trip overseas, you have any number of steamship lines to choose from. New York City alone is served by ship lines running regularly to Great Britain, to France, to Mediterranean ports, and other Continental destinations. There are our own ships of the United States Lines. American Export Lines, the Farrell Lines. There are Cunard liners, French liners, Scandinavian liners, Holland-American liners, Italian liners, Greek liners, etc. They all depart with the regularity of express trains. And each time you sail aboard any one of them, you pay tribute to the saucy little sailing packet *James Monroe* of America's pioneer Black Ball Line, which started regular service in 1818.

The Black Ball Line actually came into being in 1817, America's earliest bid for supremacy on the seas. Its founders were Isaac Wright (uncle of shipbuilding Sidney Wright), Francis and Jerome Thompson, and Ben Marshall—all substantial New York businessmen. They agreed upon an operating policy and schedule. They swore to adhere to it, regardless.

The War of 1812 had been over only three years. Its termination had brought a spate of shipbuilding—mostly of ships designed for large cargoes rather than speed. There was a reason. Under the taxing laws of those days, a shipowner paid by the vessel rather than by the ton. Hence the larger the ship, the greater her cargo and the proportionately less tax the owner would have to pay.

"What this country needs [it was Isaac Wright speaking] is a line of Liverpool packets. Dependable ships in a dependable service. I don't have to tell you men what an ordeal passengers have to go through getting decent passage to Europe. Captain advertises his ship to sail on a certain date, but nobody with any gumption expects her to sail until he gets his cargo."

"Ours will be passenger ships which also carry cargo, rather than cargo ships which also carry passengers," added one of his colleagues. "We'll subordinate the cargo to the passengers and advertise that fact."

And so it came about. The Black Ball Line started with four ships—*Amity, Courier,* and *Pacific,* in addition to the *Monroe.* Who built them? Why, Sidney Wright, nephew of the line's president! Within the next several years he'd build many more ships for the line.

The average American-built ship of that day and time was round-bellied and dumpy as a New York Dutch *mevrow.* The ratio of her length to her beam was as three or four to one. Mr. Ernest Dodge, director of the Peabody Museum in Salem, says that our ships of the early packet era had what were known as "apple bows." If you stood in front of one of them and looked at her head on, you got the impression indubitably of an apple-cheeked gal, or a maiden with mumps. Her bowsprit jutted out from this bow, tipped with a short boom. She was a brig—two masts; or ship-rigged with three masts (foremast, mainmast, and mizzenmast); square sails; and a fore-and-aft sail on the back-side of the mizzenmast—a spanker, I believe they called it. (Since I don't know a topgallant from a common marlin spike, I won't be more specific.)

Well loaded with cargo and a few passengers, such a ship would waddle down East River into New York Bay and on out to sea; roll and toss her way to her first port of call, arriving when sea and weather permitted—staying as long as her captain felt it worth his while to barter—and on to the next port of call.

Now these early ships of the Black Ball Line differed little architecturally from the type described. They were no more roomy; possibly a little more comfortable to ride in; no speedier. But they did have this merit—and in a short time the public knew it! When the company advertised regular sailing on the first day of each month, it meant it. Wind or gale, the ship sailed on the announced day, whether the captain had his full cargo or not, whether his passenger list was complete or no.

Such regularity was something new and appealing. Passengers could make their plans with certainty. So the Black Ball Line began at once to make money. Express ships—that's what they were! They got you there on time. Or if you had a special consignment for a certain delivery date, you could depend upon the Black Ball Line—all things being equal—to lay the shipment down on that date.

Soon the company needed more ships. Sidney Wright built them—the *Nestor*, 481 tons in 1820; the *James Cropper*, 510 tons; the *William Thompson*, 560 tons; the *Orbit*, 700 tons.

It must have been in the early 1820's that the Black Ball Line—and other shipowners, doubtless—began to think of ships designed for greater speed than the hitherto average apple-bow packet could attain.

The time required for the North Atlantic run began to lessen as more passengers traveled aboard the Black Ballers. How did shipbuilders achieve that objective? Without a doubt, by sharpening the ship's bow so that she would not pile up a great mass of water before her as she moved, by increasing the ratio of length to beam, by adding more canvas.

And here, say many ship authorities, we have the genesis of the clipper-ship idea—the ideal, rather—which a score of years later was to make America in reality mistress of the seas.

In 1823 the Black Ball inaugurated fortnightly sailing—the first and the sixteenth, rather than only on the first. The line had enough ships for that now.

Black Ball's success could not go unchallenged for long. Soon Great Britain established her Red Ball Line, charging 38 guineas for a crossing—which slightly undercut Black Ball's price. The average time on the eastern run for ships of both lines was 23 days; on the western run, 40 days. This time was standard for years; the customary time for average ships had previously been 60 or 90 days.

It was in 1823 that the Black Ball lads decided to set a speed record. The owners placed their new ship *New York* in service. We know little of her characteristics, but she did set a record to Liverpool of 15 days and 16 hours; and this record remained untouched for several years. Then a renowned captain, Jack Williams, did it in 15 days flat on another Black Baller, the *Andrew Jackson.* You'll find both captain and company immortalized in a well-known sea chantey:

> "To larboard and starboard on deck you will sprawl
>   With my hi, ho, blow the man down;
> For kicking Jack Williams commands the Black Ball—
>   Oh give me some time to blow the man down!"

Black Ball continued to operate its ships well into the 1870's —long after steam had supplanted sail as motive power for passenger-carrying lines. The largest of all its ships was the *Aleck Marshall,* 1500 tons, built in 1864.

The Black Ball Line ran from the old Pier 23, East River. It got its name from the insignia its ships bore—a huge black ball painted on the white fore-topsail. To the uninitiated the emblem must have looked at a distance something like the Jolly Roger—save that the ships which bore it were all trim and clean and had their hulls painted decoratively. Hulls were black from the water line up; deckhouses, lifeboats, and bulwarks, green. Later, Black Ball ships had black hulls and black ports painted on a white strake that encircled the entire ship like a belly band. Poop and lower masts, bowsprit and yards—all were white contrasting with black jib booms and upper masts.

The house flag was a long crimson swallowtail pennant with the name BLACK BALL on it. The Stars and Stripes of course flew at the peak of every ship.

There is evidence that the Black Ball Line went after the elite passenger trade in a big way—in fact, the first luxury liner may have been a Black Ball ship. "The staterooms of the Black Ball Line," announced the Liverpool *Courier,* doubtless a trifle enviously, "are fitted with great taste and with a studious regard to the comfort and convenience of passengers. Stateroom doors are inlaid with a square of plate glass. There is an arch over the doorway supported by pillars of white Italian Marble." The article failed to mention the passengers' sleeping quarters or the quality of the meals served.

Another important passenger company appeared in 1827—the Dramatic Line—and, inevitably, speed rivalry between the two lines soon reached fever heat. The earliest transatlantic race was between the Black Baller *Columbus* and the Dramatic Line's *Sheridan,* New York to Liverpool; each side put up $10,000, winner take all.

Who was the winner? The *Columbus,* in sixteen days. The *Sheridan* came in two days behind.

Meanwhile the shipbuilding industry boomed in New York, New England, Philadelphia, Baltimore. An apprenticeship system shortly assured a continuing supply of skilled artisans.

"Our ship and boatyards," wrote Tench Coxe, formerly assistant to Secretary of the Treasury Alexander Hamilton, in

1823, "are not confined to one city but are more diffused than formerly. There is no State in which citizens do not pursue the business, and it has already commenced upon Western Waters."

The term "Western Waters," of course, meant the Mississippi system. Anything beyond the shaggy Allegheny crest was, in those times, "west." Over the desolate mountain trails to that western country, a stream of settlers from the east had been pouring since the end of the Revolution. Following the end of the 1812 conflict, the migration increased enormously. The Northwest Territory had opened and brought new states into the Union. Thomas Jefferson's Louisiana Purchase already had homes and farms and budding towns and cities. Moreover, a workable type of river steamboat of entirely different design from a deep-sea ship had been perfected by Henry Shreve in 1817. Already a small inland merchant marine was plying the Ohio and the Mississippi between New Orleans, St. Louis, Cincinnati, and Louisville. And the Atlantic Coast continued to create better sailing ships.

GRANDDADDY OF THE TUGBOATS

Like many other people I have great fun in watching tugboats at work, panting officiously about a great ocean liner. A tug is so small in comparison to the great vessels she pushes and drags about that, watching her, you feel the saying about the tail wagging the dog take on a new significance. The average New York harbor tugboat is something more than 100 feet long and carries a push like the kick of a Missouri mule. The *Queen Elizabeth* is ten times as long; the *United States* nine times. Other big ships in proportion. Yet the tug pushes and pulls, bullies and shunts her huge charges around with a kind of scornful ease, as though to say; "All right! Now I've given you your start, get along with you!" and then goes waddling off to attend to other business.

49

As you look down from the forward rail of your ship at the tugs below you, you can sometimes see squarely down into the fat smoking funnel, superimposed upon the powerful upright engine. For a tugboat's all muscle—without a pound of superfluous flesh. I once heard someone call a tugboat a "power plant afloat." That's a good description. Unlike a ship, which is a carrier of passengers and/or cargo with a power plant in her innards to make her go, a tugboat is only a power plant, surrounded by nothing—and very little of that.

Tugboats are a strange breed of craft. Unlike every other type of vessel, a tug has a cocky self-satisfied way of sitting back on her haunches, her nose high in the air, her sitter low in the water. She has oversized propellers which kick up a rough little sea as big as a liner's. Graceful ocean ships are often said to resemble swans. If that is so, then the tugboat is a duckling, and a rather ugly one at that. The liners are the greyhounds of the sea; the tugs are the mules of the home waters. They infest New York and other larger harbors by the hundreds.

However, this wasn't always so. Long ago, when sailing vessels predominated in the ocean trade, a captain had to have sailors in a longboat warp his ship out into midstream. There she'd hoist her canvas and go sailing away. In about 1825, when a number of small steam craft were appearing in New York harbor (none had yet ventured on a transatlantic trip) some forgotten captain decided it would be a good idea to hire a little steam vessel to tow him out. It would be quicker than warping, and might be less expensive. The steamboats of New York then were mostly confined to ferry service between the city and the towns of New Jersey and Brooklyn, beyond New York's two rivers.

"My ship—she's the *Freedom*—sails today. Can you take us out?" the master of a big sailing packet would ask a steam ferryboat man.

The ferryman—he may have been one of the early Vanderbilts for all I know, as they ran ferries to Staten Island—would shift his quid from one cheek to another, spit loudly in the drink, and consider. "Maybe I kin," he'd answer. "What time? How much?"

"I want to get away around noon. I'll give you twenty-five dollars."

The other shakes his head.

"Hell! I kin make more'n that taking people across the river at a shillin' a head." (The American shilling was 12½ cents; that would be a quarter for a round trip.) "Noon's my busiest time—folks goin' home to dinner."

"All right. I'll give you thirty-five dollars."

"Done!"

And the wheezy little side-wheel ferry would move in and make fast to the big sailship at her dock on East or North River, and laboriously pull her out into open water.

It was in 1828 that some obscure operator of a harbor steamboat decided he'd build himself a boat specifically to take these big ships in and out. This enterprising boatman soon set before the world the first tugboat. She bore little resemblance to a modern tug. Named the *Rufus King* after a local statesman, she was an outlandish-looking craft. Her stern was square, her bow "round as a full moon." She was built rather like a sloop, though she squatted in the water; had flapping side wheels; burned wood—lots of wood!

She led a hard and busy life, pulling big ships around and rolling up a nice living for her owner. Then, in her old age, an enterprising builder bought her, lengthened her hull, slapped a new engine in her, and ran her to Albany in the Hudson River trade. For years she went cruising up and down the river preceding, by not many years, that graceful and fast-sailing lady of the Hudson, the *Mary Powell*.

The *Rufus King* is important in the story of American ships because her success bred others of her kind. Through a long period of trial and error, during which paddle wheels gave way to propellers and other improvements, the tugboat evolved into the familiar shape we know today. There are no more packets or clippers to be dragged about in our harbors, but there are plenty of liners, car ferries, and barges to keep the tugboats busy.

*   *   *

I've had a lifelong affection for tugboats. The only ship I ever christened was a tug, a Lake Michigan tug at that. I was still a long way under twelve when, in my wide hat, starched white dress, and big hair ribbons, I mounted a platform at the Chicago shipyard where the new "ship" was shored up and smashed a quart of perfectly good Piper Heidsieck over her prow while I repeated the well-conned lines: "I christen thee *Abner C. Harding*!" (That was Granddad.)

Sometimes I'd see her toiling by on the lake convoying a big tow of barges; plowing past the pier head off Hyde Park; threading the channel mazes of Chicago River.

"Look," I'd tell my playmates, "there goes *my* ship!"

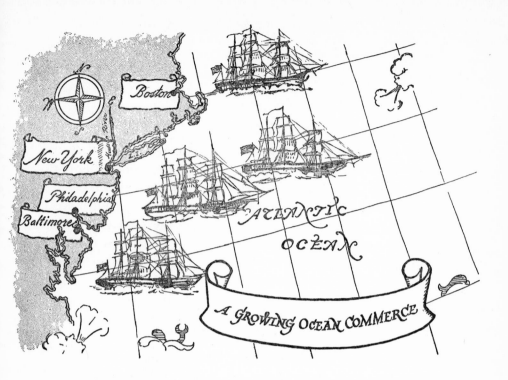

7. More Pioneer Packet Lines

THE Black Ball Line's example proved highly beneficial to early transatlantic service. Seeing the passengers coming in droves to board Black Ball ships, other shipowners decided it might be well to follow that line's example. We find newspapers of New York, New England, and Philadelphia beginning to carry an additional line in many of their daily ship notices, promising regular sailings.

Thus the hitherto proud and defiant shipmasters and owners began to abandon their sail-when-I-damn-please attitude and humbly to go after some of the passenger trade they were losing to the Black Ball.

First comes John Flack with his brand-new *Hannibal*, 500 tons, fresh from a building yard on Corlears Hook (little Manhattan Island). Flack lures Captain Wilkinson away from Black

Ball, puts him in command of *Hannibal,* and slaps her into the Liverpool trade. Well aware that a couple of ships at the very least are needed to establish a line, Flack adds the "fast-sailing *Anna Maria,* Captain Watt," and thus embarks on a very profitable venture.

Fish & Grinnell announce on July 30, 1822, that they, in association with one Thadeus Phelps, have formed the "Fourth Line of Liverpool Packets, to sail on the 8th of each month." They have in their fleet a big sailing packet named—of all things!—the *Robert Fulton.* (They naturally have no way of knowing that Robert Fulton will be one of the men most responsible for ending the sailing ship's supremacy.) Captain Holdredge commands the *Fulton* and does his job well, since he has already added luster to the North Atlantic trade. Fish & Grinnell also have the *Cortes,* Captain Decosta, and soon acquire additional ships.

About the same time the firm of Griswold & Coates, long an operator of ships to Liverpool, falls into line with the announcement that it too will provide regular sailings—and not just to Liverpool, but all the way up to London town! The Griswold & Coates fleet include *Cincinnatus,* Captain Champlain; *Robert Edwards,* Captain Sherburne; *Comet,* Captain Griswold.

A. Gracie & Co., in 1823, sends forth the *Florida* and the *Orbit* in the Liverpool run. Jacob Barber has the *Caledonia.* Hicks, Jenkins & Co., the *Mohawk,* the *Edward,* and the second *Manhattan.* All, mark you, "regular sailers." Ships that left on time.

In the shipping industry records of those days one comes across other names of importance—Franklin, Minturn, Wagstaff, Delano, Crocker, and Sketchly.

And right at this juncture of time and initiative we find the first service to France—forerunner though not direct ancestor of the great Compagnie Generale Transatlantique. Francis DePau, John Skiddy, and G. G. and S. Howland had long been

54

interested in running ships to Le Havre. To DePau, however, goes the distinction of founding the regular sailing line between New York and that port. His ships were *Stephania, Helen Marr, Montano,* and *Henry IV.* They were little ships, none much over three hundred tons, but they formed the beginning of a great and regular ship service which in 1855 became steam propelled.

"Many of these later packets," says Captain Carl Cutler in his incomparable book, *Greyhounds of the Seas,* "would continue in service until they saw the clipper ships in all their glory slipping easily and gracefully through the seas against which *their* bluff little craft would have battered in vain."

Meanwhile news had spread down to Philadelphia that regular lines in New York were doing all right, and Philadelphia followed New York's lead. The Cope Line, founded in 1821, began in a small way. Not until 1833 did this company set any sizable ships afloat. They began with two ships—the *Montezuma* and the *Susquehanna.* The latter was 573-tons, "built on a very sharp model"—so the American Lloyd's rated her as late as 1869. She was so dependable and so fast, according to Cutler, that you might call her a clipper ship and be done with it—a clipper born before her time. She was an instantaneous success. Her name betrays her Maryland origin.

From the outset—her maiden voyage was April 20, 1833—she set some astounding speed records. Over a long period of years —under the command of Captain Dixey—she averaged twenty days from the Capes to Liverpool.

And Boston—fine old Boston, center of our earliest shipping industry—was Boston to be left behind in the matter of dependable ship lines? Boston made an earnest effort. The Appletons and some fifty other leading merchants of the Hub City established the Boston & Liverpool Packet Company in 1821. The company assembled a fleet of gems—*Sapphire, Topaz, Amethyst, Emerald*—and the *Emerald* won considerable distinction.

Yet despite the probity of the owners and the quality of the ships, the adventure didn't pan out. The line dissolved.

Thatcher Magoun of Boston made an attempt in 1827 with eight good ships. After four or five years, however, his line folded too. The reason, so it was said, was its inability to attract large shipments of foodstuffs from the West. New York was a nearer port to that rapidly awakening section beyond the Alleghenies. Boston found it extremely difficult to get a paying freight to England without going all the way to the far south for cargoes of cotton. That, of course, precluded any sizable passenger traffic.

So after Magoun abandoned his line, Boston remained without a regular sailing service until the coming of Cunard and steam in 1840. About that we shall have more to say later on.

RECORDS OF FAST SAILERS

Yes, packet liners set the pattern for modern transatlantic service. The fastest of the pre-clippers made a western crossing in fifteen days, proving that safety and speed—even with a greater emphasis on the latter—could work harmoniously together. But it took a race of seamen which has not been seen before or since to bring it about.

Making fast runs meant working your crew to the uttermost on each trip. Working conditions for a seaman in those days makes one wonder why anyone would sign up. For an almost unbelievable pittance, men would haul the lines and reef the sails in fair or foul weather. Snow, ice, and gale kept no man down from the rigging. Clewing icy canvas high up on the yardarm, a hundred feet above the deck, was only one of a merchant sailor's jobs in the days of sail. He took it stoically— the American Jack did—took it in good part, apparently throve on it.

But the graveyard list—which was to attain fearful proportions when the clippers came—had already begun to mount under the packet skippers. Men falling unnoticed into the ocean. Men blown overboard in one of the Atlantic's familiar gales. Men suddenly disappearing from the crew line-up and never seen again! Arriving home in America, a ship's captain would often have the grim duty of informing some poor wife and family that their main support had been lost while the proud ship with her load of passengers and freight sped homeward in foul weather, with all sails set.

Fast sailing became the order of the day—fast sailing and big cargoes. The year 1838 ended a depression which had retarded nation-wide business for a while. Thereafter shipbuilding once more took an upward swing. The North Atlantic route was firmly established with a ship service that proved (for those days) dependable, comfortable, fast.

Speedy trips of some individual packets have come down to us giving a picture of surprising accomplishments.

Each time I cross to Southampton on the *United States* or one of the Cunard *Queens,* I marvel that the trip is made in as little as five days—or less. But I was even more impressed when I read the records of the sailing ships. To my astonishment, I found many of them outdistanced early steamships. As long ago as the end of the War of 1812, a little sail ship named *Lady Madison* made the run in 18 days, New York to Liverpool. That record remained unbeaten until 1819, when Captain Holcombe's *Triton* covered the same route in a few hours less. The *Triton,* however, never made the round trip in 37 days as the *Lady Madison* had once done. And there was Captain Fox's *Herald,* a little 300-tonner, built at Newburyport, with an unusually sharp prow for those days which cleaved the rollers like a razor. Captain Fox, to quote Captain Cutler, "weighed anchor in Liverpool and drove for Boston, arriving there on the 23rd with a 17-day record, in ample time to dock his ship and ride down to Cohasset in time for his Christmas dinner spread on an old table in the home kitchen."

Fox had the reputation of being a hard taskmaster. He

spared neither ship nor crew when making a record. He even bettered his own time when he brought his ship into Boston Harbor on March 9, 1824, in 17 days flat. He apologized later for not doing better. He had really arrived outside Boston Light in the amazing time of 15 days and 14 hours. There, he explained, he ran into a calm which held him up for a day or more. Now contrast that record of Fox's with the times of two other ships which were fairly representative "speedsters" of that era: it took the *Topaz,* Captain Calendar, 42 days to come over; the *America,* Captain Turner, 47 days, both docking at Boston.

Captain Jim Rogers' *Caledonia* almost equaled Fox's record. She arrived off the Highlands below New York in 15 days and 22 hours from Liverpool. The *Josephine,* Captain Tom Britton, knocked off the run from Belfast to New York in 15 days and 12 hours.

These and other excellent performances of the packets had a most salutary and stimulating effect on American commerce as a whole. Shipbuilding during the 1830's was a barometer of good and bad times, just as records of railway carloadings later indicated our nation's commercial health. During that depression of 1837, many of the finest ships did not even make expenses. The toughness of the time made captains take an additional hitch in their lines and hawsers, thus making a tauter ship, and strive for even faster runs.

After a time, as noted, the depression of 1837 lifted; and under brighter skies the era of the clipper ship dawned.

A vast upsurge of interest in America's midlands (then the "West") had meanwhile engaged all America. Where earlier the original states had felt their destiny lay towards the East, seaward, and had built ships to fulfill that destiny, many coastal interests now felt their attention drawn irresistibly inland. A mighty system of internal improvements, planned initially by Washington himself, began to take shape. Roads, canals, and a combination of the two provided easy access to the inland empire. The first steam engines and cars clanked along rickety rail lines.

Beyond the mountains, independent Western and Southern communities had fostered a thriving commerce of their own. It moved to the East via river steamboats and by transfer at New Orleans to the northern-bound coasting schooners.

The Erie Canal—opened in 1825—gave an added push to the growing Western interest. Manufacturing, farming, transportation—so much was happening in all these fields within the confines of the United States, that more and more attention was being drawn away from trade with the Old World.

America's sea trade was not falling off—far from it; better and better sailing ships were being built on the coast, and the nation's high point of shipping, when America was mistress of the seas, lay just ahead. But nevertheless the American interest in the hinterlands was a trend.

8. The Shipbuilding
Westons of Duxbury

AS AN industry, shipbuilding could make or break a town in those days. If it moved into a town, that town prospered. If it left—all other things being equal—the community fell on evil days. Shipbuilding made Duxbury long ago.

Though today an important suburb of Boston, Duxbury had a humble beginning. Late in the eighteenth century it had no roads of any kind. You approached it by muddy trails. Probably you'd meet some sad-looking, slab-sided, shabby local farmer coming out, astride a rawboned nag, with his weather-beaten wife riding behind him. To live, Duxbury folk caught fish and raised a little garden sass, but meat was a luxury. Then, in 1760, Duxbury's luck took a turn for the better.

Four solid Massachusetts citizens—Ezra Weston, the two Winsor brothers, and Samuel Delano—decided they'd open shipyards in Duxbury. The Winsors, their eyes fixed upon the Grand Banks—those happy fishing grounds!—built large schooners to bring in loads of cod for the Boston market. Sam Delano, an ancestor of Franklin Roosevelt, built ships of various kinds and sizes and seems to have done all right. Ezra Weston—well, Ezra took a more long-range view than the others and began to build ships for world trade.

But Ezra Weston had just got going well when the Revolution interrupted his labors. Off he went to join Washington's Army and fight through the struggle for independence. Then, back in Duxbury, he resumed work and hired a force of local workmen to build ships in a big way.

In the eighty-two years of the Weston shipyard's existence, it passed through four generations of Westons. It built more than 100 vessels: 20 full-rigged ships; 28 brigs; 2 brigantines; 27 schooners; 4 sloops; and numerous other types whose records have long ago vanished.

Ezra Weston not only built ships—he operated them, loaded them, sent them off to every part of the globe. By 1790 he had a sizable fleet plying the domestic and foreign trade lanes. Ezra Weston furnishes a fine and typical example of the prosperous merchant-shipowner-shipbuilder of those days, with something added. He employed trusted captains for his ships—men who were excellent salesmen as well.

There's a letter extant which Ezra wrote in 1793 to Captain Arthur Howland of his favorite sloop, *Jerusha,* which reveals several important facts: first, the confidential relations between an owner and captain; second, the authority and diverse duties resting upon the shoulders of a sea captain of those times; third, the flourishing trade (now that the Revolution was over and the Constitution adopted) between the former colonies. Weston had even sent his son Ezra, Jr., down to North Carolina to act as his local agent. Here's Weston's letter to Captain Howland.

Duxbury, December 11, 1793

Arthur Howland, Sir, you being at present master of the ship Jerusha, now in the harbor of Duxbury, and presently to sail, our orders to you are that you embrace the first fair wind and weather that permits and proceed to the Pascotonck River in North Carolina. On your arrival there you will deliver your letters to Ezra Weston, Junior, your consignee, and join with him in trading your cargo on board, or deliver him your cargo to trade. If an opportunity presents to freight or charter the sloop, or any part of her and you think more to the profit of your owners than to proceed with their property, you will freight or charter to such port or ports as you and your consignee think best. But if you neither freight nor charter the sloop, you will take on board such goods and merchandise as you and your consignee think proper and proceed to such ports as he, (the said Ezra Weston, Junior) and you shall think best. So that he and you have a right to act each and every part of the business in the port of North Carolina on an equal footing and he, the said Ezra Weston junior's orders shall be binding on you and your owners.

If so be that on your arrival at Pascotonck River, Ezra Weston junior is not there, you will sell your cargo and purchase such goods as you shall think best and proceed to such port or ports as you shall think most to the advantage of your owners; or freight or charter the sloop, or any part of her, and act every part of the business the most to your owners profit, so that you are on your return to Duxbury, the port of your discharge, at or before the last of July next, which will be in the year 1794. You will keep a good command on board your vessel. You will let your owners hear from you by every opportunity; and for your commissions on trade in Carolina five per cent on sales and returns, divided between you and the said Ezra Weston, junior, if there, and likewise five per cent in each and every port or ports you shall trade in, for sales and returns.

So God send you a prosperous voyage and a safe return,
We are your friends and owners,

EZRA WESTON

Captain Gershom Bradford, in some of his stimulating writings, quotes Captain Arthur Clarke, maritime historian and once New York agent for Lloyd's of London, to this effect:

"Ezra Weston, *père,* was the most famous of the old-time Boston ship-owners. . . . The Westons were easily the largest ship-owners and not only built but loaded most of their own vessels.

"If all the vessels built and owned by the Westons were to have sailed in column, with only a ship's length between them, they would have formed a line four miles long."

The building of ships was only a fraction of Mr. Weston's diversified activities. He had a big roomy house right there in Duxbury on the shores of a little navigable tidewater creek known as Blue River. About him on every side were supporting industries which enabled him to do a complete assembly job almost in his own back yard. Down from his nearby forest lands came a steady stream of ox teams dragging logs of oak and pine which would soon be sawed and shaped into ship's timber. He partly provisioned his ships with vegetables grown in big truck gardens on the outskirts of town. He also provided fish which had been brought in from the Grand Banks by his own ships, and salted down in the Weston fisheries with salt he'd brought over from Portugal and the West Indies.

A huge ropewalk a thousand feet long occupied a nearby field. There workmen were busy all day long turning out the lines and hawsers (made from Manila hemp brought in by his East Indiamen) and destined to rig new Weston vessels.

He had a spar yard where masts and spars were hand fashioned. The Weston sail loft wove the mighty widths of canvas to drive the Weston ships.

That clanking you hear at the forges down the street? Those are Weston blacksmiths hammering out chains and anchors to supply the continuing Weston demand. Weston vessels picked up and brought the iron from St. Petersburg, Russia.

With his highly diversified industry going full tilt, and all in Duxbury, every man who needed one, got a job. Soon Duxbury became a prosperous community. Duxbury folk began to have meat twice a week if they wanted it—or oftener.

Along Washington Street there arose, one after one, the big solid frame houses for which the town is now celebrated. To quote Captain Bradford again:

"In these houses one found Turkey carpets, mahogany furniture; elaborate French ware graced the dining tables which also displayed the luxury of figs, oranges, raisins and dates, all brought from the seaports of Europe. This was before the China trade was in full swing, yet Duxbury ladies appeared on occasion dressed in Italian satins, French shoes, gloves and laces. In fact, the ship-masters, owners and builders of this little town formed a community of relative affluence to the southward of Boston as Salem was to the northward."

It is pleasant to think of the old shipbuilder seated in the midst of his own little industrial empire, receiving reports from his shipmasters back with argosies from the far seas; writing detailed instructions to other shipmasters about to sail—the brig *Pilgrim* possibly, to which Dana refers in his *Two Years Before the Mast*—or *Hope,* with her three towering poles and wide spreading canvas. Or the schooner *Collector,* fresh in from the Carolinas. Or the bark *Pallas,* newly come from the West Indies.

Captain Bradford, who knows a great deal about old shipping days in New England, told me recently:

"If a modern executive had such a many-sided business under his immediate charge, he'd likely have a big suite of offices—in the Empire State Building, possibly—and a force of a dozen executive assistants, bolstered with every sort of calculating machine, filing system and office aid you can imagine. Ezra kept it all in his head. Most likely he had his office in a room on the ground floor of his home, kept his papers in a tall old-fashioned 'secretary,' and himself wrote his letters by hand."

Following is a partial list of the Weston fleet, thanks to the customhouse records of Plymouth and Boston and to Captain Bradford, who collected and tabulated the information.

Admittance	brigantine	*Herald*	brig
Admittance	ship	*Hope*	ship
Admittance	ship	*Jerusha*	sloop
Angler	schooner	*Joshua Bates*	ship
Angola	brig	*Julian*	ship
Ardent	schooner	*Julius Caesar*	ship
Baltic	brig	*Lagoda*	brig
Branin	ship	*Levant*	brig
Camillus	ship	*Lion*	brig
Ceres	brig	*Magnet*	schooner
Collector	schooner	*Malaga*	brig
Columbia	sloop	*Manteo*	ship
Dispatch	brig	*Margaret*	brig
Dray	schooner	*Maria*	sloop
Eagle	schooner	*Mattakeesett*	ship
Eliza Warwick	ship	*Messenger*	brig
Exchange	schooner	*Minerva*	ship
Express	schooner	*Mirror*	schooner
Ezra and Daniel	brig	*Neptune*	brig
Federal Eagle	brig	*Ocean*	schooner
Fenelon	schooner	*Oneco*	ship
Flora	schooner	*Oriole*	brig
Franklin	ship	*Pallas*	bark
Ganges	brig	*Panope*	schooner
Gershom	brig	*Paulina*	brig
Globe	brig	*Phoenix*	schooner
Golden Grove	brig	*Pioneer*	brig

Pomona	schooner	*Sophia*	schooner
Prissy	schooner	*Trenton*	brig
Ranger	schooner	*Triton*	schooner
Reform	sloop	*Two Friends*	brig
Renown	ship	*Undine*	ship
Rising States	schooner	*Union*	schooner
Rising Sun	brigantine	*Vandalia*	ship
St. Lawrence	ship	*Virginia*	schooner
St. Michael	schooner	*Volant*	schooner
Salunith	schooner	*Volunteer*	brig
Seadrift	schooner	*Vulture*	schooner
Smyrna	brig	*Warren*	brig

The names of many Weston ships have vanished, just as the old ships themselves have gone. Ezra Weston, *père et fils,* along with his neighbors, the Crowninshields, Peabody, and Derby of nearby Salem, no less than the big shipbuilders in New York, may be said to have brought the packet era to its zenith. They flourished throughout the period, became wealthy, their names bywords in every port of the world, just as their ships were fine examples of the pre-clipper era, which was to dawn in the mid-1800's.

Ezra Weston II was a friend of Daniel Webster, who, in common with most other people, had a mightly respect for the Weston shrewdness.

I live on the seacoast of New England [wrote the godlike Daniel], and one of my nearest neighbors, Ezra Weston, is the largest ship-owner probably in the United States. During the past year, he has made what might suffice for two or three large fortunes of moderate size: and how has he made it?

He sends his ships to Alabama, Louisiana, Mississippi, to take freights of cotton. This staple, whatever may be the price abroad, cannot be suffered to rot at home; and therefore it is shipped. My friend tells his captain to provision his ship at Natchez, for instance, where he buys flour and stores in the currency of that region, which is so depreciated he is able to sell his bills on Boston at forty-eight per centum.

Here, at once, it will be seen, he gets his provisions at half-price, because prices do not always rise suddenly, as money depreciates. He delivers his freight in Europe and gets paid for it in good money. The disordered currency to which he belongs does not follow and afflict him abroad. He (the captain) gets his freight in good money, places it in the hands of his owner's banker, who again draws a premium for it. The ship-owner then makes money, when all others are suffering, because he can escape from the influence of the bad laws and bad currency of his own country.

9. *Lovely Ladies Go to Sea*

ON Lake Park Avenue in Chicago there is a public museum, housing among other art objects some sea-battered ship figureheads. The Chicagoan who made the collection and presented it to the city was an uncle of mine, and long before he had moved it from his home on Indiana Avenue, I used to spend enchanted hours studying ship models and figureheads.

One I recall especially represented an Indian warrior shielding his eyes against the sun, his knife held menacingly at his side. He leaned forward in a stealthily threatening manner as though he stalked some unseen prey. To my childish eyes it seemed that sure as fate he'd catch that prey before long—that he was leading the ship forward on the trail. I have never seen movement and determination more vividly limned than in the lines of that old figurehead.

Action! Push Ahead! Get There! Sail On! These and other pithy and stimulating sentiments were what early American designers liked to body forth in figureheads for ships.

Figureheads, of course, were no new thing when America was colonized. Centuries earlier, the superstitious ancient navigators wouldn't think of setting foot aboard a ship that didn't have a figurehead. The Norse seamen—cousins, probably, of my worthy ancestor Olaf Hardynge!—built long ships in the form of dragons.

I've seen fine examples of those ships in a museum in Oslo. Graceful, sweeping lines. Sturdy, strong timbers, preserved with pitch and calked with animal hair. A fearsome dragon's head rearing up in front (the bow). The dragon's fiery tail curled up at the stern over the rudder. . . . The ships of those days must have frightened the living daylights out of people to whose shores they bore armies of invaders. Now add to that frightening paraphernalia two score pairs of oars moving rhythmically as the boat flew over the waves. The whole gave the impression of a gigantic, ferocious sea centipede rushing in to attack some quiet seaside town!

The old vikings knew well the value of first impressions. Frighten your enemy half to death ahead of time and you have just that much less conquering to do when you land to burn the town and carry off the loot, including the good-looking girls.

Before the vikings, however, the Greeks and Romans decorated ships' prows with daintily carved swans' heads; later, with scrollwork and spiral volutes. In mythology, the ship in which Jason sought the Golden Fleece had a figurehead which (he claimed) talked. The legend has it that it pointed and led the way to the realization of his quest. Ships bearing such classic abstract names as *Hope, Victory, Fame* carried at their bows idealized figures of those same virtues. Much later, England's warships and great sailing merchantmen had elaborate designs carved on stern frames, billet heads, and hawse holes. The hawse holes gave the impression of two eyes glaring malevolently ahead.

Look at a modern liner, bow on. You can't escape the impression of something live, with eyes looking straight at you. The ancient Chinese folk painted such eyes on the front of their ships in the belief that they enabled the ship to see where she was going in fog and darkness. . . .

No, America did not originate the ship's figurehead. Nevertheless, here in early American shipbuilding communities the art of carving—and it *was* an art!—reached a higher peak of perfection than anywhere else in the world. With the passing of wooden ships and clipper bows, passed also the figurehead.

A few years ago, Pauline A. Pinckney wrote a full-bodied volume—and most interesting it is—on figureheads.[1] She explains that the old vikings named their ships with great salt and pithiness, and then adorned them with a figurehead embodying what they thought the name indicated. Hence we have such captivating ship names as *Hawk of the Seagull's Track, Lion of the Waves, Mare of the Surf, Reindeer of the Breezes, Dragon of the Seas,* and so on. In "The Building of the Long Serpent," Henry Wadsworth Longfellow, a native of shipbuilding New England in her prime, proved he could spot a good-looking figurehead as well as the next man, and speaks of a viking ship thus:

> ". . . High above it, gilt and splendid,
> Rose the figure-head ferocious
> With its crest of steel. . . ."

In New England and New York, the demand for figureheads kept pace with the flourishing shipping industry. The Skillins of Salem and Boston and William Rush of Philadelphia attained international reputations for creating fine figureheads. Their work attracted much attention in England, especially Rush's, who was a competent sculptor, as well as wood carver, and did several fine busts of William Penn. Rush conducted a school in Philadelphia, and many of his pupils set up shops in other cities.

Imagine yourself in Salem in the 1850's. Walk down a waterfront street towards the old red-brick Derby home. Straight out in front of the home runs the Derby wharf—a long filled-in causeway against which sail ships used to tie up in the heyday of packet and clipper. (It is deserted now except for the seagulls squawking on the pilings and resenting intruders.)

[1] Pauline A. Pinckney, *American Figureheads and Their Carvers* (New York, W. W. Norton & Co., Inc., 1940).

Lovely Ladies Go to Sea

Long ago, along the head of this wharf and lining the shore of the bay, you would find the ship suppliers, the chandlers, the carpenters and occasionally a sign WOOD CARVER UPSTAIRS. (Usually he'd have his "studio" in some abandoned mold loft.) Walk up and the chances are you'd find the artist—though he'd probably be the last to consider himself as such—at work with his wood chisel, mallet, and knives on some hitherto lifeless hunk of wood, now assuming shape and actuality under his craftsman's hands.

Look! He's carving the figure of a woman—a beautiful young girl. For his model a demure Puritan maiden sits there, shapely and attractive. Possibly she's the artist's daughter or the daughter of the owner or the captain of the ship for which the figure is intended. She sits there, blushing in all likelihood, as she sees her own counterfeit coming into being before her eyes.

Turn once more to Mr. Longfellow, In his "Building of the Ships"—certainly not one of his best—we find this:

> "And at the bows an image stood,
>   By a cunning artist carved in wood,
>   With robes of white, that far behind
>   Seemed to be fluttering in the wind.
>   It was not shaped in a classic mould,
>   Not like a Nymph or Goddess of old,
>   Or Naiad rising from the water,
>   But modelled from the Master's daughter!
>   On many a dreary, misty night,
>   'T will be seen by the rays of the signal light . . .
>   Guiding the vessel, in its flight,
>   By a path none other knows aright!"

Thus the poet, in one of his less inspired moments. . . .

Individual ships came to be known for their figureheads. Often, in fact, the figurehead was a wooden representation of the person for whom the ship was named.

71

No one loved a figurehead more than the great shipbuilder Donald McKay of Newburyport, whose clipper ships live in portraits, prints, and publications. No one, unless it was Elias Derby or the Crowninshield boys.

The ship *Creole,* plying between Portsmouth, New Hampshire, and Modena, Spain, bore the likeness of a beautiful brunette in a very décolleté gown.

The large brig *Indian Princess* had the similitude of just such a dusky maiden under her bow. She was a popular and profitable vessel, but the girl looks as though she had a bad case of adenoids. You can see this figurehead, restored and arresting, in the Mariners' Museum at Newport News, Virginia. A few yards away from it stands the figure of a gentleman in a green cravat, white vest showing where the cutaway coat parts. He is Brooks Walker, who had his own likeness on the prow of the ship that bore his name. He was a Mason, and you can see the Blue Lodge emblem in his lapel. Many of the old shipmasters, and doubtless many of the owners too, were salty and lusty lads. They liked their ladies shapely and busty. As Elisabeth Shoemaker says, in a lively pamphlet glorifying old Cape Cod, "Ships' figureheads were lovely ladies who went to sea with grim Clipper Captains and salty sailors. . . ."

That is why you may see, at the Mariners' Museum and elsewhere, figureheads showing ladies with their exquisite bodies liberally exposed. There's an especially eye-catching one at Newport News—a lovely siren, rising as from a cloud, showing a fine pair of breasts, a shapely tummy, and delicious arms. But, as though to compensate for such shocking exposure, the figurehead immediately opposite is of a slender gray-clad, demure little Victorian lady, with small hat, long skirt, high neck. She daintily holds an umbrella.

The clipper *Polar Star,* 1851, had no figurehead per se, but she made up for the lack by bearing an elaborately carved billet head and sternlight with a great star encircled by a wreath.

Witch of the Wave, 1852—what a charming name!—a beauti-

Drawing by Mr Constance Brulow after photograph of Painting

73

ful airy maiden hiding her nudity with a shell, gracefully stepping along on the top of the wave.

The famous Donald McKay-built ship *Seabird* boasted a gilded eagle on the wing, and at her stern a gilded carved trailboard and arch.

The *John Bertram,* clipper extraordinary, had a long, rakish head with an outspread eagle on it.

The *Flying Cloud*—today the most widely remembered clipper ship due to dramatic paintings of her under full sail— had at her prow a full-length figure of a triumphant angel with a trumpet.

The *Bookman of Boston* had a figure of Samuel Appleton (a name well known in publishing circles) to lead the ship forward over the waves.

The *New World* bore, symbolically enough, a full figure of Columbus, painted white.

Another of Donald McKay's ships—named for its owner and builder—had a full-length figure of Donald himself decked out in a bright kilt and tartan!

The *Glory of the Seas,* one of the well-nigh forgotten clippers, carried a goddess in draped Grecian costume.

The *Nightingale,* carried a figure of Jenny Lind, who visited America in the 1850's. The figure has dark hair, and I must admit it is much more beautiful than the original could possibly have been. You can see this figurehead at the Mariners' Museum.

The *Shooting Star*—a heroic figure of liberty, all in white, spangled with gilt stars.

The *Golden Fleece*—a full length figure of a knight, plumed and in white, carved by W. B. Gleason.

Many of our early ships were named for heroes and heroines we revere today, such as Davy Crockett. The *Davy* had a figure of Davy himself in hunting garb, carved by Jacob S. Anderson. There was the *Minnehaha,* with Hiawatha's bride in all her beauty; and the clipper *Sachem,* which, naturally enough, carried a figure of an Indian chief (by Gosling Gleason).

J. W. Mason, of Boston, carved the *Anglo-Saxon's* figurehead for Donald McKay, an Anglo-Saxon warrior in battle guise. John Bellamy carved the American eagle for the *U.S.S. Lancaster.*

Few if any of the figurehead-carvers went overseas to study their art. For the most part, they got what they knew from serving apprenticeships with established carvers. Along Boston's Commercial Street were many carvers well known and well thought of; others were in the South Street neighborhood in New York and along Front Street in Philadelphia.

Famous carvers whose names have been passed on to us through the years, in addition to the Skillins of Boston and Rush of Philadelphia, are: Edbury Hatch; William Deering of Kittery, Maine; Charles Dodge of New York; William Gleason and Charles Sampson. William Deering could turn out pieces of wood carving which gave joy to owners and spectators alike. You can see his figurehead of General Warren, which graced the bow of that ship, in the Peabody Museum at Boston. The captain's daughter posed for the figure which Charles Sampson carved for the ship *Maybel.*

In the early days of America's shipbuilding, figures were painted "to life." Clipper ships by the mid-1850's, however, were carrying figures painted white against a dark background. The artists would touch them with sun-catching bits of gold or bronze.

The full figure was preferred by most shipowners.

"Be sure you carve it in motion," the owner would tell a carver, and the result would be an Indian maiden, maybe, or an angel, or just a local girl with one foot stepping forward, as though she actually walked lightly over the water. Her arm would probably be outstretched. Her garments would flow back behind her as though blown by the wind. In every line of her body would be a suggestion of forwardness and intense movement.

So to the golden age of America's sailing-ship days—packets and clippers—was given an added glow and beauty by these specimens of native art which rested just under the bowsprits of tall vessels and "personalized" each and every one.

I know now why I was fascinated by the figurehead of the stealthy Indian in the Chicago Museum.

10. Ed Collins's Sailing Packets

THREE-QUARTERS of a century ago my grandfather would frequently travel between St. Louis and New Orleans in the high old days of steamboating on the Mississippi River. Deep-sea designer that he was, he never ceased to marvel at these inland river craft. In his old age, long after the Mississippi steamboats had retired from the river, and he from business, he used to tell me about them.

"It's the damndest thing, Addie!" he once said. "Those river boats were as long as ocean ships. Some of 'em, longer. Yet, by God, they could float on a puddle!"

Many years after my grandsire had sailed away on some dim eternal river, I read the record of Mississippi steamboats—how beautiful and efficient they had been; how they came to the rivers; why they were so different from deep-sea ships—and I came to understand what Grandfather meant.

During the time the big sailing packets were plying in and out of our Atlantic ports, before the first clipper ship had spread her proud white wings to the gales, a big fleet of these light-draft steamboats had grown up on the "Western Waters," the Mississippi system. By 1840 there were 200 of them—all built on a peculiar hull model. They had specially designed light machinery. Many of them were 200 feet long or more, and carried huge cargoes of freight on their lower decks, 100 or so passengers in their ornate cabins. Their funnels ("chimneys," your inland boatmen called them) often towered 50 feet high above the hurricane deck. Yet the boats themselves usually drew only about six feet of water. That was what made Grand-dad whistle in amazement.

The river channels of our midland streams have puzzled shipmen ever since our country was settled. The Mississippi channel varies from places where you can't touch bottom with a fifty-foot pole to places where the bottom is virtually on top of the water. (*See* Mark Twain's *Life on the Mississippi*.) The prime requirement of a Mississippi craft was said to be this: "run on right heavy morning dew and turn around on a dime."

Speaking of the Mississippi steamboats of that period—and definitely they are germane to our story of the growth of our merchant marine, as you'll see in a minute—F. Lawrence Babcock, in his lively book *Spanning the Atlantic*,[1] observes: "The American river steamers were the wonder and envy of tourists from Europe." He might have added they were floating palaces to Americans who lived along the rivers!

The reason for their so-different design was this. Craft sailing the seas were *ships;* those on the rivers, despite their size, *boats!* A ship sails *in* the water. A boat sails *on* the water. The Mississippi steamboat was outlandish, speedy, ornate as an over-dressed bride, and highly practical. At her best, she could make twenty miles an hour upstream at a time when practically all ships in the ocean trade depended upon sails (though there were a number of small steam craft in the eastern harbors).

As a type, the river boat's birth was an expedient, a happenstance. Robert Fulton, shortly after his success with the *Clermont* on the Hudson, went out to Pittsburgh to "introduce steamships to the Western Waters." That was in 1811. He

[1] New York, Alfred A. Knopf, Inc., 1931.

called his river "ship" *Orleans* or *New Orleans*. She went downstream from Pittsburgh to Natchez, Mississippi, in a time of high water. But she could not come back: the rivers had sunk to their normal stage. Her draft was too great, her engines too ponderous and heavy; she dragged on the bottom.

Yet within five years after her failure, the inland-river folk had perfected a workable design of their own. She was a boat adapted to meet the demands of those swift, erratic rivers of the American midlands, light draft, almost flat-bottomed. Her machinery (weighing a fractional part of the Fulton-type engines) was carried on deck instead of in her hold.

Her creator was a forgotten genius by the name of Henry Shreve, whose name is borne by a Louisiana city. He began his career as a bargeman on the Mississippi. The steamboat he built was, to tell you the truth, nothing but a steam-propelled barge. But she proved so satisfactory as a carrier of passengers and cargo that within a very few years a sizable fleet of such boats was skimming up and down the rivers between the north and the south, delighting the riverfolk and confounding every deep-water ship builder, who swore up and down that such ships wouldn't run!

With her great side wheels flapping around, her cabin decorated like a wedding cake, her heaven-kissing black chimneys belching smoke, and her chime whistles sounding musically, the steamboat proved herself a useful old gal. She built up the West before the railroads came and while the Atlantic seaboard was still depending largely upon sailing packets—by now evolving into clipper ships. Cincinnati, Pittsburgh, St. Louis, Memphis, New Orleans—all these fine cities of the "West" and South looked to the steamboats for service because there was no other practical means of travel and transport available.

Granddad used to tell me of the big river boats he had ridden in his young days. The *Robert E. Lee,* the *J. M. White,* the fast boats of the Anchor Line, the *City of Louisville,* and so on;

79

but mostly I think Grandfather liked the wonderful meals and the fine whisky served aboard those big river boats.

"Grand boats, Addie!" he'd say reminiscently, "I can taste the fried chicken and coffee yet."

Now, how do these boats come into our story of American ocean shipping? They had a marked bearing on ocean-ship design, though the inland folk probably never knew it; the deep-water shippers, if they were aware of it, have long since forgotten. It came about in the most natural way. But first we'll have to go back a little way.

By about 1836 the earlier type of packets on the Atlantic— the kind with rounded bows, slow, roomy, and comfortable as dowagers—had about given way to newer type ships. These later vessels gave evidence—as one may very well say!—of the shape of things to come.

Oh, there was a reason for it! They had to meet the demand, becoming more insistent with each passing day, for greater speed.

Of course every shipbuilder knew that the sharper a ship's bow and the narrower her hull, the less room she'd have for cargo. Yet plenty of cargo space was a *must* in any ship if she was to make money for her owners, and the great cry for greater speed could not be ignored.

Packets from the yards in New York, New England, and elsewhere in the East began to take on the visible aspects of fast sailing. Rounded-apple bows disappeared entirely. Not only did the new ships have more pointed stems which would cut sharply through the water rather than piling it up in front as the early packets had done, but these bows began to take on a "hollowed out" appearance.

Any captain would tell you that speed was a valuable asset. A shipowner who could deliver a cargo in the East and bring home a load of high-priced perishable commodities in a short time suffered less loss and rolled up a greater profit. The ideal of course—and shipbuilders knew it!—was to strike a nice balance between speed and capacity. Among shippers who endeavored to achieve that ideal was Edward Knight Collins, early shipping magnate of New York City.

Collins's name, though it is largely forgotten now, deserves to be remembered. It was one to conjure with in those days. A year or two after the Black Ball Line's success, Collins established his own line of Liverpool packets.

One knows little of his personal life and habits, but it is easy to surmise that he was stage-struck, or at least had a great liking for the theater. For he named his packet company the Dramatic Line; and to each of his ships he gave a name that had some well-known theatrical connotation. There were the *Shakespeare,* the *Garrick,* the *Siddons,* to name only three. The largest of his packet fleet was the *Roscius,* 1,007 tons, one of the largest American sailing ships then afloat.

In his early venture some of Collins's ships had been running between New York and New Orleans. Because of an obstructing bar in the mouth of the Mississippi, all ships in the New Orleans trade had to load lightly or be of basically lighter draft than other ships. Otherwise they couldn't get up the big river to the Crescent City. One of Collins's captains was Nathaniel Palmer. A seasoned shipmaster of long experience, he was known as Captain Nat. Collins liked and trusted him, and when the owner decided to organize the Dramatic Line, he needed a ship, a new kind of ship (he explained to Captain Nat) which would go like the devil and still carry a lot of cargo.

We can imagine a conversation something like this:

"Captain, have you any ideas on the subject?" Collins inquires.

"I sure have," answered the captain. "Those New Orleans fellows build their river boats flat-bottomed and——"

"But Captain, you know flat-bottomed boats won't do any good on deep water. Flat as pancakes. High seas would toss 'em around like chips."

"But suppose we build a ship with a flat floor but with a hold deep enough to carry a big cargo; give her flush sides and a dead rise of say fifteen or twenty feet?"

"It never has been done," Collins replies doubtfully. "But it might work out at that. That would give us more cargo room in the hold."

"I'll stake my reputation as a shipmaster that they'd work all right."

"Very well, Captain Nat. I'm going to put you in charge of building my ships. Go ahead along the lines you've indicated." So Captain Nat Palmer began designing ships for Collins's Dramatic Line.

Says Carl C. Cutler, writing in *Greyhounds of the Sea:*

> All these ships [of the Dramatic Line, that is] adopted the most noteworthy innovation which had yet been developed in American naval architecture, the long flat floor of the New Orleans packet. Heretofore all vessels which were designed for fast sailing had in greater or less degree the sharp V-bottom of the frigate. In a considerable modification in theory, shipbuilders generally believed that speedy craft could not be built without a substantial dead rise. Even Brown & Bell, who constructed the Dramatic ships under Captain Palmer's supervision, shook their heads while scores of old masters and builders declared "they'd never make a passage to the west'ard." However, both Collins and Palmer had learned a thing or two about the old cotton carriers and they bided their time.
>
> The results proved an unpleasant revelation to the established packet lines. In 1839 the four Collins ships made twelve westward runs from Liverpool to New York in the average time of 28 days. It will be remembered that the average time of the first Black Ballers over the same course had been forty days. Packet sailing had improved considerably in the interval but the new flatbottoms had set a much better average than any line in existence, and in addition had increased measurably their cargo capacity—a most important consideration.[2]

[2] Carl C. Cutler, *Greyhounds of the Sea* (New York, G. P. Putnam's Sons, 1930).

Ships of the Dramatic Line had made some splendid individual records. Captain Nat once brought the *Garrick,* bound from New York to Liverpool (in 1837), to Cape Clear in twelve days. There contrary winds held his ship back, but he still made Liverpool in sixteen days.

Another time the Captain, in command of the *Siddons,* fell in with the frigate *United States,* fastest ship in the U.S. Navy, and raced her in a friendly contest. In a ten-hour run she left the *United States* ten miles behind.

"The *Siddons,* by God, will outsail any vessel in the American Navy!" swore old Commodore Hull, who had once commanded the battleship *Ohio, 74.*

To quote Cutler again, "The ships of the Dramatic Line had a most important influence on future packet design. This, parenthetically, is equivalent to saying that they had a most important influence on Clipper-ship design. From the time of their first successful voyages until the advent of the Clippers and later, no liners were built which did not follow or improve upon their new points of excellence."

Collins's largest packet, the *Roscius,* stands out among the ships of her era. She had a beautiful cabin, finished in expensive woods of contrasting colors. One may presume her passenger accommodations—for those days—to have been "luxurious." Probably no other American ships of the sailing era attained a luxury comparable to hers. More than that, she was fast—so fast and of such beautiful lines that Cutler compares her favorably with the renowned *Flying Cloud* of the clipper days.

The *Roscius* was built to go, and go she did.

Edward Collins, for all his accomplishments with his sailing ships, made his greatest contribution to American shipping later—with his steamships.

Not for nothing is he spoken of today as the American Cunard. We shall meet him again.

The Stag Hound

The Charles W. Morgan

11. *The Clippers in Grandfather's Scrapbook*

IN HIS young manhood my grandfather suffered a dreadful disappointment. He longed for a life on the sea and sought entrance to Annapolis; but he couldn't make the riffle—he was a half-inch too short. So he comforted himself by doing the next best thing. He became a ship designer and a consultant in marine engineering. Moreover, he took ocean trips as often as he could and kept the most marvelous scrapbooks of ships that childish eyes ever devoured.

They were huge things—these scrapbooks—almost as big as a full newspaper page. On the cover of each, Grandfather had pasted the date and a label indicating what was inside. He took a lot of pride in keeping them up to date, and the contents were beautifully mounted.

And was I lucky! I had free access to them as long as I was

careful, opening the books only when they were laid flat on the floor or a big table, and washing my hands before delving into them.

Inside you found all sorts of wonderful things: ship photographs; reproductions of ship paintings; old prints of ships; woodcuts of ships; lithographs of ships; newspaper clippings about ships; ship biographies and sketches of men of the sea—captains, owners, builders.

Along the margins Granddad had written in his bold, businesslike hand his comments on certain of the ships and the captains and owners. For example, concerning some big schooner, you'd find this comment: "Splendid coaster. Not much good in cross-Atlantic service."

On another schooner, the giant *Thomas W. Lawson,* a seven-master, he'd noted: "Too many poles. Too much sail."

Of the great clipper *Sovereign of the Seas:* "Grandest lady of them all! Wish I could have seen her!"

As to this captain: "A first-rate ship-master and a gentleman. Knew him well."

As to that owner: "Fourflusher! Tightwad! I'll never do business with him again."

And so it went.

It is to my memories of that scrapbook, with its sailing ships and steamships, and to the notes I took from it later, that I now turn for much of what I am putting in this volume. How I wish I had the books themselves! Alas, they were destroyed in a warehouse fire on Chicago's south side, years ago. . . .

Best of all, I remember the clipper ships.

"Addie," Granddad used to swear, "there's only two things more beautiful than a fine clipper. One's a beautiful woman; the other's a beautiful steamship. Now you take the *City of Paris,* or the *Etruria*——" And he'd be off on some reminiscences of his favorites in the ocean ferries—queens of the sea when he was a youngster.

85

America Rides the Liners

ENTER THE CLIPPER

Go back in your mind 120-odd years. On a June day in 1833 a news story appeared in the Baltimore *Republican and Commercial Advertiser* about a ship that marks a milestone in America's merchant-marine story. It read:

> The splendid ship *Ann McKim* will be launched from the yards of Messrs. Kennard & Williamson tomorrow afternoon. She is 143 feet in length being the longest merchant ship in the United States and built by Messrs. Kennard & Williamson who are among the most skilled mechanics in our country, and of the very best materials which have been selected with the greatest care and at great expense under the immediate supervision of Capt. Jas. Curtis for the Hon. Isaac McKim, for whose wife the new ship is named.
>
> Her fastenings are altogether copper, no iron being used in her construction. The bills for copper alone amount to upwards of nine thousand dollars. The carving of the figurehead and stern display great taste and are admirably executed. The lower masts are fitted in their places. The standing rigging is attached and the topgallant masts are raised at the top to serve as flag staffs, being painted with much taste and beauty. She presents a grand and imposing appearance.

Allowing for the reporter's evident flowery compliments to a good advertiser (Kennard & Williamson), we have here a fine close-up of an important American ship. Some have called her the first clipper ship. That's an inaccurate appraisal, many believe, since the packet ships being built in the North—New York and New England—had for some years been gradually assuming clipper lines. As we saw, the round-apple bow—chief speed retarder of the earlier packets—had begun to give place to sharper bows, more slender hulls, in the days of the early Black Ball Line.

Then, after Black Ball, the Dramatic Line ship designers had followed the example not only of the flat-bottomed Mississippi-type craft, but of the Chesapeake Bay shipyards as well.

From the beginning, early Virginia and Maryland yards had built ships which, though smaller, had sharp prows and narrow hulls. Such construction of course meant sacrificing a lot of cargo space; but the Baltimore builders seemed to have been willing to do that. At some forgotten time people began to speak of these sharp-pointed, narrow-hulled ladies from the Chesapeake as "Baltimore clippers."

What does the name *clipper* mean? Search me! It has no etymological standing or derivation in our national terminology (though it is accepted and used)—no more than the word *schooner* has. There's a tradition that the term *schooner* came about this way. When old Captain Robinson, in 1713, had launched his first fore-and-aft sailer, some forgotten waterfront boy saw her gliding swiftly over the waves, and shouted, "See how she schoons!"

To *schoon* a flat stone or pebble is to skip it over the water surface—a familiar pastime for lads brought up along river or bay shores.

"Fine!" answered old Captain Robinson. "A schooner she is!" And the name stuck.

Well, the name *clipper* may have come about in somewhat the same way. When your old-time seaman wanted a word, he often made it up on the spot. No one seems to be certain. It may, for all I know, have been adapted and applied simply because such sharper, faster ships were built to clip time from established speed records.

By 1833, when the *Ann McKim* glided on the Chesapeake's smooth surface, the clipper idea had already taken hold. Many big ships in the packet lines had assumed sharper and more slender lines, tending toward the clipper type.

But now came the *McKim,* finest example to date of a fast, sharp ship, and thus known to this day as the "original" Baltimore clipper. . . .

She has her place in this story and definitely! Not only did she establish enviable speed records as a fast sea lady, but she added to the trend toward faster vessels which brought in, a decade later, the real, full-bodied clipper era.

According to Captain Cutler, ship authorities place the beginning of the clipper era around 1840. Between that year and the end of the decade some fast and beautiful clippers sailed out on the Atlantic and set records in the New York–European runs.

In 1849, however, the California gold rush began. That stepped up shipping to a point never known before. The gold rush was the clipper's meat, and during the ten-year madness for California gold, the art of building clippers reached its apogee.

"The *Ann McKim*," said the Baltimore *Sun* of November 7, 1838, "made the run [coming home from the gold fields] from Valparaiso, Chile in 53 days, said to be the quickest time by nine days ever made before." (Cutler, however, believes the *Sun* is in error—that the *McKim's* margin of victory was somewhat less. He admits, however, that her run was a darn good one!)

The rise of the clipper ships brought in the golden age of America's merchant marine. At no time in the past had such magnificent ships come from shipyards anywhere. At no time in the past had such sailing records been established. America was fighting to establish her place as the world's leading maritime nation. England already possessed that title. But America had grown and achieved wealth and fame such as no other nation had, and with her fine clippers was ready to challenge Britain's claim.

Ghost Ships

Wouldn't it be wonderful if David Morton's poetic theory were correct and the ghosts of old ships did come back to haunt ports they once had known?

88

The Clippers in Grandfather's Scrapbook

What a satisfying experience it would be to walk at night along the waterfront at Salem or Boston; loaf pleasantly along South Street, West Street, and the Battery in New York to welcome such nautical visitations. Suppose we could see, coming out of the sea mists and moving majestically up the harbor, the very wraithlike semblance of once-famous American ships! Stand here with me on West Street in New York. Out there the North River rolls by, wide and mist-ridden, broadening into the bay.

The roar of the city and harbor has been muted both by the coming of darkness and the mystery of this moment. Let's see what old ships will return to us.

Ah! See there! Are those not the tall poles of a giant ship coming to port? The mists part, and she moves, ghostly, toward us—still, white, ominous. No sounds issue from her. Silently her sails are being furled as by unseen hands. There are no shouted orders from the captain's bridge.

But hold on there! Something's wrong. She comes in stern first; her bowsprit points downstream. Her sails are blown back against her masts instead of bellying forward in the wind! Good Lord, she's sailing backward! She's the *Dreadnought,* and she holds a big place in the nation's epic of ships on a number of counts. What is her record?

An old sea chantey that lightened the labor of many hard-driven seamen on her decks lives on:

"There's a saucy wild clipper, a packet of fame,
  She belongs to New York and *Dreadnought* is her name,
  She is bound to the westward, where strong winds do blow.
  Bound away is the *Dreadnought*—O Lord, let her go!

"Then a health to the *Dreadnought* and to her brave crew
  To bold Captain Samuels, his officers too.
  Talk about your flash packet, Swallowtail and Black Ball,
  The *Dreadnought's* the flyer than can lick 'em all."

She won fame in the fifties, and the strange thing is that she wasn't, strictly speaking, a clipper. Architecturally she was a bastard sort of ship, but beautiful. She had the towering masts and enormous spread of canvas that the big clippers had, but her hold was spacious for carrying cargo, her passenger accommodations were enormous and, for those days, luxurious.

To the *Dreadnought* (some say) goes the accolade for making the fastest time among all the sailing ships in the North Atlantic ferry—less than fourteen days New York to Liverpool, which beat the time of some early steamships then in service. And speaking of the speed records of early steamships, it was this same *Dreadnought* which once overtook Cunard's new sidewheeler *Canada,* saluted her, and brazenly sailed away, beating her to port!

She was built at Newburyport in 1853 by Currier & Townsend for a group of New York shipping men. There was a dispute about the spelling of her name (she was christened in honor of Nelson's fighting ship); some said it should be *Dreadnaught* and some *Dreadnought.* Only a letter to the British Admiralty, asking for the correct spelling, settled it as *nought.*

Though destined for the California gold-rush trade, her owners, after launching, decided that the Liverpool run— where cargo rates were high and the number of immigrants mounted yearly—offered better business. The *Dreadnought,* therefore, ran under the house flag of a company known as the St. George's Cross Line (largely financed by Americans) and wore a red cross on her topsail.

She had numerous experiences. Her decks knew mutiny once, but her intrepid master, Captain Samuels, a lad still in his twenties, faced up to the troublemakers, bolstered by many of his passengers who swore they'd stand by him; and the mutiny fizzled. Probably no other master would have dared to take a full-rigged ship from Long Island Sound through Hell Gate at night. Samuels (said the old salts) "done it and done it noble!"

As to her ability to get through the water, no other ship had made as many consistently good runs. Liverpool to New York in fifteen and fourteen days was common in the *Dreadnought's* epic. . . .

Her best authenticated run was made in 1859. She left New York at 3:00 P.M. on February 27, and arrived Liverpool—3,018 miles—13 days and 8 hours later.

It may be that she actually did better on a later voyage. Captain Samuels lived until 1908. In his old age he swore: "I made it from Sandy Hook to Queenstown (now Cobh) in 9 days, 17 hours." Such a run, it is admitted, was possible for a fast clipper, even probable; though no one has ever produced logs to clinch such a claim. There are no records to prove Captain Samuels right; none to prove him wrong.

But whether true or not, her other quick trips, for which written evidence exists, hoisted *Dreadnought* high on the scale of famous American ships. She deserved it.

Her most outlandish accomplishment—a freak voyage, due to necessity—has brought her even more fame than her more substantial deeds. Here's what Frank Braynard, marine authority and artist, once said about her:

The *Dreadnought's* feat of sailing backwards for 280 miles took place in 1862. A huge sea put the dauntless Captain Samuels out of action with a fractured leg. The wheel would not work. A jury rudder failed and it was found impossible to turn the ship about. So what happened? Under Samuels' orders her head sails were taken in, and those on her foremast. With her main and mizzen yard braced until every sail was flat aback, she slowly gathered stern way in the direction of the nearest land—280 miles away. A second jury rudder was finally fitted on her bow; the *Dreadnought* finally reached port. It was eleven months, however, before the Captain was able to take command again, so serious was that compound leg fracture.

Old seamen would laugh and say, "Nobody but Samuels could have sailed a ship backwards!"

She wound up her days—the brave old *Dreadnought*—in the California trade, New York to San Francisco around the Horn. On one of those trips, however, she struck a calm in the midst of heavy seas off Tierra del Fuego. Her sails proved completely useless. As a last desperate effort, the crew got off in longboats and tried to warp her clear—a futile effort. They had to abandon her. The aged sea greyhound of the clipper days crashed into shore and flung her fine old bones down wearily on the desolate South American coast in the neighborhood of Cape Horn. . . . Peace to her!

As we stand here on the New York waterfront and see her cloudy wraith disappear again into the mist, we turn to see if another ship is coming from out of the past. . . .

Sail ho! There she is, a clipper of clippers—*Sovereign of the Seas*—her masts unbelievably high, her canvas spread so wide she seems fearfully top-heavy. Her main yardarms have extension sails run out—known as studdingsails or, as seamen call them, "stuns'ls." She has four flying jibs to her bowsprit and even a small spritsail under that. She seems to race toward us—for that was her particular forte, racing. Knifelike prow, with pointed bows deeply convex, she seems to be flinging the seas to each side as she rushes through ghostly waters.

How beautifully she embodies Cutler's description of the ideal clipper: "Clean, long, smooth as a smelt. Sharp arching head. Thin, hollow bowl, convex sides; light, round and graceful stern. . . . Aloft, large-built, iron-banded lower masts; taut tapering smaller masts, long proportioned spars from lower to skyrail yards. Aboveboard, she towers up with strong, fibrous arms spreading a cloud of canvas to the gale."

Donald McKay, one of New England's most noted builders, created *Sovereign of the Seas* in 1850, and Donald's brother, Lauchlin McKay, commanded her. She was built for the San Francisco trade around Cape Horn.

No less a person than the distinguished Pathfinder of the Seas, Matthew Fontaine Maury, credited the *Sovereign* with making the fastest day's run in sail-ship history: 427.6 statute miles between two sunups. McKay himself, however, claims better than that. His official log entered a run of 495 statute miles. Even Maury's lower figure would set the *Sovereign* up as a queen in that sphere. The matter is still in dispute among old shipping men who love to hark back to early speed records.

Cutler, however, comments that no matter how you consider it, this fast trip of the *Sovereign of the Seas* ranks among the world's greatest voyages under sail. She also did 374 miles a day for four consecutive trips, and 330 miles a day for eleven days in succession.

It was these performances of the proud *Sovereign*—was she a queen or a king?—that focused world attention on Donald McKay as the prime shipbuilder in America. It is claimed that fine as he was, his contribution to the clipper's development was no greater than that of some others; that, in fact, "he did not lay down a keel until the clipper design had been perfected after severe testing."

McKay claimed otherwise—that he actually designed his ships along lines that made them beautiful and fast. Well, let's not withhold from the gifted old Scot and his brother (Captain Lauchlin) his just meed of praise and honor—whatever it is. He had a most pleasing personality, so it was said, and fine discrimination. He was well grounded in the fundamentals of his difficult profession, shipbuilding. More too he had undeniably a high sense of the dramatic. If you doubt it, look at old prints and portraits of his *Flying Cloud* and *Seabird*.

The fame of the *Sovereign* did not long go unchallenged. And here, out of the past, comes the challenger—appropriately named *Young America*. For America was then young indeed—not yet a century old on that day in 1853 when *Young America* took to the water at an East River building yard between Fifth and Sixth Streets. Right away she drew attention because she carried no figurehead, though her billethead and trail boards were handsomely carved, the latter "with emblems of the nation." She had an elliptical stern, with slightly more over-hang and counter than most American ships. With her long sharp bow, this gave her, it was said, a racy appearance. And she lived up to that adjective in the speed records which she achieved.

The year 1853 was the peak of clipper-ship building. There were forty eight big clippers and numerous ships of other types running regularly in the California trade around the Horn. *Young America* stood out among them. She was a big ship for her day—293 feet long. She cost her owner $140,000 to build—a large sum, as costs went then. But it was money well invested, for she was a money-maker from the start—not only in her fast freight and passenger returns, but in the sums that sporting men wagered on her speed achievements.

In the year 1853 William H. Webber, chief owner of *Young America,* came out with his challenge, which appeared in the New York *Herald:*

> I wish to state that I am ready to bet the sum of $10,000 on the *Young America,* Capt. D. S. Babcock . . . now loading at the foot of Dover Street, East River, against the ship *Sovereign of the Seas,* the trial to be from New York to San Francisco—both vessels to be loaded and sail together.

Whereupon the owner of the *Sovereign* backed down. "The state of the freight market," he said, prevented him from accepting the challenge—whatever that meant! And so the *Sovereign* disappears.

Once more the mists part. The ghost ship which now bears down upon us has a familiar look. You've seen her likeness many times—in paintings and old lithographs. She's the *Flying Cloud,* and aptly named, too! For those mighty billows of canvas on her sky-raking yards look as though they were in truth part and parcel of the natural elements.

Indeed, so well known is the *Flying Cloud* that we'll not go too deeply into her record. She was fast and she was beautiful—

mainly beautiful. True, in the California run she achieved some records that still live. But many old-time sea-wise gentlemen maintain that she was not the fastest clipper. Her fame, they say, rests to some extent upon the beauty of the paintings that have been made of her. She was so dramatic-looking when under full sail that artists loved to portray her.

Granddad, when I once asked him which was the fastest clipper, threw up his hands.

"Lord, Addie," he replied, "I don't know. Over there in Salem they're still arguing about it. All clippers were fast."

Well, I'm certainly not going to get into an argument on speed records. The clippers as a breed were fast ladies—beautiful, reckless, somewhat cruel in their demands upon the men who worked them. All America owes them a debt.

If we chose, we could stay here all night on New York's waterfront and conjure up the ghosts of more than a hundred clippers which docked on these same river shores. To name a few more, there were the *John Gilpin;* the *Flying Fish;* the *Contest;* the *Wild Pigeon* (a bird as extinct now as the clippers themselves, and as fast and as beautiful, too); the *Flying Dutchman* and the *Trade Winds;* the *Dauntless* and the *Westward Ho;* the *Northern Light; Queen of the Sea; Grey Feather; Meteor; Telegraph; Whirlwind; Golden Fleece; Winged Racer; Defiance;* the *Black Squall;* the *Mermaid;* the *Hornet;* the *Victory. . . .*

But time runs out. Night wears thin. The river mist grows chilly. With the first streak of light in the east, the spell breaks and the ships we have been summoning out of the past disappear silently and more swiftly than on any run they ever made in their own colorful careers.

Let them go! Their stories are recorded again and again in authentic and well-known volumes. A mere lover of ships and sea travelers such as I, born years after the last clipper had departed, may only pay a passing tribute to them, one and all.

When they passed, America's supremacy of the sea also went,

despite the new age of steam which dawned immediately after their departure. Thereafter, our nation yielded place to England. England had, during our preoccupation with fast sailers, been devoting her time and efforts to steam. Soon we shall see what she accomplished.

But first, what had the clippers done for America's foreign trade? A few figures speak volumes. In 1840—roughly the year in which the clipper era began—America's total foreign sea commerce amounted to only 762,898 tons, valued at over $221,000,000.

In the year 1860, when the clouds of fratricidal strife darkened the national horizon and the impending conflict was soon to take the biggest sailing ships for transport and fighting work —the tonnage had risen to over 2,378,000 tons, the value of which was more than $687,000,000.

Not only that. The clippers have left their mark on modern ship design. Clipper builders had brought the long narrow hull to its peak of perfection. To that, no less than to mighty spreads of canvas and hard-driving skippers, they owed their swiftness. The steamships which followed the clippers had hulls designed on clipper models; in modern liners ratio of length to beam is even greater. The clippers set the pace, showed the advantage: when the steamships came, they followed suit and did the clippers one better. . . .

And here it is that I reluctantly close this volume of Grandfather's sailing-ship scrapbooks, and take down from the shelf another labeled simply STEAM.

PHOENIX · June 10th 1809

COL. JOHN STEVENS of HOBOKEN

12. Steam Up on the Atlantic

A VENTURESOME shipowner first decided to navigate
the Atlantic by steam because two other Americans held
a monopoly on the waters of the Hudson River.

The year was 1808. John Stevens of New Jersey was the
venturesome shipowner. The ship was a little side-paddler by
the name of *Phoenix*. The first course she sailed—the stretch
of ocean between New York and Philadelphia. That made her
the first steam vessel in the world's history to navigate the open
sea. . . .

In our oft-reiterated gratitude to Robert Fulton for giving
us a practical steamship, we must not lose sight of other historic facts. First, that Fulton merely utilized and combined into
a successful vessel what some earlier gifted men had long before
invented. Second, that Fulton and his financial backer—shrewd
and rather grasping old Robert Livingston of New York—demanded a fearfully high price for running their boats on the
local rivers.

"Here's our proposition," Livingston had announced. "We'll build our ships and operate them on the Hudson, East River, and the other waters of this state and New Jersey. But we'll do it only if we have a patent to the exclusive right to do so."

It was monopoly with a capital *M;* but Livingston had a way with the state legislature. Robert Fulton was known and respected. They got the patent.

In 1807 New York harbor was dotted with white sails and the dark weathered hulls of sloops, barks, brigs, and schooners —most of them flying the American flag. Now imagine the scene: down the wide river, between rows of such proud ships with their towering masts, comes Fulton's *Clermont,* noisily puffing, as though saying in effect, "I'm the forerunner of a new era in navigation! Get ready to retire, you old canvasbacks!"

Many a year, however, was to pass before steam would present even a slight threat to the fast-sailing American ocean ships. Seasoned seamen were not worried—not in 1807.

For use on rivers and harbors, they admitted, sure! Steamboats were all right! But as for sailing the ocean— Loud, long, and scornful rang the ridicule of shipowners, builders, and seamen. Steamboat? An expensive and dangerous toy for visionaries to play with in shallow water! Someday it might be a useful handmaiden to the big ships. But never anything more!

And yet the very next year after the *Clermont* made her first trip, John Stevens's steamship *Phoenix* actually ventured out into the ocean, steamed a course of 150 miles, and reached her destination safely.

Stevens was a New Jerseyman who had for years been experimenting with steam craft. Two or three of his early ventures had run along rather successfully. He was a brother-in-law, by the way, of Chancellor Robert Livingston. But the two apparently had no love for each other. They were rivals. Can't you imagine their discussion?

"No sir! I don't care if you did marry my sister!" roars the old Chancellor. "I'll give you no right to run your steamboat on our waters! Mr. Fulton and I hold the sole right to do that!"

John Stevens probably told him to go to the devil. Then he set about getting his little *Phoenix* to Philadelphia—away from monopolized waters. As we read of that timid little paddle-wheeler on her first voyage—her fight against big seas, her fear of storms—we are tempted to laugh. But we have to admire her spunk, too. She was only forty-four feet long. Her machinery was complicated and heavy. Down the Narrows she huffed and puffed her way. Up on his own front lawn, above the water, Colonel Stevens watched with his telescope. He had put his son Robert on board as his representative. The *Phoenix*'s master was Captain Moses Rogers, a seasoned old salt of vast experience.

The *Phoenix* got as far as quarantine.

"Let's tie up for a while," says young Robert Stevens, cautious man that he was.

We can imagine old Captain Rogers shrugging and saying, "You're the boss!"

So the *Phoenix* drops anchor. She stays for two days. On June 13, the weather seems all that one could desire—and the sea, calm. Off chugs the *Phoenix* once again. But hardly has she got going strong when the engineer begins to swear. He has reason: the ship's fly-wheel has dropped off!

They warp the *Phoenix* into shore and replace the fly-wheel. Underway once again, Bob Stevens feels the wind freshen. After about three and a half hours of steady steaming, her starboard paddle snaps a blade. The *Phoenix* ducks into Cranberry Inlet and the ship's carpenter repairs it. On Friday, the air is sunny once more, but a high wind has sprung up.

"We'd better wait a few hours," young Stevens insists. Toward midafternoon the *Phoenix* cautiously pokes her snub nose into the big swells once again. For three more hours hand-running she proceeds on down the coast, "giving Neptune his first taste of the many steamers that were to crawl across his bosom."

Next day the sky is cloudy. The *Phoenix* sneaks into Barnegat Bay. There she remains for three days while the wind blows hard.

Later, we find her anchored at Cape May. The next day saw her off shore at Newcastle. Then on Friday, despite some high winds, the *Phoenix* kept right on going and tied up at the foot of Market Street, Philadelphia, on the thirteenth day after leaving New York. . . .

Timorous though she was, and frail as a Victorian spinster, she had shown that steam could push a vessel over and through the ocean's waves—an accomplishment not to be sneezed at in those days.

THE AMBIGUOUS SAVANNAH

In the ten years after the *Phoenix* made her historic voyage, other toiling little steam craft ventured out occasionally into the ocean proper, though not for any great distance. So far as I can learn, they did all right. But not until 1819 did a steamship venture on the long, rough transatlantic run. This dauntless seafarer was named for her home port, *Savannah*. Despite her southern name and ownership, she was built in New York. Her designer was a young man of Morristown, New Jersey, named Stephen Vail. Whether the Georgia firm which financed the *Savannah* intended her originally as a steamship or whether the idea occurred as an afterthought during construction, I can't say.

In any case, she had the lines of a sailing vessel. Full-rigged, small, and compact, she spread plenty of canvas and had a long bowsprit. When at last she was completed, however, she had, inside, an added means of propulsion—a crude steam engine of the Watt & Bolton type which Fulton had used. She had a pair of big side wheels, of course; but unlike those of other steamboats of her day, they were movable. When not in use, you could pull them over on deck and let the crew work the sails.

In Granddad's scrapbook of ships which entranced my childhood fancy, I used to see pictures of the strange early ships that had both smokestacks and sails. There was something anachronistic about them, as though the past and the present met in such a ship.

"Look, Granddad," I'd ask, "why did they have sails on a steamship? Were her engines too weak to make them go by themselves?"

Granddad's eyes would twinkle.

"No, honey. They had to have 'em along in those days so when the engines broke down the sails could take over." I noticed he said *when* and not *if*. I never knew whether my grandsire was joking, but the fact is that the *Savannah's* engines functioned for only three days during her twenty-five-day voyage to Liverpool. Sails carried her the rest of the voyage.

First, her builder took her from her building yard in New York down the Atlantic coast, loaded her up to capacity with coal, cordwood, and a miscellaneous cargo, and then shoved her out to sea.

She could do only six knots an hour under steam; and how those old sailors must have roared with pleasure when they heard it! Any half-decent sailing vessel, they swore, could do twice that speed.

The *Savannah's* captain was the same Moses Rogers who had taken the *Phoenix* down to Philadelphia—America's first ocean-going steamship captain.

Remember that story about Sir Walter Raleigh, introducer of tobacco to England? His valet saw smoke issuing from the noble nostrils, thought his master was on fire, and doused him with a pitcher of water. The *Savannah* came near to having a similar experience.

A Royal Mail cutter lying off Cape Fear, Ireland, saw her

coming up over the horizon. The *Savannah's* poles were bare. Smoke rolled from her stack, enveloping her in a black cloud.

"Egad, she's on fire!" shouted the skipper of the British cutter. "We'll have to go to her assistance! Man the hose, boys!"

Kindly meant, but entirely unnecessary, they soon found out: and the American newcomer pushed on into Liverpool. She did not tarry there long. Her owners had a fixed purpose in mind. The Czar of Russia, they knew, was a steam enthusiast. They'd sell the *Savannah* to him at a whopping good profit! So it was Ho, for St. Petersburg!

But although Nicholas expressed his great interest and sent the captain a gold snuff box, he proved no purchaser. He may have offered a price, but if so, it did not meet the owners' requirements. And so the *Savannah* toiled back—alternating steam and sail—to her home port in the American South. Her owners removed her engines; she became an out-and-out sailing ship, and in 1822 she was wrecked off the coast of Long Island.

So much for America's initial adventure in transatlantic steamshipping. You could not call it a success; it wasn't an outright failure. Sir Thomas Graham, of Glasgow, who had boarded the *Savannah* at Stockholm and ridden over to Russia with Captain Rogers, presented the captain with a gold teakettle inscribed:

> "Presented to Captain Moses Rogers of the
> Steam Ship *Savannah* (being the first steam-
> ship that had crossed the Atlantic), by
> Sir Thomas Graham, Lord Linedock, a passenger
> from Stockholm to St. Petersburg, Sept. 15, 1819."

Despite that recognition and admission from a Britisher, English seamen as a whole rather discount the *Savannah's* accomplishment. These Englishmen point out that she was not really the first vessel that crossed the Atlantic by steam. She was merely a sail vessel with steam equipment which had crossed the Atlantic, using her sails more than she used her steam machinery.

In 1827, a small forgotten Dutch ship, the *Curacao,* with steam equipment, made several trips between Antwerp and the Dutch islands off South America. Now neither we Americans nor our British cousins apparently like to admit *Curacao's* accomplishment because she did not ply between England and the United States! But I have always thought that the little Dutch steam girl has been wrongfully ignored in our histories. Even the Cunard Line now admits: "Despite their isolated place in history, these several trips between Antwerp and South America gave Holland the distinction of having initiated practical steam navigation."

The *Caracao* was only 433 tons register. She had three schooner-rigged masts and paddle wheels driven by independent engines like our own Mississippi steamboats.

But, the English will tell you, "You see, old chap, after all she was *built* in England."

This is a fact. She came from a shipyard at Bristol and was originally called the *Colpé.* Then Holland bought and used her as a warship in the Netherlands Navy. All the passages she made were under steam, carrying passengers, mails, and costly freight. Let's give the little *Curacao* a real big hand!

Canadians claim the first vessel to cross the Atlantic by steam power was a product of the yards of Quebec—the *Royal William,* built in 1830. In the Canadian House of Parliament there's a tablet recording just that. I have found no satisfying evidence of it, however.

At first, the *Royal William* ran between Quebec and Halifax. And several times during the year 1831 a young Canadian came down to the docks in Halifax and examined *Royal William:* studied every beam and spar; every cylinder-head, boiler, shaft, piston, and gear; walked her decks from bow to stern; devoured with his eyes the lineaments of *Royal William.*

A grave-faced young man he was, resident of Halifax, who

attracted the attention—so oblivious was he to his surroundings—of fashionable folk, of travelers, crew members, and sailors.

"Who's that young chap?" one visitor asked curiously. "I've seen him around here for two days in succession now."

"That?" their escort most likely replied carelessly. "Oh, a young fellow named Cunard—Sam Cunard."

The name meant nothing in those days in the shipping circles where the man was seen most often. But later on it was to mean a great deal indeed. And further along in this book, we shall meet Mr. Cunard again.

13. More Steam

THE name *Cunard* has always signified to me things typi-
cally British. Three times I've crossed on the *Queen
Elizabeth;* twice on the *Queen Mary;* once, on the *Parthia.*
I've made one cruise on *Caronia;* one on the *Britannic.* All are
Cunarders.

On these trips I've had a chance to observe close up the sea-
going spirit of old England which pervades each ship. It's there
—very definitely there—from the aloof master down to the low-
liest deck steward of the Cunard fleet. Sometimes it rather palls
upon one—as though the ship's company were trying to make
certain that passengers do not for a moment lose sight of the
fact that the steamship company providing America with its
most extensive passager service is owned by an English company, officered and manned by a British crew in a most un-
mitigated English manner.

More than once, in the face of such overwhelming British-
ness, I've been tempted—thoroughgoing American that I am—
to laugh and say, "It's all right, boys. At ease! I know you are
all Englishmen and exploiters of the great sea tradition. So
take it easy; you're doing all right!"

But when I came to read the story of the Cunard Line, I
found out some interesting facts about the founder, Samuel

Cunard. His family wasn't English at all. They lived near Germantown, Pennsylvania. His ancestor was a sturdy German immigrant who came over and took up land which William Penn was selling cheap. The family name wasn't even *Cunard*. It was *Kunders*. Sam's grandfather changed it to *Cunard,* and some of his brothers chose *Conrad* instead. Sam Cunard got his first shipping-business experience in Boston.

The Cunards, though Americans, had strong Tory leanings, as did many another American family in pre-Revolutionary times—in New York, in Pennsylvania, in Virginia, in North Carolina, and elsewhere. With the onset of the Revolutionary War, they left Pennsylvania and went to Halifax, Nova Scotia, then a young seaport city of vast activity and commercial importance. There Sam was born and got such education as he could. One finds him, in his teens, holding down a draftsman's post in the civil branch of the Canadian Engineering Establishment. Between times he'd hang around the busy docks, watching the ships, talking to shipping folk, and doing a little private merchandising—peddling probably—on the side, to make extra money.

He was still in his teens—he'd been born in 1787—when he took part with other Halifax folks in celebrating Nelson's great victory at Trafalgar. Then off he went to Boston to work for a while in a ship broker's office—a job which fostered his interest in navigation matters. He was back in Halifax, however, when the War of 1812 broke. By that time Sam Cunard had large ideas of being an export merchant.

He and his father established the firm of Abraham Cunard & Son and secured the agency for several sailing ships. Even with the war going on, Sam wangled from the Lieutenant Governor of Nova Scotia a permit to trade with any port in the United States—a fact which shows that although America and her sometime mother country beyond the Atlantic were belligerents, there were really no hard feelings between the United States and Canada. In short, that both Canada and the

United States had a bond of common interest which not even such a war could break.

Sam was twenty-seven when he got a contract to carry his Majesty's mail between Halifax, Newfoundland, and Bermuda. There is nothing to show that he did not give entire satisfaction. The Cunards, *père et fils,* bought the little sailing ship, the *White Oak,* as their mail boat. That brought Sam into even closer touch with shipping folk and gave him further opportunity to trade.

There was plenty of freight to be carried, too, and apparently some passengers; for we find Sam advertising: "There are good accommodations to be had on the ship *White Oak* sailing for London, with the first convoy." (The war, you see, was still going on).

Sam was making money. There was no question about that; and as a young man of means, he began to take part in the social life of Halifax—joined up with the local "fire laddies" and the county militia, and married a fine woman.

His portrait at middle age shows him a steady-eyed man with a good jaw and firm lips; straight nose, a pensive and thoughtful countenance as though he were a dreamer as well as a man of business. He wore his side whiskers well down on his cheeks. From his portrait, you would say that he resembled a cross between a bishop of the established church and a successful New York banker who had not yet acquired his "faire round belly with good capon lined." At forty he was worth a couple of hundred thousand dollars (Canadian) in a day when wealth was reckoned in thousands rather than in millions. And, although continuing to merchandise, Sam's interest in ships and the sea (awakened by his owning the *White Oak*) mounted. He began to dream ambitious dreams of what he would do later.

Through his exertions, ships of the Honorable East India Company began to dock at Halifax, bringing tea direct from the Orient. Next, Sam assumed the agency for a large coal-mining company which in later years would supply coal for Cunard steamers. More and more he became interested in steam: those first crude railroad lines built in the United States; the *Savannah* which had only recently crossed the Atlantic.

In the last chapter, we glimpsed him haunting the Halifax docks to examine the *Royal William,* pioneer steamer to Canada. Soon afterwards he came to the conclusion that "steamers properly built and manned might start and arrive at their destination with the punctuality of railroad trains on land."

Patently, he wasn't going into such an enterprise hastily. That we know, for he writes to some Nova Scotia promoters that he'll have no part in a scheme to build ships for transoceanic service. However, he didn't forget the matter—not Sam Cunard!

The British homeland was most anxious for a steamship connection with America. Hard times in England and the 1837 financial crisis emphasized the need for such a new avenue for trade and emigration travel. But Americans apparently were not interested in steamships. Fast sailing-ships satisfied America's needs. Year by year the quality of American sail packets and clippers improved. Moreover, Americans were so busy building railroads to join the East Coast with the rapidly growing Midlands and West that they didn't have much time to give to ocean steamshipping.

England, on the other hand, was going in strong for steamships. She has established the Peninsular & Oriental line, running through the Mediterranean to her eastern possessions. (That line still operates.) During the same period America, clinging to her sailing ships, was building railroads to her western states.

One observant historian commented, "While England built the P & O, American built the B & O!"

However, one New Yorker, Junius Smith, tried in 1838 to organize a steamship line to run to England. America was just not interested. So Junius turned to England, having heard that the British Government and businessmen favored steam service to America.

Finally Junius Smith succeeded in organizing the British & American Steam Navigation Company. Curling & Young of Limehouse, London, built their first ship, the *British Queen*. But construction problems delayed her completion so that two other British-built steamships, the *Sirius* and the *Great Western,* had already made voyages to America before the engines of the *British Queen* first turned over.

The *Great Western*'s reception in New York seems to have been more vociferous than the *Sirius*'s, although the latter arrived a few hours earlier. I can't see why, unless it was because the *Sirius* was only a 700-ton ship, much smaller than the *Great Western*.

Anyway, the *Great Western* threshed her way up to the Battery, under the command of Captain L. Hoskins, R.N., to the tune of a twenty-one-gun salute from the harbor defenses.

"She's a benefactress of all that relates to the communication of intelligence, to the spread of liberty, to the certainty and convenience of traveling!" proclaimed a local orator.

The *Great Western* must have been a pretty efficient little ship, at that. She arrived in New York with a five-day supply of coal left in her bunkers after a fifteen-day voyage.

Sam Cunard watched with interest, meanwhile continuing to carry Her Majesty's mail from Falmouth on his own schooners. He also had some interest in coastal steam vessels, and may even have had some financial interest in the *Royal William*.

This association and the comparison of time and dependability of steam vessels as against sailing ships awakened in him the determination to create a steamship line to England.

He tried American businessmen first. But his efforts to find financial assistance in Halifax and Boston proved futile.

"Steamships?" a Boston merchant would shake his head after Sam had made his proposal. "Just look out there"—pointing to the docks where serried lines of clippers and sailing packets were tied up, loading and unloading. "What do we need steamships for?"

14. The First Atlantic Ferry Boat

I T WAS a gala occasion in Boston. The staid old town
had put on her party attire that July day in 1840 to welcome a friendly visitor from the British Isles. She was a little
paddle-wheel steamer, *Britannia*.

Citizens by the thousands, marching eight abreast, swung
down to the waterfront. At their head rode the mayors of the
principal New England cities, the foreign consuls, the business
moguls—predominantly those in the export-import-shipping
business. They had gathered, as one reporter announced, "to
show their fellow-countrymen and the world that they knew
how to appreciate the magnitude and importance of the under-
taking so successfully commenced by that gentleman, who, it is
well known, is one of the most enterprising and public spirited
merchants of today."

They toasted him—these New England folk. They wined
him. They dined him. He received 180 invitations to dinner.
Boston people subscribed money for a silver loving cup as big
as a bathtub. Never had the staid old town seen such hilarity
and enthusiasm.

Who was he, this man whom Boston delighted to honor? Why, Sam Cunard, the young sometime merchant from Halifax whose interest in shipping had led him to found the steamship line which bears his name today—though on that day in Boston, long ago, the line consisted of only one ship, *Britannia*. Later we shall discuss the struggles through which young Cunard passed to inaugurate this North Atlantic ferry.

Right now, let's listen in to what the Boston people are saying as they welcome the first liner over the Atlantic. At a big party tendered him, Boston's elite gathered in Faneuil Hall, the same hall in which American patriots sixty-seven years earlier had planned the Boston Tea Party. Josiah Quincy proposed a toast:

"To the memory of Time and Space—famous in their day and generation—they have been annihilated by the steam engine."

"England and America!" shouted Mayor Chapman of Boston forensically. "May neither forget that they stand in the interesting relationship of mother to daughter!"

The Reverend Ezra Gannett, Rector of the Federal Street Meeting House, opined that the new steamship service was an illustration of the power and wisdom of the Creator.

"I confess that no event which has occurred since the beginning of the present century," continued Gannett, "seems to me to have involved more important consequences to this city. With its lines of communication terminating on the one hand on the shores of Europe and on the other mingling with the waters of the Mississippi,[1] it is impossible that it should not draw to itself a large amount of capital and industry of the most productive kind. . . .

"It will strengthen the bonds of kindness and just consideration between the Eastern and Western continents . . . and we

[1] The Erie Canal, completed in 1825, furnished through water connection from our East Coast via the Great Lakes to the American Midlands.

believe it is fraught with issues of spiritual moment to the whole world."

Boston crowded down to the wharf where the *Britannia* lay tied close to the pier—her long jib boom poked up as though it still pointed to America (America, her ultimate goal, now achieved); her engines quiescent, though live enough to keep a slender spiral of smoke above her tall stovepipe funnel. Her great paddle wheels in their ornamental paddle boxes were weary and still after her long battle with the Atlantic's rollers. Her canvas was furled. Her three masts—one forward of her wheels, the other abaft her smokestack—towered stark and bare above her deck. She lay still, resting after her fourteen-day "dash" from Liverpool.

Look at her well, this little wooden *Britannia!* As she lies at her berth, she is flanked by clippers and packets far larger and more powerful-looking than she, but all are slated for oblivion within the next few years. The *Britannia* is vital to any story of America's merchant marine, for she is the originator, the progenitor of regular service between Europe and the United States.

American-flag ships today make up only a fractional part of the whole passenger fleet serving our ports. The rest of the total number are owned in other nations.

Where once American shipping, in the days of sail, led the world, we are today—in point of fleet size—about fifth from the top in the list of nations operating passenger ships in and out of American ports.

Before we go further, let's see what we mean by the term *passenger ships.*

The earlier American ships, as you recall, carried cargo and passengers, emphasizing the former. Later, when the Black Ball Line came into being (1818), the emphasis changed so that passengers, their welfare and comfort, came first. Vast cargoes, however, still continued to move in the same ship with passengers.

Somewhere along the line between the start of steamship operation and the rise of the luxury liner, shipbuilders began to turn out vessels designed primarily and almost exclusively for passengers. Today, the largest of the ocean ferries are passenger ships. They carry little freight—and that of a specialized "express" sort.

In addition to these—the mighty passenger liners, the super-liners, the luxury ships—there are other very excellent ships known as "combination vessels." They are designed to carry both cargo and passengers, the importance of each being about equal. They have fine accommodations for a limited number of passengers, ranging from about 26 up to several hundred. Service on the combination ships is impeccable—comfortable, even luxurious. The Maritime Administration classes them as passenger vessels, and in speaking of them I shall do the same.

But there is yet another class of ships—and America has as large and fine a fleet of these as any nation on the face of the earth—which likewise carry some passengers. These are the cargo ships, the freighters of many types and kinds. Some of them are stodgy, commonplace, lacking in beauty. Others are built along lines which would do honor to the finest sail clipper that ever floated. Many such ships carry twelve passengers each. Their accommodations are comfortable, neat, well ventilated. The food, while not as elaborate as on passenger liners, is nevertheless ample, wholesome, and delicious. As a passenger on these freighters, you mess with the officers. Being primarily cargo carriers, the freighters do not come within the scope of this book. They are not classed as passenger ships, as their passengers are merely "something added"—a means by which the owners take in some revenue over and above the returns for freight carrying.

I've taken one of these freighter trips, and I want to tell you

I had the time of my life. (Fortunately my fellow passengers were friendly and congenial.) However, since the Maritime Administration does not place such cargo ships in the passenger class, I shall follow suit. When I speak of passenger ships, I refer merely to the luxury liners—the all-passenger ships—and to the combination carriers which take 26 passengers or more.

Now, with that explanation, let's turn to the unfolding story of American shipping. Time has wrought great changes since the passing of the sail ship.

Boston, Salem, Newburyport, Duxbury, New Bedford—these were all once ports of vast shipping activities, as we have seen. Their docks are now empty, their shipping days past. With the passing of sail, Boston for a while retained her prestige when Sam Cunard brought his first liner there as the first port of call in the United States. Later, however, the Cunarders transferred their terminals down to New York City when that mighty port became the seat and center of East Coast shipping activity.

We saw how Sam Cunard tried without success to interest Boston merchants in his plans to establish a regular line of ships between England and America. That was late in the 1830's.

Now if that Boston merchant—or a New York merchant or a Philadelphia or Baltimore merchant, for that matter—had added, in his talk with Cunard, that America's sailing ships were larger, faster, sturdier than any of the steam vessels that braved the ocean, he would have spoken no more than the truth. No one doubted it. The fact was accepted because everyone knew that England had ceased to be a large factor in the building of sailing ships, whereas America was building them bigger than ever before. Bigger, better, and speedier.

But what was England doing to maintain her prestige as mistress of the seas? She was busy, all right. England's mills

115

and forges and factories were humming. Her coal mines, close to the seacoast, furnished all the fuel she needed, and her iron mines provided the metal. Her attention to steamships increased. With the success of the *Great Western*, British firms built steam craft to run to the Isle of Wight, up the coast to Glasgow, over the Channel and the North Sea to the Continent.

Samuel Cunard, British subject over in Halifax, meanwhile pondered his plans for a line of transatlantic steamers and debated how best to get the needed financial backing.

Fate aided him—aided him in the person of a couple of wealthy Haligonians (residents of Halifax)—Joseph Howe and Sir Thomas Chandler Halliburton. Both were on their way from Halifax to England on the brig *Tyrian*. As they nosed out of Canadian waters, they saw the steamer *Sirius* (which had got to America a little ahead of *Great Western* and was now running regularly) returning from a New York trip. A passenger on the *Tyrian* wrote to a friend:

> To our astonishment we saw the great ship *Sirius* steaming down directly in the wake of the *Tyrian*. . . . You will recollect the prompt decision of Commander Jennings (of the *Tyrian*) to carry the mail on board the steamer, and our equally prompt decision not to quit the sailing craft, commanded as she was by so kind and excellent an officer: and the trembling anxiety with which we watched mail bag after mail bag hoisted up from the deep waist of the *Tyrian;* then lowered to the small boat below, tossed about between vessels, and finally all safely placed on board the *Sirius.*

There it was! Sail bowing to steam in the matter of carrying the mail—a significant and prophetic occurrence. Mr. Howe went over for a visit to the *Sirius* as the two ships lay close together, and "took a glass of champagne with the captain."

These two Haligonians, arrived in London, hunt up the

S.S. SAVANNAH, 1819

First steamship to cross the Atlantic, *Savannah* was really a sailship with auxiliary engines. Still, she set the pace for the later conquest of the stormy North Atlantic. *Courtesy of Peabody Museum of Salem*

S.S. GREAT BRITAIN, 1845

England's first iron-hull ship in the New York–Liverpool run. It had six sails, one steam engine and one propeller. *Courtesy of Peabody Museum of Salem*

TWO EARLY CUNARDERS

They helped establish the Ocean Ferry between England and America.
Courtesy of Peabody Museum of Salem

S.S. ARABIA, 1852

S.S. AUSTRALASIAN, 1860

S.S. LILIAN, 1864

A Confederate blockade runner—a service that demanded fast, light-draft ships such as this one. *Illustrated London News*

S.S. INDIANA, 1879

In Delaware Bay. *Bon voyage* to General Grant off on his world tour.
Courtesy of Peabody Museum of Salem

PAQUEBOT TAMPICO, 1862

Inaugurated Atlantic service by French Line between Saint-Nazaire and Vera Cruz.
Courtesy of French Line

PAQUEBOT WASHINGTON, 1864

Inaugurated Atlantic service by French Line between Le Havre and New York.
Courtesy of French Line

S.S. OHIO. 1870's

A 3,014-ton, 600-horsepower ship operated by the American Steamship Company, the Pennsylvania Railroad-backed line.

Copyright, S. Walters, Liverpool

NEW YORK HARBOR ABOUT 1850

Era of the clippers. Tall masts against New York's skyline! Side-paddlers in midstream.
Courtesy of The Mariners' Museum, Newport News, Va.

S.S. L. D. BAKER, 1903

Tall, spindly stack and auxiliary sails. Early ship of the United Fruit Co.
Courtesy of United Fruit Co.

S.S. NEW YORK, CIRCA 1894

The vessel after her auxiliary sails were given up. *Courtesy of Peabody Museum of Salem*

WILLIAM INMAN, ESQ.

Head of one of the largest shipping companies serving America prior to the turn of the century. He built and ran the beautiful *City of New York* (1889). *Courtesy of The Mariners' Museum, Newport News, Va.*

EDWARD KNIGHT COLLINS

The "American Cunard," who built and ran the pioneer American luxury liners. Can be said to have founded the American passenger merchant marine. *Courtesy of The Mariners' Museum, Newport News, Va.*

STEPHEN BARKER GUION

Founder and head of the Guion Steamship Line, Liverpool–New York, in the 1870's. *Courtesy of The Mariners' Museum, Newport News, Va.*

S.S. HAMMONIA, 1882

First-class dining saloon, with small-group tables. *Courtesy of The Mariners' Museum, Eldredge Collection, Newport News, Va.*

S.S. MAJESTIC, 1889

First-class dining saloon, with the long tables. The furnishings as well as the food were notable both for quality and quantity. *Courtesy of The Mariners' Museum, Eldredge Collection, Newport News, Va.*

S.S. SANTA ROSA

One of the largest of the "Good Neighbor Fleet" in New York Harbor. *Courtesy of Grace Line*

S.S. CONSTITUTION AND INDEPENDENCE

American Export Lines' "Heavenly Twins" of the New York–Mediterranean service, in Genoa.
Courtesy of American Export Line

S.S. CITY OF NEW YORK

Ever-memorable liner built by Inman of London, but later transferred to the American Line, where she built up a devoted and discriminating following in the 1890's and early 1900's. *Courtesy of Peabody Museum of Salem*

S.S. QUEEN OF BERMUDA

An Atlantic queen in the "Little Abroad" service—Furness-Withy's *Queen of Bermuda* on the New York–Hamilton run.

COMMODORE HARRY MANNING,
UNITED STATES LINES

Master of the nation's largest merchant ship, *United States*, when she set a new speed record (still untouched) on the Atlantic. *Courtesy of The Mariners' Museum, Newport News, Va.*

GENERAL JOHN M. FRANKLIN,
PRESIDENT OF THE UNITED
STATES LINES

Courtesy of The Mariners' Museum, Newport News, Va.

JOHN E. SLATER,
PRESIDENT OF THE AMERICAN
EXPORT LINES

Courtesy of Pach Bros., New York

S.S. QUEEN MARY

Cunard Lines' New York–Southampton speedster. *Courtesy of Cunard Line*

S.S. UNITED STATES, 1952

The *United States* proudly enters New York Harbor for her maiden trip.
Courtesy of Copic, Inc.

Colonial Secretary for Canada and through him urge the British Government to back a line of mail steamers.

Very well, says the Secretary, and within a matter of months an advertisement appears in the London and Canadian prints. Desired: bids for the conveyance of mails by steamships of not less than 300-horsepower each, between England, Halifax, and New York. All tenders for the contract to be received by December 15. . . .

Two offers came in pronto: One from the Great Western Steamship Company, and the other from the St. George Steam Packet Company, owners of the *Sirius*.

But the Admiralty was choosy. Neither of these bids seemed acceptable. And while the matter was hanging fire, Samuel Cunard—now aged fifty-two and still eagerly on the trail of capital to help him establish a line of steamships—registered at the Hotel Piccadilly in London. Before long, through the efforts of Fanny Kemble, the famous actress, and the well-known Mrs. Norton, arbiter of society in those parts, Cunard was dined and presented to the right Government folks. In time Cunard got the contract. Then he cast about for good shipbuilders and makers of steam machinery—boilers and engines. He made a deal with Napier & Wood of Glasgow. With them Cunard signed a contract to build and supply him with:

"Three good and sufficient steamships, each not less than 225-feet keel and fore-rake; not less than 32-feet between paddles, not less than 21-feet from top of timbers to underside of deck amidships, properly finished in every respect."

There were to be cabins furnished in a "neat and comfortable manner." Accommodations for from sixty to seventy passengers or more, "if the space will conveniently and commodiously permit thereof." These were to be 960-ton vessels and would cost 32,000 pounds each. In return for carrying the mail on these ships, Cunard was to get 55,000 pounds per year. That was certainly more than the actual cost of carrying the mail. But England was eager to see a regular steamship service established between her shores and the United States and frankly proffered a subsidy.

As it turned out, the three small ships Cunard had planned were never built. Instead he built four "mammoth" steamers in Glasgow, the *Britannia,* the *Caledonia,* the *Columbia,* the *Arcadia;* it was the first of these which caused Boston to stage her grand celebration of welcome that day in 1840.

This is primarily a book of American ships. Yet I have spun out rather lengthily on this Samuel Cunard matter for good reasons. The Cunard Line (originally called the Royal Mail Line) gave America its first dependable North Atlantic line of steamers. Cunard remains today the largest steamship company to provide America with North Atlantic passenger service. Someday we hope American ships in the ocean ferry will once again outnumber those flying the colors of other lands.

At that time America's door was open wider than ever before or since. America needed the laboring folk—from Germany, the British Isles, Belgium, and the Scandinavian countries—who sought new lands in which to grow up and fulfill their individual destinies. American shipping men, ready to build up their business with big sailing vessels, went after passenger trade and made increasing profits.

An immigrant in those days had to undergo a fairly rough fifteen, twenty, or more days between decks en route—in the steerage.

But if he survived that, he knew he'd find a new country and a good job waiting for him in the United States. To escape military service at home, to breathe the air of freedom known to circulate throughout America, to earn bigger wages, buy a home for a growing family under different skies—all these drew immigrants by the hundred-thousands.

An immigrant could get passage on a *regular* sailing packet for from 3 to 6 guineas. On one of the many with *irregular* sailing times, he could get it from 5 pounds down to 40 shillings. Of course he had to furnish his own food, which represented about 50 shillings more.

In all European ports there were stores along the waterfront which supplied passengers bound for America with food, clothing, and other necessities. It was for the most part spoiled food of the worst sort at outlandish prices. The fleecing of immigrants went to such lengths that protective associations arose in Europe to aid the plight of outbound families and put a stop to this pernicious practice.

The steerage bore a sinister reputation even on the later and better sailing ships—and to all accounts it was well deserved. Sailing first class on a clipper, you fared somewhat better; your bunks were softer and the food was plentiful and good, though not of a great variety.

When the first steamships came, they brought slightly better accommodations—but not much. From what I've read of early passenger accommodations, first class on pioneer steamships fell so far short of what the present lines offer as tourist (once third class) as not to be mentioned in the same breath.

Take the case of Cunard's pioneer—the famous little old *Britannia*. She and her three sister ships each had two decks. On the upper deck were the officers' cabins, the galley, the bakery, the padded cow-house where Bossy spent days and nights.

You see the *Britannia* was considered a "luxury liner" of her day. She boasted that her passengers had fresh milk from port to port; hence the cow was carried. But from the way *Britannia* tossed and heaved about on the rough North Atlantic voyages (see Charles Dickens's *American Notes* if you want a pertinent comment), Bossy's milk must have been churned to butter inside her before "she yielded her udders to the milkmaid's hand."

So Britain, with her Cunard ships, started the ocean ferry, giving us our first regular steamship service. As we shall see, America in time set her own steamships going: a fleet small in numbers but top rank in quality.

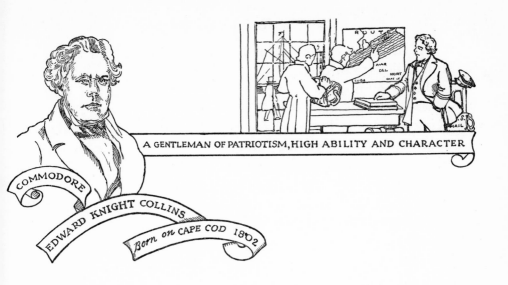

A GENTLEMAN OF PATRIOTISM, HIGH ABILITY AND CHARACTER

COMMODORE
EDWARD KNIGHT COLLINS
Born on CAPE COD 1802

15. *Granddad Was for Subsidies*

WHEN England boldly helped subsidize Sam Cunard's ships, she established a precedent, and America looked on with mixed feelings—mostly disapproval. We were an independent nation devoted to the exercise of free enterprise. Many senators and representatives, even then, saw red at the mention of Government subsidies, just as they do today when they feel the Government dares to venture too far into the realm of private industry. Let Britain help pay to run her little steamships! But not America—we're hard-headed businessmen, we are! We want no help from the Government! Look at our shipping—hundreds of fine clippers and packets, faster, sturdier, more dependable than ships of any other country in the world. Why do we need Government aid? We're doing all right. . . .

Others said it was just like England! She's handing out cash to her shipping companies simply to make it possible for British ships to leave American ships behind!

... And besides—others maintained—we've got our hands full building railroads.

But a number of thoughtful men—in Congress and elsewhere—held different ideas. There was Senator Thomas Butler King of Georgia, for one. King, an able and convincing talker, said we ought to encourage shipping with good hard cash subsidies. Set aside a million dollars annually to pay for ships carrying our mail! Sure, that's more than the actual cost, but what of it? Our steamships need encouragment. If we don't encourage them, England's going to cop the cream of the maritime trade. King, in proposing a subsidy bill, said further:

> It's sufficient to show that they [the British statesmen] are resolved, as far as possible, to monopolize the intercourse between these two important points. This movement shows clearly that the time has arrived when we must determine whether we will yield this essential branch of navigation and this direct means of extending our naval armaments to our great commercial rival [England] or whether we shall promptly extend to our enterprising merchants the necessary means to enable them to bring American energy, enterprise and skill into competition with British sagacity and capital.
>
> Of all the lines of sailing packets that cross the Atlantic, not one is owned in Europe. And it is not to be doubted that American merchants, properly encouraged, will assuredly excel in that field [that is, in steamships] as they have done in sailing vessels. And when we reflect that this may be accomplished to the mutual advantage and advancement of our commercial and military marine, it would seem that no statesman ought to hesitate to give his support to this measure which is demanded alike by prudence and the necessities of our position.

President James K. Polk was then in the White House—likewise a Southerner. He too favored the measure to subsidize our merchant shipping: "An enlightened policy by which a rapid communication with the various parts of the world is established by means of American-built steamers, would find an ample reward in the increase of our commerce and *in making our country and its resources more favorably known abroad."* The italics are his.

President Polk added that in this way we'd make our naval officers more familiar with steam vessels. That, you see, was just at the time when our Navy was "getting up steam" and retiring the old canvasbacks as they wore out. It was the custom then in America and England to have a Navy man on board each of the pioneer steamships for the dual purpose in aiding in *her* navigation and teaching *him* the mysteries of the steam-propelled craft.

Our first transatlantic mail contract went to the Ocean Steamship Company (some authorities speak of it as the Oceanic Steam Navigation Company). This American company inaugurated steam service from New York to Le Havre and Bremen and was given $200,000 for twenty trips ($10,000 per trip). This was about half of what Cunard received from Parliament for his first venture. The Ocean Company built two steamers at the yards of Westervelt and Mackey—the *Washington,* 1640 tons, and the *Herman,* 1730 tons. They both had the lines of the traditional sailing packet; each had the customary crude but effective engines of those days and also, of course, "lofty spars with great spreads of canvas which were used when the winds were fresh and fair." The *Washington* and *Herman* made fairly good time—14 to 17 days (to Bremen) on the eastbound run; 15 to 19 days on the westbound trip. They were strong ships with heavy frames and fastenings.

And right here we find the beginning of another interesting ocean trade—to California via the narrowest strip of the Western Hemisphere—Panama. The clippers, as we saw, years earlier had begun to sail around Cape Horn: fur and gold-rush shipments had built up that trade enormously. Soon California-bound travelers by ship, however, would get off on the Atlantic side of Panama and cross the Isthmus by foot or horseback. (The renowned Collis P. Huntington, railroad builder, once did so in his young days.) There they would board another ship on the West Coast and on up to the gold fields.

Well, Congress took cognizance of that shorter route in 1848 when the United States decided to exploit its new western territory received by treaty at the end of the Mexican War. Contracts were made with George Law of New York, who agreed to build and run three ships from New York down the Atlantic Coast to Aspinwall (now Colón), Panama. Another contract went to C. H. Aspinwall to pick up our mail and passengers on the other (western) side of the Isthmus, take them in his ships up to the American West Coast territories—to San Francisco and Astoria.

Law's line built the great ship *Georgia,* 225 feet long and 2700 tons; the *Illinois,* 267 feet long and 2123 tons; the *Ohio,* 248 feet long and 2432 tons—the biggest steamships yet built in America, or anywhere else to that time.

Aspinwall's ships for the Pacific Coast run were the *Panama* and the *Oregon.* So there you had it! American ships running down to Panama—the narrowest link in the Pan-American stretch of continent—and American ships running from Panama northward to our new possession on the Pacific side.

Next—to connect them at the Isthmus! Whether anyone entertained any idea of the canal across that narrow strip in those days, I can't say. But this much is certain. The railroad bug had got hold of America, and so American capital built a little one-track jerk-water line across the Isthmus (the distance is about 125 miles) to connect the ships of two oceans.

Into the California trade in 1849—height of the clipper era —sailed the game little steamer *Senator* on a venture no one believed would succeed—no one but her owners, Grinnell and Minturn, and her master, Lieutenant Richard Bache, who had asked to be detached from Navy service and detailed to the *Senator.* She was a tiny 750-ton vessel built for the New York and New England trade, via the Sound. In response to advertisements that she would sail for the West Coast, passengers crowded to the wharf. But when they saw the diminutive ship, all backed out. When the *Senator* also backed out—of the harbor, that is—she had only one passenger and a lot of freight.

Down at Panama, however, she picked up several hundred passengers eager to get to the gold fields and willing to sail on anything that would float.

Around the toilsome and dangerous Horn and up the West Coast labored the *Senator,* paddles whipping strange seas, engines fighting fierce currents.

On October 27, the *Senator* reached San Francisco and at once established a new steam service—San Francisco to Sacramento. Those were the days of easy money and high prices. The *Senator* charged $35 for the trip each way, plus meals at $5.00 each, plus berth at $5.00 per night. She carried freight, too, at $40 to $80 per ton. She kept up this service for years, making as much as $50,000 on a single trip.

The *Senator* probably earned more money than any ship that ever floated.

Within ten years after the start of the steam service on the Atlantic and Pacific coasts, twenty-nine fine steamers were running in both branches of the trade, with Panama transfer.

Law and Aspinwall later joined interests and formed the Pacific Mail Company—then the greatest of American steamship operations. In those ten years steamships in this trade carried 175,000 passengers, brought home $200,000,000 in gold bullion. Not until 1866, however, was the Trans-Pacific Steamship service to be established—California to the Orient.

Though not strictly within the scope of a book dealing with the ocean ferry, these pioneer coastwise lines deserve mention because they show a growing though belated interest in steam vessels—the belief by many that the big clippers (then in their heyday) would soon be relegated to the limbo of things past.

Also, the use of steamships as mail carriers shows that Uncle Sam was willing to pay rather well (though he would not "subsidize") mail-carrying ships.

And while we are on the subject of steamship subsidies, I recall that Grandfather—a staunch protectionist Republican of the deepest stripe—held out nevertheless for subsidizing the ships. (There's a reason—ships were his business!)

" 'Y God, Addie, they need it!" he'd tell me. "You see, running a steamship line to foreign ports costs a hell of a lot of money. It's not like any other business. Merchant ships running between our country and foreign lands are really ambassadors; they help build good will between two countries. That means they are an aid to our Government, and should be paid for it. Oh yes. I'm a Mark Hanna Republican, but I'm for ship subsidies! If the Congress hadn't later taken it away from Edward K. Collins, we'd have licked the breeches off England as mistress of the seas."

Granddad had his metaphors a little mixed in the matter of Britannia's breeches, but I knew what he meant.

For carrying the mail down the East Coast to Panama, Uncle Sam paid $276,000 for the year 1852; for 1855, $290,000. For carrying the mail north up the Pacific Coast, Uncle Sam paid $308,000 in 1852; $346,000 in 1855. Let's see what Prescott Marvin [1] has to say about it.

"These two services together did not draw as much support from the United States Treasury as the Cunard Line drew from the Treasury of Great Britain. Both concerns were 'protected industries' but the British protection was much earlier, more generous and more persistent."

Meanwhile the Ocean Company's service to Le Havre and Bremen had proved a sound money-maker. So successful, indeed, that the Government was encouraged to take another step forward—or backward, if you were an anti-subsidy man. Remember Edward K. Collins, whom we met once before as the founder of the Dramatic Line of sailing ships, and as the producer of a new type of vessel modeled somewhat on the

[1] Prescott Marvin, *The U.S. Merchant Marine* (New York, Charles Scribner's Sons, 1902).

hull of the Mississippi steamboat? We meet him again, in 1847, in Washington, where the matter of steamship subsidy is again before the Congress. Collins is after a mail contract. Let's listen in:

"Now, Mr. Collins, what do you plan to do? What kind of service will you offer in return for a contract?"

"Well," Collins answers, "the Government says that ships to carry the mail must be at least 2,000 tons each. I'm prepared to go further than you require. I have the capital and the backing and the experience. I want to build a fleet of American steamships of about 2,500 tons each—ships such as the world has never seen before. They'll be faster than the Cunarders; they'll be finer in appointments. They'll have comforts and luxuries that no ship has ever had yet."

"I see. If you can do all that, Captain Collins, I can think of no reason why you should not have the contract. The Government is prepared to pay $385,000 a year. That's smaller, I realize, than Cunard received for his first contract—eight years ago—but it's the best that can be done."

So Collins got the contract. And thus steps upon the scene of American steamshipping the man who did more than any other to make America, for a time at least, the leader on the seas; who brought new ideas of design and equipment into the practice of the profession of shipbuilding, and outdid the English Cunard line. There is reason for his being spoken of today as "The American Cunard." There's an unmarked grave in one of the cemeteries in the Bronx. There Collins lies, but he is not forgotten.

As I write this, American shipping interests and societies everywhere have joined in a movement to honor him on what is known as Maritime Day—May 22, the date (by the way) on which the little *Savannah* began her trip to England in her pioneer effort of 1819. The United States Merchant Marine Academy has unveiled a bronze plaque to him.

Just who was this Collins, and whence did he come? of what

stock and stamina? Since he is a towering figure of our early shipping days, we can afford to take some time out to look into his story.

From Maine to California his name was then (1850) on the lips of men who shipped and men who ran ships. While yet he sent his fast sail packets flying over the waves, his reputation as a dependable, generous-minded gentleman went before him. And that, mark you, was in a day when most of the seas' fraternity was hard-fisted, rough-talking, and rampant—more than a trifle uncouth.

"He was a gentleman of patriotism, high ability, and character," Marvin states in *The American Merchant Marine*. "He knew perfectly the sea and its affairs. He had a remarkable power of convincing and directing other men, and a genius for the shaping of great enterprises. As between the two chiefs of the international steamship enterprises [Cunard and Collins] which were to vie with each other on the important route between New York and Liverpool, the advantage lay overwhelmingly with the experienced, ardent and ambitious American."

Collins inherited his learnings toward the sea. His ancestors had come to New England in 1635. His father was born while the Revolution was just getting underway, and at twenty-one got his papers as a shipmaster. He must have had persuasive ways—this Israel Collins, father of E. K.—for on one of his trips to England, as a young shipmaster, he married and brought home a high-born young lady who had also inherited a sea tradition. She was the niece of Admiral Sir John Knight of the Royal Navy.

They lived on Cape Cod, and there Edward Knight Collins was born in 1802. Maybe the hard New England climate was too much for the English girl. At any rate, she died while Edward was still in kilts.

His father kept on seafaring until Edward was grown. Then the boy went to sea. The Mediterranean pirates almost got him on one voyage; but he safely showed up again in New York.

There the elder Collins had remarried and was prospering as a shipping merchant—that is, an importer-exporter who owned and operated his own ships. Soon the firm on South Street, known as I. G. Collins, became I. G. Collins and Son.

"The price of cotton has skyrocketed in the British markets," a forgotten packet captain once told Ed Collins. Ed passed the information on to some of his clients—men whom he represented as a purchaser in foreign markets.

"Look!" his customers as a body told him. "You get down there to Charleston as quick as you can, and buy up all the cotton you can lay your hands on."

"Very well," said Ed Collins, "it's pretty late in the day. But I'll see what I can do."

When his factors had left, young Ed Collins hastened down to the waterfront. Too late! The weekly Charleston packet ship was just moving out from her dock. Glancing around the harbor, he glimpsed an idle pilot's schooner lying hard by.

"Captain!" he called to its master, and then went aboard her to bargain. What inducement he offered, we don't know. But his offer was successful. He chartered the schooner. An hour later she was streaking down the bay hard on the track of the Charleston packet.

"I figured it this way," Collins said later. "Having a lighter-draft boat, I could keep closer inshore than the Charleston ship. The men in my crew knew their job all right and we avoided the northerly Gulf stream current. So we were able to beat our rival to Charleston by some hours. I bought up every bale of cotton in the city and was heading out to sea again on the pilot schooner when we met the Charleston ship just coming in with its load of prospective buyers."

Edward Collins's career is definitely not an Horatio Alger epic. True, he did rise high in his profession, but he did not have to start from scratch. He had an excellent patrimony, and on his father's death headed the company they both had owned.

With such a background and experience—sea knowledge and

ability to size up the qualities of a ship after a cursory examination of her; an ability to deal with men; a reputation as a keen and trustworthy businessman—Ed Collins was the very man to provide America with its first fleet of steam greyhounds—ships which could fling down the gantlet to Cunard and the other foreign shipping lines.

With his mail contract in his pocket, Collins went back to New York and set to work. To construct his "Yankee leviathans" (as the press called them) he chose George Steers, head of a firm whose name is still familiar in shipping circles. It is to be supposed that Steers whistled when he heard of the kind of ships that Collins wanted and the amounts he was to invest in them; but if so, it was a whistle of astounded admiration.

There were to be four ships, all having names ending in *ic,* as the White Star Line (now a part of Cunard) did in later years—the *Arctic,* the *Baltic,* the *Pacific,* the *Atlantic.* They were to be 277 feet long on the keel; 282, on the main deck. Beam was 45 feet. They each had four decks; white oak frames, strengthened with timbers of live oak; bottoms filled in solidly with oak timbers to the turn of the bilge; their keelsons were more massive than a battleship's. Zinc covered the hull below the water line. Copper bolts held the timbers in place above the water line.

I got these details from Granddad. I don't know how he got them, but he always delighted in reciting them to me, dwelling particularly on the luxurious interiors of the ships, which we'll get to presently.

16. High Old Days
in the Ocean Ferry

S OMEDAY I shall build ships that will make the run from
New York to Europe in ten days or less."

This magnificent boast came from the lips of Commodore
Edward K. Collins in 1840. The now defunct title "Commodore" rested fittingly upon his shoulders, for no man in
America knew more about ships and the sea or had had more
ships under his charge.

It took Collins ten years to fulfill his boast. But fulfill it he
did, and magnificently, as we shall soon see. In 1840 Collins
had said there was no longer any money to be made in sailing
ships and had turned his full interest to the support of the idea
of steam. He must have known that he was in a fair way of
realizing his ambition when George Steers, his architect,

showed him the plans for the *Baltic* and the *Atlantic*—the first two ladies of his fleet. For they surpassed in splendor and comfort any dream the most ambitious designer of early steamships could have envisioned.

I wonder if, like me, you have a feeling of lift and exhilaration each time you walk into an ocean liner's cabin and observe the masterly manner in which beauty and restrained luxury have deftly been combined. There is a certain fitness and finish about the large rooms of a modern liner that can be found nowhere else in the world, I believe. And I also believe this is true of all modern liners which serve our ports. My grandfather lived to see this trend to a more subdued type of elegance following the Victorian era, but he didn't like it.

"If they're going to build 'em luxurious, why don't they show it?" he'd ask me as he scowled at some lithograph advertising current steamship sailings. "Look"—pointing to a picture in his scrapbook showing the interior of the old *Hammonia* or the first *Mauretania* or the *Kaiser Wilhelm der Grosse*. He'd known and loved all those ships whose deep cushions, tapestry, rococo wood carving and colors on walls and ceilings of their saloons and grand ballrooms were surpassed only by the elaborateness of the "bridal suites" and the de-luxe first-class staterooms.

"You were getting luxury then when you paid for your ticket and you could damn well see what you were getting! And the *City of New York* and *City of St. Louis!*" And once again he'd regale me with a tale of the glory of his youthful favorites.

Ship luxury and beauty today find expression nowhere more satisfying than on the United States Lines, the American Export Lines, the Cunarders. Yet the earlier Cunarders had no particular distinction in that direction. Far from it! Back in 1842, when the Cunard agent sold Mr. & Mrs. Charles Dickens their passage on the *Britannia* for their first trip to the United States, the agent exaggerated the ship's accommodations to such an extent that the great Victorian author came aboard expecting to find something really impressive. And what disillusionment he was in for! Dickens walked into the main saloon and asked if it was the butler's pantry. He swore afterwards that his stateroom was nothing but an "utterly impractical, thoroughly hopeless and profoundly preposterous box," rather than one of the "chaste and pretty little bowers sketched by a masterly hand in the highly varnished lithographs in the agents' counting house in London."

Well, it must be said for Mr. Cunard that he himself made no claims for grandeur or sumptuous quarters. Nor did he admit he was out to beat all other ships afloat in the Atlantic run. He had said he would build his ships for "neatness and safety." This leads us to the conclusion that steamship luxury as we know it today came, not from the pioneer English Royal Mail Line (Cunard), but from the first of the fleet of four big ships which Edward Knight Collins built in 1849 and 1850 to carry the United States mail.

THE FIRST COLLINS SHIP

She was the *Atlantic* and was completed only a short time before her sister ship *Baltic*. As she lay at her pier in North River, crowds stared at her, open-mouthed, from the shore. They'd never seen such a long ship. From cutwater to taffrail she measured 282 feet. Her three masts shot slantingly aloft, their very rake imparting to her the sense of speed. The Collins house flag flew from her foremast and mainmast; the national emblem from her mizzenmast. She had a rather short, fat smokestack. If you'd laid it down, a tall man could have walked through it upright from end to end. Through the fancy carvings on her paddle boxes, the people on shore could catch glimpses of the giant 35-foot wheels at rest.

Maybe some old salt in the crowd yelled out, "My God,

where's her bowsprit?" and a landlubber answered, "Yes, she *does* look funny—out there in front."

They would have been right: the *Atlantic's* bow was unlike any other the world had ever seen. In his design the Commodore had given her an entirely new "wrinkle"—a straight up-and-down bow, sharp as a knife. Hitherto all ships—sailing craft as well as steam vessels—had been designed with the familiar clipper bow—that is, the bow cut gracefully back from the sharp point where the timbers met (I believe shipping men call it the *knighthead*) from which the bowsprit and jib boom jut slantingly forward.

But sail was passing—had already passed as far as Collins was concerned. Hence, as we've seen, he put his faith in steam. There was no need for sail save to augment or replace steam in an emergency—no need for so much canvas. Besides, Collins wanted his ships to look different from Cunard's—and all other ships too, for that matter. It may be that Collins had an early sense of public-relations values: he wanted to fix and lodge his ships and their appearance, no less than the service they offered, in the minds of his present and potential patrons. He wanted people to talk about his ships!

Whatever his reason may have been for building his ships with straight stems, he set the pattern for the future shape of ships. Practically all ships today are built with a straight stem —save that some of them in recent years have developed a curve or rake for appearance's sake, not utility's—witness especially Cunard's cruise ship *Caronia,* some ships of the Italian Line, and the *United States.*

Not all shipbuilders, however, were ready to follow Collins's lead at once. Some did adopt the straight stem in their ships; but most other builders refused for a time to abandon the graceful clipper bow. As late as World War I there were steamships afloat which had no sail equipment at all, but which had clipper bows and small bowsprits for no reason in the world save that the builder and owner liked them. . . .

But to get back to the *Atlantic* and what she was like. When the gangplank was let down for a procession of admiring visitors to come aboard and inspect her before her first voyage, they were left speechless—so it was said. The interior fittings were done in white holly, satinwood, rosewood—combined, diversified, blended into a rich and impressive costliness.

In the drawing rooms were mirrors—mirrors on door panels, on ceiling supports, stanchions, and in the ceilings, too. Intricately wrought bronze sea shells served as bases and tops of the mirrors. In the center of each frame were scenes representing the ocean mythology of the ancients, done in bronze and burnished gold.

More bronzework—hand wrought into intricate design—served as metal supports and light *torchères*. I have read somewhere—though I've forgotten the source—that the *Atlantic* had oil lamps rather than the customary tallow candles. She may have pioneered in that respect.

And paintings too! In the spacious cabin—into which the sunlight filtered through stained-glass windows—hung portraits done by skillful local artists—likenesses of the founders "of the Confederacy" (as the very early Americans like to speak of the Union, thereby possibly suggesting to the Southern people a name which, a decade later, would mark the gallant but ill-starred effort to found a nation bearing that name in truth). "The paintings are done in the very highest style of art," commented a local paper of that era, and added that they were hung in rosewood frames to match the pillars of the cabin.

"She's the most handsome, most luxuriously fitted out steamer ever built," commented an open-eyed visitor as he walked from the comfortable smoking room into the well-stocked library. Thence he passed into the main lounge which likewise was paneled in handsome wood, with stained-glass windows. The *Atlantic* even had a grand piano "for the pleasure of the passengers."

The *Atlantic* likewise pioneered in making her staterooms

comfortable. Staterooms and public rooms were both steam-heated. There were baths on the ships, with hot and cold running water. As her contribution to greater safety, the *Atlantic* bore on her foremast a powerful magnesium searchlight—the first to grace an ocean vessel.

It is to be supposed that the *Atlantic* had a good bar: no self-respecting passenger-carrying ship was without one in those times (nor in our own). But when the gentlemen who were among the first visitors to the *Atlantic* came to the barber shop —with shelves of colored bottles and big upholstered chair— they must have fingered their beards or side whiskers appreciatively, remarking, "By George! Getting a shave and a haircut while you are at sea! Think of it!"

The dining saloon was spacious and airy. In each first-class stateroom there was a call bell leading to the steward's quarters by which a passenger could summon assistance when needed— another innovation in ship equipment. As to her cuisine—I find little or no reference to the meals served. One may justly suppose them, however, to have been in keeping with the rest of the vessel.

Sam Cunard, conservative though he was, was not to be left behind in the creation of beautiful ships. In the *Arabia*, built in 1852, he took a leaf from Collins's book. She was the first Cunarder with two stacks. She was 285 feet long, had two paddle wheels, and, as it turned out, was the last wooden vessel built for Cunard. She had handsomely painted paddle boxes.

In her cabin her "sofas, covered with Utrecht velvet," caused wide comment. On the cabin floor, fore and aft, ran a deep-piled velvet carpet, into which were woven Arabian scenes. The stained-glass skylight and painting on the wall carried out the Arabian theme.

Thus we see that the traveling public was becoming more discriminating, more demanding with each passing year, and the two rival steamship lines in the North Atlantic stood ready to supply that demand.

High Old Days in the Ocean Ferry

The purpose of the mail subsidy—one of its purposes at least, according to its proponents—was to encourage the building and running of more steamships. And did it work? It most emphatically did. Let the figures convince you.

In 1847, just before the effect of the mail contracts was felt, merchant steamships flying the American flag amounted to only 5,631 tons. England had four times that tonnage. Most of these American-flag steamers ran to the West Indies, Mexican ports, Panama. But with the starting of the New York-Le Havre-Bremen subsidized service (Ocean Steamship Company), American deep-sea tonnage shot up in one year to 16,068; in two years, to over 20,000; in three years, to 44,000; and increased each year until 1855 saw us with 115,000 tons. By 1851 we had nearly caught up with Great Britain in shipbuilding, and our ships were running to many foreign ports. There was an understanding that in time of war every one would, if required, convert to a warship and fight for the nation. That was one of the provisos, of course, of Congress-extended aid.

Now what was Cunard doing all this time? He was building ships—new and finer ships—and running them in the New York trade and making money. Cunard recognized a good case of competition when he saw it, and acted accordingly with good fat subsidies at his command.

As to the new Cunard ships. Besides the original four— *Britannia, Arcadia, Caledonia,* and *Columbia*—Cunard built the *Hibernia* in 1843: ship by R. Steele and Company, Greenock; engines by Robert Napier. She was 217 feet long— ten feet longer than the other four. She carried 110 cabin passengers, was bark-rigged, with a couple of extra large paddles. She ate forty-three tons of bituminous coal a day. Bravely she threshed out of Liverpool and headed for America, arriving in a little less time than the *Britannia* had set.

But sad news awaited her docking in New York: the *Columbia* was lost at sea. The *Columbia* had been dogged by the unkindest fates ever since she came out. For instance, in 1842, on a westward passage, she broke a shaft of one of her paddle wheels; and because her sails alone were inadequate, she had to return to England and be refitted. Running down from Boston to Halifax the following year, the *Columbia,* while in charge of a coast pilot, ran in a deep fog onto Devil's Limb, now known as Rock Ledge, near Cape Sable. She had eighty-four passengers aboard. Most of the women were saved and some of the men; the majority of the latter remained on board to try to save the ship—a futile effort.

This is one of the few peacetime accidents in Cunard's long history. Momentarily, it put a damper on the British company's efforts, but not for long. The "flying" *Cambria* glided into Boston harbor in 1845. Her engines were said to have been finished so beautifully that one newspaper suggested they be put under glass. This was really not as silly a suggestion as it may have sounded. Grandfather told me that some of the older ships had a glassed-in deck space through which passengers could look down and see the giant pistons thrusting in and out.

Cunard, however, needed a larger subsidy. So . . .

"For an extra subsidy, I'll run my ships to New York as well as Boston," he offered. No sooner said than done. Parliament came across with a ten-year subsidy of 149,000 pounds sterling per year, Cunard agreeing to run his ships on alternate Saturdays into New York and Boston harbors. *Hibernia* inaugurated the New York service for Cunard, and Manhattan repeated the kind of reception (though on a lesser scale) which Boston had accorded the *Britannia* eight years earlier.

So now the rivalry mounted—Cunard vs. Collins; America against Britain. It seems to have been a good-natured contest with neither side apparently objecting to a joke at its own expense. Wrote the London *Punch* with a friendly dig at honest Sam Cunard:

> "A steamer of the Collins line
>   A Yankee Doodle notion
> Has also quickest cut the brine
>   Across th' Atlantic ocean.
> And British agents, no way slow
>   Her merits to discover
> Have been and bought her just to tow
>   The Cunard packets over."

It became the fashionable thing to ride the new Collins ships. The *Atlantic* cut the America-to-England time to nine days plus a few hours—far faster than anything Cunard could show. When Cunard's passenger traffic fell off alarmingly because of his American rivals, he set his jaw and ordered two more ships. In 1850 the *Asia* and *Africa* appeared—more than 2,200 tons each, with an indicated horsepower of 2,400. They were each 266 feet long. They could do up to 12½ knots an hour—a figure which fell far short, however, of what the Collins opposition liners were doing.

But there seems to have been no real enmity between the rival lines. Says Lawrence Babcock, historian of the Cunard Line, in *Spanning the Atlantic*: [1] "Intense as was the competition for the supremacy of the Atlantic, encouraged by national pride, though restrained by conservatism of the Cunard partners, it was characterized by a fine sportsmanship." And he proceeds to cite several instances.

On one occasion the Cunarder *Hibernia* was held in New York harbor. The Customs lads charged that her crew had violated the Customs laws of the port, and demanded a bond of $150,000 before they would release the ship for sailing. When Collins heard of it, he had his agents post the bond and

[1] New York, Alfred A. Knopf, 1931.

stood security for that amount, thus permitting his rival's ship to depart on schedule and continue the contest.

Not to be outdone, the Cunarder *Africa* came racing into New York harbor one day not long after the Collins liner *Atlantic* had sailed on her maiden voyage. As the *Africa* came within a mile of the Battery, she commenced to fire her signal gun over and over again. New Yorkers raced down to the Battery in great crowds and saw the majestic Cunarder sweeping up toward her North River dock. With his megaphone, the *Africa's* Captain shouted, "The *Atlantic's* quite fit! She arrived safe!"

Later he explained that the Collins ship had been detained by a broken shaft but would be along soon. That is what New York had been waiting for—news of the *Atlantic's* safe arrival on her first transatlantic voyage. And the city went wild with rejoicing and relief. . . .

"Yes," says Babcock, "both lines played cricket."

17. Sea Tragedy and a
Slow Congress

TO ME Ed Collins has always seemed the most gallant, the most tragic figure in American maritime history. Had Grandfather known him, I wager they would have been close friends. As it was, Granddad read everything about Collins he could lay his hands on and he talked about him frequently.

"Seemed to have been born under an unlucky star," Granddad would say, shaking his head mournfully, biting his cigar, walking nervously up and down the long drawing room of the old house on Indiana Avenue, as was his habit when interested. Outside the wind and rain might be swirling around the corners; old Lake Michigan might be doing her rough stuff. That was before they'd filled in so much of the lake shore that you couldn't see the lake from Grandfather's house. But I knew he didn't see the lake as he talked. In his mind's eye he was seeing the plunging Atlantic and those fine early ships of Ed Collins's. I would be sitting on the floor poring over the scrapbooks, thinking right along with him.

"Yes, sir," Grandfather went on. "He was a shipbuilder that was way ahead of his time. Americans—that damned Congress especially!—didn't appreciate him. Give him half a chance and he'd have kept America mistress of the seas instead of leaving it for the British. Didn't he make her that for a while? . . .

I have since found out about Collins.

As is nearly always the case when you set out to build houses or ships, Collins's ships cost much more than he had intended. About $675,000 apiece, considerably more than the $575,000 which Cunard had laid down for each of his fine new ships *Asia* and *Africa*, both less elaborate.

Atlantic was the first to sail. Her initial voyage to Liverpool began April 27, 1850. Ten years ago, Cunard's *Britannia* had first nosed into Boston from London, inaugurating regular transatlantic service. *Pacific* was the next Collins ship to sail; then *Baltic*, then *Arctic*. The *Atlantic* made it westward to Liverpool in 9 days, 17 hours—about an hour faster than the Cunarders. Collins's officers and crews introduced what is known as "liberal management" (whatever that means—extra perquisites for passengers? A larger show of courtesy? Greater attention to their comfort? More elaborate meals?). In any case, whatever it was, it won patronage with a bang. Between January and November 1852 the Collins ships carried 4,308 American passengers against Cunard's 2,969.

"Just wait!" warned Sam Cunard, and gave them his new *Asia*—16 horsepower more than the *Pacific* and *Atlantic*.

What really accounted for the Collins ships' superiority? One authority says, "Effective boilers and ability in their preparation."

Meanwhile, Congress in Washington looked benignly on, just as though it had been the first to think of aiding Collins in his efforts instead of holding off until the eleventh hour. In 1852, however, Congress gave a tangible gesture of approval; it increased the mail subsidy to $858,000, which even topped Cunard's by a couple of thousand. "Fine!" said Collins.

Sea Tragedy and a Slow Congress

Today our Post Office Department pays more than $10,000,-
000 annually to Atlantic steamship lines to carry its mails. And
that despite much of its first-class mail-carrying having gone
to the airlines. Collins deserved the increase.

"We can run the best ships and beat the Cunard ships—
beat 'em by a day and a half each trip, but it costs us nearly a
million more a year," announced Collins.

The faster time, and the extravagant luxuries and comforts
of his ships, drew passengers by the thousands.

Collins and his ships had introduced the wholesome element
of competition into the Atlantic ferry, which Cunard had
hitherto controlled. Now, to meet the American rivalry, more
Cunarders appeared, as we mentioned in the last chapter.

The decade of the 1850's opened auspiciously for American
shippers and shipping. America had at last met England's (and
other European countries', too) subsidy arrangements with
American subsidies almost equal. America didn't want to do
it. She preferred free and untrammeled enterprise, each business standing on its own feet, or—since we're speaking of ships—
each tub on its own bottom. But there was no choice. Europe
started out by giving its shipping interests subsidies. The only
way American shippers could offer any sort of adequate competition to foreign ships was by a similar gesture. And yet in
the face of that knowledge . . . But we are getting ahead of the
story.

For the shipping world, 1854 dawned clear and cloudy. Clear
with the consciousness that we had the finest fleet of ships
afloat, rolling up the business to a king's taste. Cloudy because
of the portents of tragedy to come. On September 27, 1854,
the *Arctic*—finest of the Collins fleet—was heading northward
along the northern track to England. Just off Cape Race on the
southern tip of Newfoundland, she ran into a fog which old
seamen said was the "heaviest ever seen in them parts."

It was then that a small French ship, *Vesta,* rammed her.

Feeling no immediate concern for his own great ship—the *Arctic* was so large, the *Vesta,* so small—Captain Luce turned his first attention to the *Vesta's* crew and passengers, to render what aid he could. But then some of his crew told him that the *Arctic* herself had a big hole in her bow. She was filling fast. That, you see, was before the days of transverse bulkheads, which serve to confine leaks to a small part of the hull. The *Arctic* started to fill from prow to stern. Captain Luce headed his ship straight for Newfoundland's nearest port. It was a sixty-mile race. Could those fine engines that were the *Arctic's* pride push the big vessel to shore before the hold filled with seawater? Officers, crew, and men passengers fell to at the pump and attempted to plug the leak, working with a desperate will. The water rushed in through the gashed side. The seas ran rough. The wind rose high. It was a losing fight.

The crew then turned to the lifeboats and tried to launch them. But as has frequently been the case in sea tragedies, the davits did not work properly, the launching proved slow and cumbersome. "Rough cowards and coal heavers," says Winthrop L. Marvin, "seized the one or two boats which were actually got afloat."

Of those on board, 212 passengers and 110 of the crew went down with the *Arctic.* The *Vesta?* Oh, she went on about her business. She was damaged and lost thirteen of her company, but at least she was able to crawl into St. John's.

The *Arctic's* loss cast a cloud of gloom all over America. There was no rejoicing on the other side of the Atlantic. The Cunard people—although a formidable rival was put out of the running for good and all—were good sportsmen, too chivalrous to rejoice in their rival's misfortune. Cunard knew what losing ships was. He'd lost two. He sent messages of friendly sympathy to Collins.

The man hardest hit, of course, was Ed Collins. The loss of a fine ship was bad enough; the loss of 212 people on board was worse. Worst of all for him personally—his own wife, his son, and daughter had been aboard and they too had gone down with the ship.

Collins turned from mourning his personal loss to the continued operation of his remaining ships. He still had three fine vessels—largest, fastest, strongest, and most beautiful afloat. They continued to ply the sea lanes from New York to Liverpool and, despite the *Arctic's* fate, to do a good business.

January, 1856. There was little travel in the winter months, but freight consignments filled the *Pacific's* hold as she cast loose from her Liverpool berth on a homeward voyage, with only 45 passengers and a crew of 141. Out into the Atlantic's mists and storms she sails—never to be heard of again. There was no wireless in those days to send rescue ships or planes speeding to a sinking vessel's aid. There were no rescue ships— there were no planes. All the owners could do was to wait. They waited in vain. When the *Pacific* was lost—or where she was lost, or how—these questions remain unanswered. Her story remains a mystery of the sea—a sister tale to the loss of the famous sailing ship *Mary Celeste,* which one day was found by the crew of another ship, floating undamaged, without a soul on board.

But more bad luck was in the offing. . . .

In early 1855 Collins had yet another ship in the stocks—a giant she was, larger, swifter, more luxurious than any of his others. She was the *Adriatic,* 4,144 tons and the first ship ever built to cost more than $1,000,000. The figure in the contract was $1,100,000. George Steers had designed Collins's other ships for other shipyards to construct. Meanwhile Steers himself had become a shipbuilder. So he both designed and built the *Adriatic,* the fifth of the Collins fleet. She was 345 feet long, of 50 foot beam, bark-rigged, side-wheeled—and, says Marvin, "the noblest of all wooden steamships [to date]." She had barely made her initial crossing, fulfilling completely her owners' and builders' expectations, when the next piece of ill luck hit Collins and American shipping: slavery, disunion, and war.

Back in 1847—after a considerable dispute—all parties had united in backing the subsidy mail protection for the steamship lines. The policy was initiated by the Southern Democratic leaders. A Democratic President enforced it. The North and the South favored it, though the interior offered some opposition.

But now things were reversed. Much of the North and interior was for subsidy. The South opposed it! The tenor of the South's argument was: The shipping interests are all in the North and East. Subsidized mail steamers all sail from northern ports (save one line running from Charleston to the West Indies). The entire country, said the Southerners (who had probably just listened to some hosanna-ing, crusading Northerners inveigh against their section because of slavery) contributed to the great shipping enterprise; and who profited by it? The North and down East! Some Northern writers, looking back, say that the Southerners were afraid that these great new ships, built in the North, owned in the North, might be used against them—when and if civil war came.

They would be a formidable addition to Yankee seapower! Well, I wouldn't know about that. I question it, for there were still some Southerners who were for the subsidies. The favoring element was small, however. The great majority, joined by the agricultural West, swayed the Congressional mood when, on that day in May, 1855, it voted for "abolishing the present ocean steam services."

That meant the end of ship subsidies for Ed Collins—the end of mail contracts—and was the final big blow to the Collins enterprises.

The ROBERT E. LEE
BLOCKADE RUNNER LENGTH 350 FEET
BEAM 31 FEET TONNAGE 2000

18. Paisley Shawls
and Blockade Runners

IN HER old age, my maternal grandmother McCain—of the Georgia McCain's if you please!—used to wear a soft, vividly colored Paisley shawl. As a child I wondered about that shawl. Never have I seen another like it—so soft, so richly colorful, and yet so evidently old.

"Where'd you get that shawl, Grandma?" I once asked her. She was then well into her eighties, but she could still blush. Her cheeks took on a slightly pinkish hue.

"Addie, my dear," she answered, "an old admirer of mine gave it to me." Then, sighing, she went on quickly, "No, my dear, *not* your grandfather. It was long before I met him. This shawl, I would have you know, ran the blockade into Savannah the last year of the War." What Grandma actually said was,

"The last yeah of the Waw." There was only one waw for Grandma—that was the Waw of the 1860's.

"I came mighty near not getting this shawl," Grandma continued reminiscently. "His ship barely made port. She was the *Flamingo,* and her captain was my dear friend. Ah, that was long ago. . . ."

Well, of course, I was glad to know about Grandma's boy friend. But what interested me most in the episode was that a ship was able to slip into port through the Federal blockading cordon. That started me thinking about the blockade runners and wondering what distinctive qualities they possessed that enabled them, even down to the last weeks of the war, to continue to carry on the thriving commerce between England and the Southern ports which, I soon discovered, they did—all the while figuratively thumbing their noses to the Federal blockading ships. In the course of my ship reading I had come across items about the blockade runners. Our school histories told how, during the War of the States, the North blockaded every Southern port with cordons of Navy ships, denying vessels of other nations, as well as of the Confederacy, both entry and departure. With her means of supply from the interior and from the sea shut off, the South resorted to the only course left open to her—privateering and blockade running.

The North protested, vocally and vehemently. "You can't use privateers! It's forbidden by International Law!"

"Rats!" the Southerners rejoined. "Remember the Revolution and 1812? Didn't our good Yankee privateers roam the seas destroying British commerce? If it was good then, its good now! . . . International Law, he says! You Yankees have shut up our ports and that's illegal under International Law, because only ports of a belligerent can be blockaded. You won't recognize the Confederacy as a belligerent. You say we're nothing but states in insurrection to be brought back by force and punished. And yet you keep your damned old ships out there on the coast, shutting off our trade!"

To that the North had no reply. But she did have the ships necessary to do the blockading—and that was what counted.

Not all the North, however, agreed with "Mr. Seward's blockade."

Commenting on the situation in April, 1861, the New York *Herald* stated, "No Government blockades its own ports. Moreover it cannot legally and commercially prevent the ships of other nations from entering its ports while it is at peace with those other nations. . . ." But the *Herald* was a lone voice crying in the wilderness.

So the South went right ahead. She placed her experienced naval officers in command of daring privateers. Luckily she had a high-class diplomatic representative in London—an officer of the old Navy who was now a commodore under the new flag—James B. Bullock. (Bullock's daughter had married into an important New York family and had a small son who was someday to make an impress on the nation's history which would possibly have made his granddad proud of him. The lad's name was Theodore Roosevelt.)

The South had need for speed! Bullock, working feverishly, arranged in England to have some fast steam sloops and frigates built. This he did under the very eyes of the protesting Charles Francis Adams, U.S. Minister in London. You probably recall having heard of these first ships—*Sumter, Florida, Shenandoah,* and the renowned *Alabama*—all steamships with auxiliary sails. Each rolled up an astounding total of captures on the high seas which intimidated the North and sadly restricted her commerce.

Ironically, however (as it turned out), these rich captures aided the South very little. Not many of the captured cargoes reached her hungry population. There was then no way to bring captured prizes into Confederate ports. The growling dogs of the blockade effectively saw to that. When they could, the privateer captains would use what they needed on board and sell the rest for gold. Most nations, however, feared to buy captured prize goods from the Confederacy. The United States might not approve!

Some way must be found, the Southerners well knew, to pierce that closely linked chain of ships hovering off their ports. How? Bullock and the other Confederate commissioners went into a huddle and came up with the answer—*runners!* Ships that would sacrifice almost every other virtue—cargo space, size, a large degree of safety—to speed! In recent years we have heard the expression (applied to our own wartime shipbuilding supply efforts), "a bridge of ships."

This is what the Southerners planned, though in a small way—enough ships to keep cargoes coming in and cotton moving out despite the losses which must inevitably occur. Through skillful arguments and diplomatic representations Bullock sold the British in Glasgow on the idea that they were to build the ships. The Confederacy had no shipbuilding plants of its own.

It was in the month of April, 1861—the war had hardly got under way—that Lincoln established the first blockade. It covered the ports of South Carolina, Georgia, Alabama, Florida, Mississippi, Louisiana, and Texas. Ten days later he gathered the ports of North Carolina and Virginia likewise into his net. Hardly was the ink dry on the Proclamation of Blockade than Bullock began to get definite action. He used at first such existing vessels as he could lay his hands on. Then he planned for new ships specially and admirably adapted to the service.

Since they must of necessity be very light-draft vessels, the full transatlantic voyage—between England and the southern ports of the Confederacy—would be too great a hazard to undertake. Old Navy man that he was, Bullock well knew the rough Atlantic would have little mercy on the kind of ships he must use. But fortunately England possessed some colonies on our side of the Atlantic—Bermuda and the Bahamas. Fine! The plan thus adopted was: British ships would bring the needed cargoes of supplies to St. George and to Nassau. There the runners would pick up the cargoes—and it was Ho! for Wilmington or Charleston or Savannah—as inconspicuously as possible.

Outbound ships, carrying cotton, the South's only product, would simply reverse the process: Confederacy to the islands by runners; from the islands to Britain by big ship. The Confederacy depended largely upon its printing presses for money. However, as is now well known, it did have a small treasure in gold coin and bullion (a few millions) for just such needs as this. . . .

You could build a good runner, the South soon found, for $150,000: average length, 300 to 350 feet; draft, 7 to 8 feet; tonnage, 1,000 to 1,500. Many of the earliest ships used soon went out of service, were wrecked or captured. They had not been designed for the service; they were makeshifts. The shipyards of Scotland then turned out new vessels built especially for blockade running.

So from the shipyards on the Clyde and the Tees came ships that, for speed, literally left behind anything that had ever tied up at American ports. They were a unique fleet among America's ships.

America was even then proudly vaunting its fine clipper ships and the Collins Line had only recently gone out of service. Fast and sharp and slender, they undoubtedly were up to that time the fastest American ships afloat. But the Blockade Runners! . . .

Most of them had side wheels—very necessary adjuncts too! They served as stabilizing and balancing factors, keeping the ships on an even keel. Otherwise, because of their great slenderness, the ships might have toppled over. Every ship, of course, had auxiliary sails. The typical blockade runner lay low in the water (the average runners as finally developed had only six or seven feet freeboard). Painted a dull, inconspicuous gray—the first American use of camouflage—the runner also had a pair of telescoping smokestacks. These would close together in a matter of minutes so that even the tinest wisp of smoke from the burning anthracite coal could hardly be discerned. The runners had two masts—usually with little rigging—only enough to support a little sail if it should become necessary to augment the engines. At night she carried no lights above the deck. She carried some live chickens for use in the galley (as all ships did in those days), but no roosters! A cock crow from the darkness would be sure to give away her presence to some waiting Yankee ship!

Among the early runners was the *Emily of London*. She had excellent passenger accommodations as well as a fair-sized freight hold, and was a favorite for conveying Confederate commissioners, envoys, and other V.I.P.'s back and forth. The *Ella* had propellers—one of the few. The *Georgiana McCain* (no kin of Grandma's) was of Glasgow nomenclature—a sidewheeler, and a fairly good one. Then there were the *Wild Dayrell* and the *Phantom;* and the *Fanny & Jenny* (one ship despite the double name), which was speedy and dependable. All she asked was a dark night, a dependable pilot on board, a hold full of cargo—and away she'd go! The open sea between our coast and Bermuda was no problem. The South had plenty of good navigators among its naval personnel. Many of these they released from the Navy for blockade-running duty, to pilot the runners in and out.

The real tug-of-war came when the runners had to cross the two lines of blockading ships—within only a few miles of the home port—the Cape Fear at Wilmington, the Savannah River at Savannah, the twin rivers at Charleston.

No ordinary pilots would undertake running through this blockade even if permitted. It remained for those who were at home in those waters—who knew each secluded bayou, each hidden inland passage behind sandy islands, every forgotten and well-nigh filled-in old mouth of the rivers through which no big ship would dare to fight her way, but which gave easy going for the light-draft runners.

These earlier blockade runners I name—while they differed in appearance and architecturally—all had one thing in common. They each came to a grievous end, casualties—victims of Federal gunfire or of beaching to escape northern ships. You see, when attacked and fired on, the runners could, because of their shallow draft, run spang into shore and pile up their bones on the beach if the worst came. Their crews usually escaped. . . . For years after the war, it is said, coastwise and incoming foreign ships to Southern ports used the stark rusting remains of many an old blockade runner as a shore mark to steer by and avoid.

A demand next arose for the type of vessel constructed specifically to elude Yankee ships. It was in response to this demand that the records of the American Merchant Marine added one other type of vessel to its calendar of ships—packet, clipper, liner, etc. This strange and long-forgotten type was the blockade runner. She stands out distinct and different from every other ship that has served our ports. She adds a colorful off-the-track chapter to the nation's maritime epic.

Over in Glasgow, some forgotten shipbuilding genius—I don't know who—excitedly said, "We've got the very type of vessel those Americas need right here!" And pointed out his office window. Out there on the Clyde River, steamers went riding past or lay tied up at the Glasgow docks. And so it was the Clyde River steamer became the accepted model for running blockades.

She had what it took—a long, sharp nose of almost de Bergerac proportions (save that it tapered to a razorlike edge); a wily look; and she was rakish, too, her masts and funnels and bowsprit slanting delightfully. And for slenderness! Friend, in comparison to the Clyde-type blockade runner of 1864 and

1865, the average extreme Baltimore clipper was a fat and waddling dowager!

The runners stand alone in the history of American ships, of ships that have served America—a marine architectural phenomenon. The South had more than a hundred of them plying in and out of her ports in those last months of the war. The North raged; as well try to stop the pompano, fresh up from tropical waters, as the fast little runners.

So it was the Clyde River steamer which modeled the blockade runner, but an improved type of Clyde River steamer: more strongly built, more powerful. Two at least, possibly others, had iron hulls—the *Robert E. Lee* and the *Kate*. Both proved high-stepping gals—which was what they were intended for. *Kate* ran afoul of a Federal gunboat, took a few solid shells in her hull, and tried to keep headed homeward. But another Federal ship hove in sight over the horizon; and defensively *Kate* headed straight to shore, piling up her valuable cargo and herself on the beach. A *Kate II* soon took her place.

When the "bird" ships steamed into Wilmington and Charleston late in 1863—*Falcon, Flamingo, Condor, Ptarmigan, Vulture*—the Confederates thought they had a fleet of winners.

Construction posed a problem to the Confederates no less than to the British shipbuilders. To be fast, the ships had to be attenuated—slender as a willowly debutante, breadth a fractional dimension of the length. Yet how to build them slender and at the same time roomy enough to carry sufficient cargo?

In these five ships with the bird names, the builders came nearer, perhaps, to reaching their objective than at any other time. They kept the hulls slender, built the holds roomier, but increased the furnace draft in the engines by adding a third funnel (smokestack) to each, thus giving America her first three-funnel steamships.

There was a *Banshee*, too—the *Banshee*, with her 214-foot length of hull and only twenty feet of beam; with her tall poles and skimpy sail; with a crow's-nest lookout high up. For every ship he sighted and called, the man on watch received an extra dollar. But woe to him if he failed to spot a sail and a sailor on deck saw it first! In that case the lookout had five dollars deducted from his pay!

Aboard the *Herald* on one of its runs from Carolina to Bermuda, Commodore Matthew Fontaine Maury rode as a passenger, his presence largely unknown; he was on an important diplomatic mission for President Davis. Maury—his fame, as is well known, rests on his charting of the seas and oceanographic work for the Federal Government—had resigned his commission in 1861 to go with his state into the Confederacy. Richmond, realizing his ability and quality, sent him on many overseas missions for the Southern Navy.

On this trip the *Herald,* plowing the blue South Atlantic waters, missed her course, but her arrogant captain would not admit it.

"Why, you fool!" one of his friends told him. "Missing your course when you've got the world's finest navigator on board! Why not ask the Commodore to help you?" Six days the *Herald* had been plowing her way—ordinarily the run could be made to Bermuda in less than forty-eight hours—and land nowhere in sight. Someone at last told Maury.

"Bring me the sextant," Maury told his son, who accompanied him. To the captain he ordered quietly, "Slow your course. Wait."

The *Herald* drifted. Lying flat on his back on deck, the Commodore began his observations and kept them up for an hour or more, from various points, recording them as he proceeded.

"Here," he finally told the captain, handing him the course he had charted. "Steer this course at fourteen knots and you'll be in St. George by two A.M."

The captain heaved a sigh of relief, but it was a grudging sigh. He did not take much stock in these "scientific fellows," he muttered.

No one on board slept that night. The *Herald's* paddles sloshed the waves behind her as she rode through the night on the course indicated. One o'clock came—passed. Two o'clock came—passed. At 2:10 some one on board (it may have been the captain) grunted, "We'll be headed for Yankee prisons instead of Bermuda—too damn much science on board this ship!"

But just then the lookout up in the crow's-nest shouted, "Light ho!"

Maury's reputation was justified. Within an hour the *Herald* steamed into St. George harbor.

The Confederacy lived off the blockade runners during the final fearful months of its life. It might have continued to exist longer had not the blockade-running business—a large percentage of it—got into the hands of speculators. Besides paying enormous wages to captains, the Confederacy agreed to let the captains use a portion of the cargo space to bring in goods of their own—luxuries such as wines, perfumes, silks, satins (yes, and Paisley shawls!) for which only the illegal rich in the South had money to pay. A black market of blockade runners' goods flourished in the South while the things actually needed by armies and loyal Southern civilians were neglected.

Only when the last Southern port had fallen to Yankee arms, when Richmond lay in ruins, when out on the seas only a few raiders remained flying the Stars and Bars (because there was no one to notify them that peace terms had been signed)—only then did the blockade runners (those that escaped) steam away to foreign ports to take up peacetime pursuits.

But they had justified their existence. If you don't believe that, you ought to have asked Grandma.

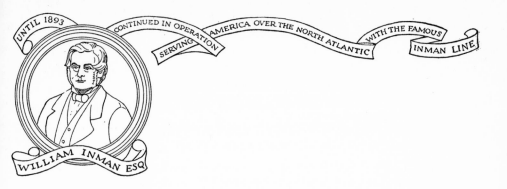

19. *Valiant and Forgotten Liners*

THE record against Edward Collins, by the late 1850's, had
read this way:

> *Arctic,* lost with 322 drowned.
> *Pacific,* lost with 186 drowned.
> His own wife and two children drowned.
> Mail subsidy, which had formed the basis of his ability
> to operate a potentially profitable and elaborate line of
> ships, suddenly withdrawn by a bull-headed Congress.

The loss of two ships—even two fine ships such as the *Arctic*
and *Pacific*—would not have shaken the general public's confidence in Edward Collins, so firmly had he established his
reputation in the American mind. The American public has
an inherent common sense. It trusted Collins—knew that the
loss of these ships resulted from acts of nature and was in no
way attributable to negligence on his part or on the part of the
officers and crews he employed.

"Why, look at the matter logically," they reasoned. "England
has lost ships. What about that sunk British liner, *President?*
And the *Isis,* sunk off Bermuda in 1842? *Tweed* killed on the
reefs of Yucatán in 1847? *Solway,* wrecked off Curruna in 1843.
The *Forth, Medina, Acteon*—all British steamships. All sub-

sidized. All sunk, with greater or fewer casualties. But Britain didn't stop subsidizing their owners on that account, did she? Lords and Commons both upheld the principle."

British steamshipping, growing with the years, had been marching right along with its iron-hulled ships, and American shipping, with Government subsidies to Collins withdrawn, fell by the wayside. Such few ships as were built in America had wooden hulls, and that has proved—in the light of the years —a terrific mistake.

Many Americans meanwhile protested Congress's action.

"My own belief is that the policy of England in subsidizing lines of steamships to various parts of the world has given her a prestige which is almost unsuperable." So remarks a hard-headed New York businessman by the name of A. A. Low, father of one of that city's great mayors, in 1860.

"Subsidies," Low added, "should be given as an inducement; and these subsidies, while they would cost the Government something in the beginning, would cost the Government nothing in the end."

Winthrop Marvin comments that it is a pity the War of the States came along just at this time to put an additional fearful crimp in our steam merchant marine. Yes, I think we all agree with him on that. It's a pity the war came at all. But come it did, and it played hob with our merchant ships—what was left of them. Our tonnage was declining fast. In 1856 American merchant shipping began to fall off—from 115,000 tons in 1855 to 89,000 tons in 1856, to 86,000 tons in 1857, to 78,000 tons in 1858.

All this, mark you, was before the war started—and was the result of the withdrawal of subsidies. What that action did not destroy, the war (when it came in 1861) did.

Congress, however, said in effect, "Cheer up boys! We'll pay you the regular postal rates for carrying the mail."

But it didn't work.

*   *   *

The above hiatus represents the War of the 1860's—War of the States, the Rebellion, the Civil War—whatever you choose to call it. It forms no part of my yarn since it was a time of merchant-ship destruction rather than merchant-ship building. A time when, in the North, just about everything that could float and had an engine was requisitioned into the service as a blockading ship or as a navy auxiliary. And, as I have mentioned, the clippers which ventured forth were frequently destroyed by Confederate privateers.

In the South, the Confederates also seized and reconverted everything that floated. Tugboats, river steamers, excursion boats, freighters, a few ocean-going passenger ships, coasters, and sailing vessels—all became fighting ships or auxiliaries. But the total number was small.

The only new merchant ship type to evolve from that struggle was the sharp-nosed blockade runner discussed in the last chapter.

Therefore, we pass over the war and emphasize only that what the withdrawal of the subsidy began, the war completed—the destruction of our merchant marine, both passenger and freight.

But Americans have a way of rebounding from discouragement and defeat. Hardly had the guns ceased booming and the smoke of battle cleared when some Boston merchants, well known, well thought of, and well heeled, decided to inaugurate a passenger steamship line to England.

"If we can't get subsidies, we'll go it alone!" said these residents of New England, stronghold of free enterprise. "There's business to be had, both passenger and freight. Let's go after it!"

This company's two ships were ready by 1867—the *Ontario* and the *Erie*. Good American names, both, and built at the famous old town of Newburyport! They had wooden hulls, like all other American merchant ships. Why in the name of heaven didn't America fall in line with the modern shipbuilding practice of England and other countries and build ships with iron hulls? One finds it hard to understand such a lack of foresight.

Iron mining had begun in Mesabi in 1856. Furnaces and forges were going all over the States. Already the Navy had at least one iron ship—the *Michigan*—a picturesque little side-wheeler with auxiliary sails and guns which never were used. She was built in 1842 to defend us (God save the mark!) from Canada! The *Michigan* had a charcoal-iron hull—a hull so tough that until about six years ago (as I write this) she was serving as an excursion boat out of Presque Isle Park in Erie, Pennsylvania, under the name of *Wolverine*. Mother once took me for a ride on her, years ago. . . .

But no, America, the home of progress, fell short in the matter of steamship building material. She still clung to her wooden hulls.

Now to get back to the *Ontario* of Boston. She was 350 feet long, 44 feet in the beam, 3,000 tons—a fairly large ship for the 1860's. She had an innovation, too—five transverse watertight compartments and bulkheads. This is a safety precaution all modern ships boast today—and a great saver of life it has proved, too!

Ontario steamed bravely out of Boston harbor with the good wishes and prayers of the community. She made a pretty good trip too! Twelve days en route wasn't bad, though far from a record. She was a full-rigged sailing ship and had also a powerful pair of engines.

"She aroused much interest and admiration in Liverpool," wrote a newspaperman of that day, "because of her symmetrical hull and powerful machinery."

American ships always *have* been the envy of Englishmen, say what they will to the contrary!

We have no record of *Ontario's* passenger list or her freight consignments. She made a few voyages. But soon the company announced that the terrific overhead—no less than the actual cost of the mere sustenance of the ship and crew—proved too much for the firm's effort. They found themselves "financially embarrassed." Therefore, before *Ontario's* sister ship *Erie* had even felt the salt waves beneath her keel, the company sold both ships for just about half of the $1,500,000 the two had cost, and folded up.

A Philadelphia company had meanwhile popped up in 1866. The stockholders had a shrewd idea.

"We'd like to give our shipbuilding business to an American yard," they explained apologetically, "but hang it, the cost is prohibitive! Besides, the expense to officer and man the ships over here at home would be beyond our power to meet."

So what do they do? They send a representative to Belgium to make a deal with some businessmen in Antwerp. There they organize a Belgian company to build and own their ships. They take in the Belgians as stockholders, retaining for themselves, however, the major slice of the stock to indicate their unswerving faith in the enterprise. They maintain an office in Antwerp, with Belgian directors in charge. Next they hire Belgian employees and doubtless crews of Norwegian and Dutch seamen. . . .

To the astonishment of their fellow countrymen, these Americans even wangled a neat little subsidy from the Belgian Government—$100,000 for ten years with wharfage and perquisites amounting to an additional $30,000—and merrily embarked (as one may very well say) on their venture. This line, through several mutations, became the Red Star Line, which continued operations until 1935 between Antwerp, Southampton, and New York.

In Liverpool, one day in 1850, a young couple boarded the new Inman liner *City of Glasgow*, New York bound. They had steerage accommodations and, with other emigrants, entered the close and stuffy confines of those far-below-deck areas devoted to the "lower classes." Though poorly dressed, they didn't look like emigrants; rather they looked like once well-to-do folk dressed up as emigrants. Their fellow passengers looked at them curiously and wondered what bad luck had sent them out over the Atlantic in the steerage accommodations.

These two were Bill Inman, president of the Inman Line, and his wife Elizabeth. They were making this voyage to find out firsthand what steerage conditions were actually like, with a view to improving them.

Bill Inman was among the first Britishers to offer a real threat to the hitherto undisputed Cunard supremacy. He began his operations in 1850 with the *City of Glasgow* and *City of Pittsburgh,* challenging not only British Sam Cunard, but American Ed Collins, as well. Soon, however, it appeared that Inman had designs on a specific trade.

"Competition," said he, reiterating a truism which must have appeared first in our vernacular about then, "is the life of trade. Mr. Cunard and Mr. Collins are getting the cream of the high-class passenger business. I'm going after the steerage folks."

Hence Bill and Elizabeth Inman's trial trip.

Apparently he found out plenty. Reports come down to us, through books of that period, of what a fearful experience "poor passage" travel was on the ships of that day. Mr. Dickens, in his vivid way, gives us brief but graphic glimpses in *David Copperfield* and *Martin Chuzzlewit.* Ventilation was poor, indeed, far below decks. The portholes were few and far between. A tall man had to walk stoop-shouldered to avoid bumping his head on the deck above him. The space allotted to each passenger had the suggestion of a rabbit-warren congestion. The food—well I've never read anything to contradict the oft-repeated statement that steerage passengers got the leavings from the first- and (for all I know) the second-class tables, too.

Valiant and Forgotten Liners

Gone were the days when emigrant travel made it necessary for "poor passengers" to lay in supplies at the port of departure. But conditions, even on the new steamships which now plied back and forth across the Atlantic, were little better than before in this matter of food while aboard.

Getting back to Inman. Exactly what steps he took to improve steerage conditions, I have no way of knowing. But improve them he most certainly did. I like to believe that he added more portholes for better ventilation, gave steerage passengers better food. Beyond peradventure, he gave them more space. For example, take the *City of Glasgow*. She was altered shortly after Inman made his trip so that she could care for a larger emigrant trade. She was not a large ship, even then—227 feet long and "had the power of 350 horses." She could accommodate only 52 first-class and 85 second-class passengers. But she had room for 400 steerage passengers. Soon the reports spread and Inman's emigrant business mounted.

Through the years—indeed until 1893—Inman's Line continued in operation, serving America over the North Atlantic. All told, he built twenty-four ships, naming each after a large city and using the *City of* —— form of nomenclature. Apparently he wanted to win the good will of America and showed his partiality for American cities in the names of his ships. Besides, there was plenty of American capital invested in his line. Some of his ships were: *City of Pittsburgh, City of Washington, City of Baltimore,* three *City of New York's* (successively, not simultaneously; one in 1861, one in 1865, and one in 1888). There were also the *City of Brooklyn,* the *City of Chester,* and the *City of Chicago.*

Next entered Stephen Barker Guion, American-born but long-time resident of England. Guion had worked on a windjammer in 1851 and was no stranger, it is said, to the steerage of current steamships. He had accumulated some capital and, with a Britisher named Williams, formed a partnership in 1856 and began building a couple of iron steamships at a yard on the banks of the Tyne. They started running in the New York and Liverpool trade. First there was the *Manhattan,* followed within a few months by the *Minnesota.* Guion never forgot his American birthright! His next ships were the *Nevada* and *Idaho.* In 1870 the *Wyoming* and *Wisconsin* steamed into New York harbor.

The Guion Line lasted until 1890, its ships contributing to its reputation.

For example, the *Arizona* broke all speed records on the Atlantic in 1877. She was strong as well as fast. On one trip she ran bow-on into an iceberg off the Newfoundland banks and returned to port to tell the tale. Transverse bulkheads were the reason. Haltingly she crept into New York, her bow smashed to smithereens, without loss of life, cargo, or prestige.

Guion's business increased. "The line must be good," said Mr. and Mrs. Public, "if it has such strong ships."

The *Oregon* put out to sea in 1883. She, too, established a record, bettering the record of her sister ship *Arizona.*

Stephen Guion died in 1885. His ships passed to Cunard.

Here in America, the great Pennsylvania Rail Road system decided to extend its activities from land to sea in 1872: a logical thing to do. The Pennsy was hauling plenty of freight, and passengers by the hundred-thousand, in and out of its eastern terminal city, Philadelphia. Why not add a line of steamers as an extension to its land service?

The railroad planned to give all its export business to the ships of such a line and receive in return all their imports, both freight and passengers. More than that, the company officials determined that there would be lots of additional business, and planned to run the line with the same organizational efficiency with which they operated their railroad. Think of it! You could buy a ticket in Pittsburgh straight to Liverpool with only one change—at Philadelphia.

Valiant and Forgotten Liners

The new line called itself the American Steamship Company of Philadelphia. It operated four ships—*Pennsylvania, Indiana, Ohio,* and *Illinois.* Well adapted to the service, they were fast for those days, finely built, and luxuriously furnished. Did not President Grant himself, "with admirable patriotism" (see the current press notices) make the first lap of his world tour on the *Indiana* of this same line?

Philadelphia had made an occasion of Grant's departure, a holiday. Any ship's departure then was much more of an occasion than today; and when a great soldier was sailing on a fine American ship, that was really something to celebrate! Delaware Bay had never witnessed so gay a scene. The harbor was full of tugs, pleasure boats, excursion craft, and these, in turn, full of cheering, flag-waving people. The people were full of—well, skip it.

Out there in mid-current lay the great *Indiana* in all her mighty, shapely iron length, ship-dressed for the festive occasion. Tall masts, fore and aft, flew hundreds of streaming pennants. Huge cross-yards bore the furled sails. Giant funnel amidships belched smoke from Pennsylvania bituminous. Her propellers churned slowly in the bay's waters as she jockeyed with the current. Everyone felt that America once again was enjoying a burst of fame as a maritime nation! . . . .

The American Steamship Company continued to operate for several years. It received no subsidy, and asked for none. Its four iron ships bore the Stars and Stripes to many foreign ports and were just about the only American ships to enjoy that distinction. The railroad backing ensured a certain amount of business, and the ships themselves won more on their own merits.

The company rolled up an astounding record. In all the years of its operation, it lost not a ship, not a passenger, not a mailbag. The railroad's backing, it is said, proved the line's main prop; it was further bolstered by the absence of a competing North Atlantic line running out of Philadelphia, unlike the situation in New York and Boston.

But, after a time, the Pennsy decided once again to concentrate its attention on land transport, augmented only by its tugs and car floats at its port cities. The good ship *Indiana* and her three sisters hauled down the American ensign. Up went— you'll never believe it!—the British flag. Oh yes, John Bull was on hand for any desirable merchant-marine bargains to be had, and when these four fine American ships were put up for sale, the International Navigation Company of London—it controlled Bill Inman's line and the Red Star Line running to Antwerp—snapped them up.

Ship men still talk about these four American liners. Many authorities claim they were among the "most graceful, elegant and commodious" ever to ply the North Atlantic.

America was sending her sailing ships to the Orient as late as the seventies and eighties,—a new type of ship, for the most part, known as the "medium clipper." Many a good New England shipowner was still making money out of them. But even in the decaying period of sail, America was not long to enjoy a profitable supremacy. Early in the 1870's Great Britain opened the Suez Canal. At once the route for voyages between the Atlantic ports and the far East was cut to far less than half. Steamships, however, received the bulk of the benefit. The heavily subsidized Peninsular & Oriental Company now began building up its already sizable fleet into the mightiest merchant-ship corporation the world had ever seen. Ere long these steamers had cut the life out of what remained of the American sail-ship trade with the Orient.

Out on the West Coast, in the meantime, the Pacific Mail Company, which had been operating wooden steamships to Japan and China, went modern. In the yard of John Roach of Chester, Pennsylvania, on the Delaware River, this company built two fine big iron ships, *City of Pekin* and *City of Tokyo*

—5,000-tonners, each more than 400 feet long. America did have a few, a very few, shipyards which knew how to turn out iron vessels with competent steam engines. There was Cramp of Philadelphia, Roach of Chester, Harlan & Hollingsworth of Wilmington.

And Lord, where are they all now?

THE CITY OF NEW YORK *FIRST TWIN SCREW STEAMER*

20. *Transition and Increasing Ship Luxury*

SINCE the days of E. K. Collins, comfort and luxury on an increasing scale have marked the progress of ocean-ship building. Long ago Collins pointed the way, set the example. He gave his passengers the best that could be had in the way of luxury, as luxury was known in his day and time, and devil take the expense!

Other ship operators soon took leaves from the Collins book; and before long each and every passenger ship running in and out of American ports (and other world ports, too) had something to boast about—some added comfort, convenience, or gadget which aimed at making people more comfortable and sea travel pleasanter.

One of the best-informed men on this subject is Mr. Ralph Cropley,[1] assistant curator of the Museum at Seamen's Church

[1] Mr. Cropley has presented to the Smithsonian Institution in Washington his incomparable collection of steamship historical material. The authors acknowledge their indebtedness to him for much of the information set forth in this volume.

Institute, New York City. Sitting where he can look straight out the window across South Street to the ships and tugboats on East River, and within a few feet of a fine collection of ships models (some of them in glass cases eight feet long), Mr. Cropley spends his time now in writing about the one subject he loves more than all others—ships. He knows a great many interesting things about improvements in the ships of the ocean ferry.

He can tell you, for example:

1. That the *City of Tokyo,* running in the Pacific and Orient trade in the 1870's, was the first ocean vessel to have a flush toilet on board. Before that, all vessels, even the finest, had had the old-fashioned uncomfortable open-bottom variety. General Grant—whom we saw departing from Philadelphia aboard the *Indiana* on his world tour, returned via the Pacific route to San Francisco on board the *City of Tokyo*—and lost his false teeth via one of these new fangled "sanitary comforts." Mr. Cropley points out that history repeats itself. Did not President Wilson have somewhat the same experience on board the *Mayflower* on one of his crossings?

2. That the electric arc light found its way onto a ship in 1873 (use of the incandescent light had not yet come about). The *City of Berlin* was the first to use it. She was an Inman liner, not a particularly big ship, being only about 5,000 tons, though nearly 500 feet long. She also took great pride in her dining saloon amidships—the first ship to have it so placed in order to avoid excessive roll.

3. That the *City of Berlin* had a long and useful life. Launched in 1873, she ran until Inman went out of business in 1893. Whereupon the United States Government acquired her as a naval auxiliary ship and five years later used her to transport troops in the war with Spain. She had a new name by that time—*U.S.S. Meade.*

Once she was just about to cast off from an American port with a load of troops bound for the Philippines when fire broke out. She very nearly gave up the ghost. But the Navy thought it worth while to rebuild her, and until World War I she served as a training ship for young merchant seamen at Boston —a fitting and dignified close to a worthy life of service. She was a fast ship, as indicated in the next chapter, and once held the Atlantic speed trophy.

4. That the Cunarder *Lucania* was the first ship to use wireless communication. (A sister ship to the *Campania*, *Lucania* entered the New York service in 1893, and kept up a 22-knot clip, voyage after voyage. She burned in 1909.)

5. That White Star's second *Oceanic* (17,000 tons, 689 feet long), built in 1899, had two claims to distinction. She was the first to exceed in length the renowned and much written-up *Great Eastern,* and she furthermore set a new fashion (and a very healthy and wholesome fashion it is, too!) of passengers taking long walks on decks, breathing in the sea air and building up king-size appetites: she had a 400-foot promenade deck. Who knows, she may also have started the fashion, as a result of this appetite building, of serving superlative food while at sea. What became of *Oceanic II?* She was stranded on Foula Island in 1914—a total wreck.

6. That the *Homeric* (built, 1914—34,000 tons), another White Star lady, was the first to have hot-and-cold running baths in every first-class stateroom. She was the last of the big coal burners. The age of petroleum was dawning. In her late years, she was converted to burning oil as fuel.

7. That the Cunard's *Carinthia,* built in 1925, a 20,000-tonner, was the first to put hot-and-cold water in *second-class* staterooms!

8. That the great Italian liner *Rex,* built in 1932, went one step further. She provided hot-and-cold water facilities in third-class staterooms. She also had a built-in outdoor swimming pool—the first. She was a noble and competent old gal, the *Rex.* In 1944, she was sunk tragically while in service of the Central Powers in World War II, by a British torpedo plane.

And for a long time thereafter, she lay on her side in shallow water near Trieste, a pathetic part of her hull showing.

9. That the Holland-American *Nieuw Amsterdam* was the first to have modern flushing toilets in all second-class staterooms.

Now let's glance at a few more outstanding ships. Go back to 1889. The Hamburg-American Line launched its mighty *Columbia,* a British-built ship of 7,300 tons. She could do 18 knots and had three masts and two funnels. Spain bought her and used her against us in 1898. *Columbia* had this distinction. She was the first ship to have her own electric generating plant aboard.

Stephen Guion's *Arizona,* an Atlantic speedster which survived storms and iceberg collisions, could do 17 knots. The United States bought her and made her into a transport; she served right royally through the war with Spain and the first world war. Carrying Marines was her specialty. Many a Leatherneck today, middle-aged or over, must recall her with loving gratitude. She had a kind of crank engine and a couple of attenuated funnels, four masts and two propellers. The scrapheap got her in 1926.

Another famous Inman liner, *City of Rome,* built in the early 1880's, attained fame as a great beauty because of the devil-may-care slant of her three funnels, and because of her four tall masts and her seventy-two-foot dining saloon—the longest any person of that day had ever cast eyes upon. When Inman retired from the scene, the Anchor Line of Glasgow bought the *City of Rome* and ran her in the Liverpool—New York trade. And yet despite her excellence, she never made money. Mr. Cropley explained that she burned too much coal, and her bunkers took up too much space which should have been used for pay-load. *City of Rome* had also another distinction. She was the last of the iron ships. Steel was coming into general use.

The great ship *City of New York* (whom Granddad, along with thousands of other men of her day, loved devotedly) was the first steel-hull ship in the Atlantic service. She was also the first to eliminate auxiliary sails completely as a means of propulsion and depend entirely upon her engines. (See her profile at the head of this chapter.)

Mentioning the *City of New York* brings us back to the subject of our own merchant marine, of which she became a great and shining part. We saw in an earlier chapter how the American Steamship Company, backed by the Pennsylvania Rail Road, operated for some years with marked success and later went out of business. By 1891 the mood of Congress had veered again and was such that ship men felt a reasonable subsidy might be had for carrying the mails.

These men pointed out that Presidents Washington, Adams, and Jefferson had all favored the general idea of encouraging ship operations with subsidies. They pointed back to the fine vessels which Collins had built and operated as mail carriers. That same year, therefore, Congress reverted to the subsidy idea and agreed to pay shipowners a graduated scale for the service, based on mileage. The rates ran from $66\frac{2}{3}$ cents to $4.00 per mile, according to the speed of the ship.

True, such a figure was far below what Great Britain and other European countries were paying the shipping lines with whom our ships had to compete. It would yield a top of only about $12,000 a trip. But at least that was something—something sure and tangible to proceed upon. To get such assistance, however, vessels had to be 8,000 tons or more.

Among the first to go after the new subsidy was a company that rose on the ashes of the old American Steamship Company. It was called simply the American Line and came into the picture in 1893 at a most auspicious moment.

It happened that just then Great Britain, feeling that Cunard and White Star were all the shipping facilities she needed in the North Atlantic, withdrew subsidies from Inman.

A poor return, certainly one would say, for his successful accomplishments! Inman had two ships then abuilding—two beauties—at a big shipyard in Glasgow. These were the sister ships *City of New York III* and *City of Paris II*.

In short order the American Line bought both these vessels and slapped them in the Liverpool-Southampton-New York trade. New, beautiful, fast, and eye-catching in their graceful lines, they became increasing favorites. *New York* was fast; *Paris,* a little faster.

They were each about 11,000 tons. Each had twin screw propellers, a clipper bow, a figurehead, and long bowsprit (for the simple reason that Inman loved these relics of the past). *New York,* however, had something that *Paris* lacked—a curved and domed dining saloon of large proportions on the upper deck, just forward of her funnels. Old-timers who rode aboard her said that the soft light filtering down through the stained glass ceiling imparted an almost ecclesiastical look to the ladies seated in the first cabin at the rows of long tables with heavily upholstered chairs, intricately carved.

These were the two fast sister ships with which the American Line opened the new sea ferry. Up from Washington came President Benjamin Harrison to raise the new house flag of the company: a great blue spread-eagle on a white background.

Both ships became money-makers. Next, the heads of the American Line proceeded with their future plans. In 1894 the Cramp shipyards in Philadelphia started building two additional ships for American. These were to be the largest ever constructed in the United States to that time, and those who saw them when they came from the yards in 1895 were ready to swear that not even the *New York* or the *Paris* could touch them.

Allan Nevins, professor of American history at Columbia, avers that they became objects of "great national pride."

Frock-coated Congressmen, snappy businessmen in Wall Street and executive offices, the sporting fraternity—these and

Americans in general held their heads higher because America once again had demonstrated her ability to rival any ships in the ocean ferry. Grover Cleveland came from the White House with his beautiful bride, nee Frances Folsom, who did the champagne-and-keel honors at the launching of the *St. Louis* while thousands cheered and the sturdy Grover made a few pungent and fittingly characteristic remarks approving the subsidy.

For thirty years the *St. Louis, St. Paul, Paris,* and *New York* performed finely on the great sea lanes between America, England, and France. None loved them better than the men who served as officers and members of their crews. There was Captain Felix Riesenberg, to name a shining example. Riesenberg, whose name is a legend in the merchant service, not only as a shipmaster but also as an author, came aboard the *St. Louis* in 1898 and remained for years. Long afterwards, writing nostalgically of the ship he loved best, he commented.

> One day in 1923 I walked through Erie Basin [in New York harbor] and saw the blackened rust streaked hull of the old American Liner—*St. Louis.* Her upper works were charred, her masts and funnels blistered; wear and tear and fire had assaulted the fine old hulk lying tied outside of a bank of useless ships. But an aura clung to her, her great proportions could not be effaced, short of complete destruction. The jaunty rake of masts and stacks, the line of her historic bridge and the long and graceful sweep of her shear were there. Once she was covered with spotless, flawless decks, holystoned to perfection during the watches of the night, and fine ladies and gentlemen walked the length of her or lounged luxuriously in deck chairs. . . .
>
> There was the binnacle of the great standard compass; in those days we steered magnetic. . . . A lump rose in my throat.
>
> Great sailormen commanded her, Randal, Jamison, Passow. . . . Herbert Hartley had her and ship and man made history. . . .
>
> In 1898, late in the fall, fresh from an overhaul at Cramps,

she steamed into the Empress Dock (Southampton) a shining beauty with "American" written on every line of her build. . . . She was typical of the great transatlantic service; smart with the relentless glitter of the keenest competition in the world. And the men who commanded her were the best. . . .

In those days she knew the caressing swish of silken petti-coats and the gay laughter of the elite. Her passenger lists were like the social registers of two continents. Fame and riches chose her because she was famous and swift and smart. The black funnels with the white band were the hallmark of West-ern Ocean [2] perfection, and her white house flag, with the blue spread-eagle, stood out stiff and proud from the main truck, as distinctive as a naval pennant. . . .

Her famous saloon, with its deep toned organ, was to hear the voices of celebrated men and women, to know the splendor of those fine dinners of the past sparkling with wit and wine and the flashing of jewels. Beauty chose her because she herself was beautiful and young.

Those were the days when languorous-looking pea-green ladies with large hips and ripe breasts, dressed only in semi-discreet poses, filled the walls in *bas-relief;* it was the height of decorative art. To the last these voluptuous sirens clung to the insides of the ancient liner. . . . She was a bully ship, the crack *St. Louis,* rescuer of the passengers and crew of the sinking *Veendam* in a day when Providence, and not the radio, brought her to the side of a foundering ship. The sea was full of mystery and romance then. . . . In those swift days the great liner carried the mail. And her sailing . . . signaled an event of the utmost importance. Gangways were then attended by a junior officer in frock coat and white gloves, and an old quarter-master and two youngsters in the Company uniform stood by to give the gangway an appropriate air. . . .

Fortunes were made on the old *St. Louis.* Hundreds of thou-sands of miles of ocean knew the course of her keel . . . great tragedies of the sea clung to her in the course of her voyage. But with it all she was a lucky ship.

2 Old mariners speak of the North Atlantic as the Western Ocean.

Year after year passed over her head and her new competitors of greater tonnage wrested from her the laurels she once wore. . . . Our fine old ship shuttled back and forth across the sea, year after year, a great-hearted old dame, eager and still beautiful, but forgotten. . . .

In 1917 her second youth began. . . . In her old age or in her perpetual youth she took on a jaunty air . . . the old girl stepped out across the war zones, thousands of soldiers crowded her sides, voyage after voyage, with Hartley on the bridge. . . . Hartley was her lawful, if not her first husband, and to him she was faithful through and through.

Lying in the mouth of the Mersy, quite still, so they say, with engines stopped, she suddenly forged ahead a hundred yards. Was she crazy or inspired? Her engines were started astern to stop her when lo—a German torpedo coursed close across her stern feathering white on its baffled errand of destruction. Again and again she justified the natal prayer of that fine lady who launched her on that memorable day in 1895. Had she cost a thousand times her building price, all would have been repaid over and over again. . . .

Glancing over marine reports in the spring of 1924, down the middle of a long column of vessels cleared . . . flamed the name *St. Louis*. . . . She had been towed from the basin to the Hudson and for many months lay at her North River pier; . . . from there towed to Staten Island. She was sold to Italian shipbreakers. Her last appearance in the ship news of the world was this:

Cleared May 20, 1924
St. Louis, Hart, Genoa, in tow of
Dutch Tug *Zwartee.* Philip Van Ommeren Corp.[3]

[3] Felix Riesenberg, *Vignetter of the Sea* (New York, Harcourt-Brace & Co., 1926).

21. *Speed Queens of the Atlantic*

B ACK in the 1920's I was in on my only steamship race. It was entirely unexpected, unpremeditated, and had no commercial significance or official status. Two great ships—the one I was traveling aboard and another of a rival line—encountered each other on the way home from England, and a little spurt of racing rivalry ensued. . . .

Since ocean shipping began, there have been (and probably there will continue to be) efforts to claim the speed crown as

Note: The speed records of the successive Atlantic Liners, as given in this volume, are based largely upon information presented by Eugene W. Smith, in his excellent little book *Trans-Atlantic Passenger Ships, Past and Present* (George H. Dean Company, Boston, Mass., 1947). There are doubtless many people who will differ as to the speed calculations, just as there are many other historians still debating the relative speed of clippers. Smith, however, is recognized by most shipping men I have talked to as an outstanding authority on the runs made by the various liners in the North Atlantic lanes.

the fastest ship in the North Atlantic service. These official contests, however, are quite different from the unheralded, chance racing such as I refer to above.

As I write (1955), there is no question about which is the fastest liner afloat. Every couple of weeks the mighty *United States*—America's newest merchant flagship—pulls away from her pier on North River and points her lovely Grecian nose toward England. Then her mighty propellers begin to pound out their rhythmic full-speed-ahead and she throws the salty miles easily behind her with each revolution of those gigantic blades.

The world's fastest steamship, *United States,* averages 31 knots per hour on her regular runs. She is known to have made 35 knots without effort. The full speed potential of the great ship, however, has never been disclosed. She is built to fill a war role, should that be necessary. She came from the Newport News Shipbuilding and Drydock Company, world's largest shipyard, and her designing engineer gave her not only the quality of speed, but a strength and modern beauty that does honor to the land of her creation. Her accomplishment has imparted a new lift and a mighty forward surge to the entire American merchant marine. Once again our nation has regained respect as a maritime power.

Speed queens of the Atlantic! . . . We read earlier how the great clippers raced to establish records. The coming of steam merely enhanced the zest and determination to achieve faster and ever faster time. Through the years since 1840, steamship companies have been launching and running faster and faster ships to gain the blue ribbon. "Of all forms of racing," commented Mark Twain long ago, "I prefer two mighty Mississippi Steamboats going it neck and neck up the river while on shore crowds cheer, drink, wager hundreds of thousands of dollars and salute the contestants with cannon at every port."

Such, for illustration, was the famous race of the *Robert E. Lee* and *Natchez* in 1870, from New Orleans to St. Louis—

something over 1,200 miles. (Grandfather saw that race, by the way. At least he saw the end of it. He was in St. Louis as a boy and climbed up a tree on the levee so as to catch the first glimpse of the approaching winner.)

Well, it would be hard to conceive of any two types of contest more thoroughly dissimilar (save that both were exciting experiences) than a steamboat race and a steamship race. And that brings me back for a moment to my one such experience mentioned above. We left England on board the Cunarder *Berengaria*—a mighty, spacious, potbellied old sister, formerly the *Imperator,* which England had taken as part reparation from Germany at the end of World War I. On the second day out of England we were lumbering sedately along at a fair rate of speed when one of my fellow passengers pointed and shouted, "Look yonder! There comes the *Olympic!*"

Everyone rushed to the rail, and sure enough! There, only a mile behind, came the pride of the White Star Line, *Olympic.* And living up to her name too! She was racing along, swift and dainty as a gull, and even to untrained eyes such as ours, the difference between the two ships was apparent. The *Olympic* had "racing lines"—sharpness of stem, length, and slenderness of hull. The *Berengaria,* aware of the rival's approach, quickened her pace: We could feel the tension mounting as within the mighty muscles of a giant.

Slowly the *Olympic* drew on. Slowly she came abreast of us. Slowly she passed us. I use that word *slowly* with intent. Both ships were so long, both of such speed, as to require a full hour for the *Olympic* to pull far enough ahead to compel the *Berengaria's* passengers to admit defeat.

Meantime, during the time that we were abreast, vociferous cheers bounded from ship to ship as partisans of each racer let off their steam of enthusiasm. We sighed with disappointment as the *Olympic* steamed off.

"Oh well," a man at my elbow remarked comfortingly, "the

Berengaria wasn't built for speed, but for capacity!" She certainly had that!

I imagine many steamship passengers have had the same kind of experience—a brief contest of speed with a rival ship. But these were not premeditated, official races.

Establishing an official record of fast time on the Atlantic, however, did have definite implications. The fastest ships usually got the lion's share of the passenger business as well as the most coveted mail contracts. Moreover, the contest of two rival ships was always flavored with the spice of international sportsmanship. Whenever a new contender announced that she would enter the lists to make a try for the Atlantic speed crown, the event was heralded far and wide and long in advance. In such cases there was no neck-and-neck racing such as the little spurt of speed which the *Olympic* staged for our benefit. Setting a record was a serious business. Captains, owners, and crew bent every effort toward bringing the ship to her port in less time than her rival.

The first steamship to establish a record crossing was, as we saw, the original Cunarder, *Britannia*. On her 14-day run (plus some hours), Liverpool to Boston, she made "a brief stop en route at Halifax" (of what duration we do not know). That happened in July, 1840. Then for the next decade Sam Cunard held all the tricks. The *Arcadia, Britannia's* sister of about the same tonnage and appearance, made it to Boston in 11 days, 14 hours. Winning the accolade meant little to *Arcadia,* however, since it was all in the family—no well organized outside competition. In 1849 Cunard sold *Arcadia* to the Federated German States, which made a warship out of her and renamed her—heaven save the mark!—the *Germania*.

Next, *Britannia* whirls in and betters *Arcadia's* time, making it to Boston in 10 days flat. Still not satisfied, Sam Cunard puts *Hibernia* on the run in 1847 and rolls up a record of 9 days, 1 hour, 30 minutes—Liverpool to Boston. . . .

Hibernia could do 11 knots—the fastest afloat on salt water

180

at that time. But Cunard, a great trade-in artist, poorly repaid her by selling her to the Spanish Government. Gallant and mistreated little side-paddler out of another era! Whatever became of you? On what forgotten coast did you cast up your worn-out carcass? In what unremembered seas did you go down to your doom? Or did you die battling for Spain, with your guns booming to the last? In those days, ships often came to violent ends. . . .

Cunard's next move was to put *Asia* in the trade. She at once snatched up the laurels which *Hibernia* had cast down, knocking off the watery miles from Liverpool to New York in 8 days, 17 hours.

"Cunard's raking in all the honors!" Sea-minded Americans swore loudly. "What's the use of trying to buck the British? We can't beat 'em!"

Ah, but wait! Here come those Collins liners in their impressive but all-too-brief burst of speed and beauty. In the matter of a year, Ed Collins's ships had clipped the time of all the Cunarders' runs. We have already told something of their speed record. Their individual time achievements are not available. But this we do know:

For five years the Collins ships held undisputed the speed trophy of the Atlantic. Then, as already recorded, tragedy struck. Collins lost his ships; civil war came; America lost her place in the maritime sun. And once more Sam Cunard, who had all along continued to follow his rather stodgy but effective policy, took over the supremacy of the North Atlantic.

Cunard's next ship, *Scotia*—last of the Cunard side-wheelers (built by Napier of Glasgow while our own North and South were slashing at each other's throats)—floated into the picture in 1862. She is said to have had more powerful engines than any paddle-wheeler ever built—4,000 indicated horsepower. Her run was from Queenstown to New York, and her time was less than 8 days, 4 hours. Twice in succession she bettered her own time.

In some of his preceding ships Cunard had embodied variations and improvements aimed at greater speed, safety, and passenger comfort. These he continued in later vessels. To illustrate: In *Etna* and *Jura,* two well-nigh forgotten little vessels running in other ocean lanes, he embodied several novelties which soon induced other shipowners to follow suit. Lawrence Babcock tells us in *Spanning the Atlantic:*

> Each of these two had a compass fitted up at the head of her mizzenmast, isolated from the magnetism of the iron hulls. These served as a check upon the variations which there were then no other way to correct. Each also had a "donkey engine"—a separate engine and boiler used as a sort of servant of all work. The donkey provided power to heat the cabins, to draw off bilgewater, to distill fresh water for use on board and—in case of emergency—to put out fires. *Etna* and *Jura* also had geared propelling machines—used for the first time in Cunard's ships—a novelty that would take hold fast.

From Babcock's description, their machinery must have been something wonderful to behold. Listen:

> The forward end of the propeller shaft was fitted with a large spur wheel with wooden teeth [*sic*] by which the slow speed used on paddle-wheelers was adapted to the screw propeller which made four or five times as many revolutions per minute.

Iron hulls and wooden cog wheels! That was really something! But *Scotia* was well built and for three years, 1863–1866, held the scepter as Atlantic's fastest. Meantime Cunard had come safely through the Crimean War. The Government took over many of his ships for transport service, but he maintained the New York–Queenstown–Liverpool run intact. His next contender was *Russia,* which left all her sister ships behind in 1867 when she clocked up the full run in 8 days 25 minutes.

Bill Inman, who did so much to improve steerage travel in his own ships, was running ships of his own on the New York lanes, and some good ones too. Up in Glasgow the firm of Todd and McGregor built Inman a 2,600-tonner, *City of Paris,* which outran Cunard's *Russia* in 1867. This first *City of Paris* seems to have had no other distinguishing qualifications, however. In 1869, a jealous sister of the Inman fleet, *City of Brussels*—some forty feet longer, "with many new elegancies of appointment"—made the same run from Queenstown in 7 days and 22 hours.

In 1872, the White Star Line put in its appearance. It was a propitious time to enter the shipping lists. America had by then largely turned her face from the coast and was further developing her wealthy inland empire, with its mines, its forests, its factories, its railroads. White Star entered the running with the *Oceanic.*

We who remember White Star liners of a later date—*Homeric, Olympic, Titanic*—find it hard to realize that the White Star sprang from such a crude beginning as the *Oceanic.* Her picture shows her to have been a rather tubby craft with both sails and steam engines—four tall masts pointing skyward, decks cluttered with cargo. But she was fairly long for those days and she foreshadowed the later custom of building most of the ship's cabins above the main deck. That provided more ventilation and general comfort. *Oceanic* lived to be a right old gal—until 1896. Then her owners retired her and the wreckers got her.

Another White Star liner, *Adriatic* (second steamship of the name) appeared in 1873. She had four masts, sails, and one funnel, showing that shipowners did not yet feel it safe to depend entirely upon engines.

Adriatic achieved a 7-day, 21-hour crossing—Liverpool to New York—and put past performances in the shade. But not for long. Up steams White Star's new *Baltic* the following year, cuts in on *Adriatic*'s time and cops the honors.

Now for two more years, 1875 and 1876, Inman's *City of Berlin* remained untouched for speed because of her 7-days,

18-hour record. She herself, however, shortened it later by 3 hours and some minutes.

White Star next countered with the *Germanic* in 1877. On her eastward run she outsped *City of Berlin* by about 15 minutes, only to be beaten by a sister White Star liner, *Britannic,* which made the run in 7 days, 12 hours, and 41 minutes. *Britannic* and *Germanic* were the first ships of as much as 5,000 gross tonnage and the first to have compound tandem-type engines which could develop 5,000 horsepower. Each ship could carry 220 first-class passengers and 900 third-class passengers.

So there we have the record of Atlantic racing through the late 1870's—Great Britain far in the lead with her Cunard, Inman, and White Star liners. About this time, Stephen Barker Guion slapped his new *Arizona* into the contest. Without apparently great effort she reduced the time to New York by 7 days, 6 hours in 1877. Next Guion's *Alaska* grabbed for the victor's wreath with a westward record (a much more difficult accomplishment than the eastward) of 6 days, 22½ hours. Guion put his new *Oregon* in the trade—the first ship to make as much as 17 knots per hour—with a 6-day, 16-hour record.

And so it went on down through the years: rivalry between America and England and rivalry between the ship men within the British Empire.

Meantime, from Germany, the *Elbe* of the new North German Lloyd showed herself a speedster from Continental ports to New York, although her exact figures are not available. After *Elbe,* Sam Cunard once again appeared in the picture with two fine new liners, *Umbria* and *Etruria.* We'll meet them again in the next chapter.

22. More Speed Records

S TEPHEN GUION ran into financial difficulties in the late 1870's when a partner in his steamship enterprise lost heavily in some outside investments and withdrew from the company. This happened while the *Oregon,* his biggest ship, was abuilding. Guion couldn't meet the remaining payments; subsequently and as a final disaster, the builders had to take her back in place of the defaulted payments.

"I'll buy her," announced Sam Cunard, "she's a good ship!" Sam was not a man to let so fine an opportunity slip by. That was one way of making sure the fast *Oregon* became no competitor of his. If you can't beat her, buy her—that was Cunard's motto.

So Cunard laid down 616,000 pounds for the *Oregon* and threw in two old ships, *Parthia* and *Batavia* to make up the balance. Then he set to work to alter the *Oregon.* He retained her four masts, which aided her 1,300 horsepower engines. She was a big girl—8,000 tons—and carried 342 first-class passengers, 92 "intermediate" (second-class, somewhat like cabin today?), and 100 steerage passengers. She acquired and retained her speed crown for three years—then bad luck!

On one March night she came bustling toward New York flying the Cunard house flag—gold lion rampant on a red field. Nearing Fire Island, Chief Officer Matthews and his lookout beheld a sudden bright white light off her port bow.

"There's the pilot boat," said Matthews very naturally. Only pilot boats carried white light; all other ships, red and green. But something was wrong! The intruder took no notice, apparently was off her course. The *Oregon* swung hard-a-port to avoid her, but it was no use. The intruder proved to be a big schooner which loomed suddenly out of the darkness, slammed into *Oregon's* side, and stove her in.

"Stop the engines!" Matthews ordered, and altered his course to render aid to the schooner, not realizing the extent of his own ship's injuries. Fatal unselfishness! The *Oregon*, though iron, had two death wounds in her hull—wounds "large enough, either of them, to render her transverse bulkheads ineffective," said a contemporary account.

"Lower the lifeboats!" shouted Captain Cottier, commanding the *Oregon*. The unloading began. The *Oregon* had 990 passengers aboard. Through some miracle, although she was settling fast, each and every one of them was brought safely to land by a number of nearby vessels which came in answer to the *Oregon's* distress rockets.

The last passenger to enter the lifeboats was a traveling salesman possessing apparently all the enterprise that traveling salesmen are supposed to have, for he was still gripping fast his sample cases!

Cunard suffered from *Oregon's* loss, but held on tight to his two famous racers—*Umbria* and *Etruria*. Both won speed reputations, reaching the 19-knot-per-hour peg. *Etruria* came over to New York in 6 days and 5 hours, went back in 6 days, 4 hours plus. Whereupon *Umbria*, just to show the stuff she was made of, equaled, though she did not better *Etruria's* figure.

These two Cunarders reached new heights of speed and luxury, and for many years retained their justly won fame.

But times change. Cunard is having trouble with his government. Those pesky mail subsidies! Suddenly Parliament ups and cuts them out. When Cunard's quick service and dependability begin at once to languish, Parliament hastily puts the subsidies back in force again.

Then an American ship enters the speed picture once again. In 1884, *America*, a 5,000-tonner of the short-lived National Line, snatches the crown from *Etruria*'s prow but immediately loses it and is turned over to the Italian Government, which makes her a war cruiser. For a brief period of time, *Umbria* once more takes over the championship.

In a later incarnation, *America* became a cruising yacht for the Royal House of Savoy. In 1925, forty years later, she finished her career on the scrap heap. The National Line by then had long been out of existence.

In the epic of the Atlantic sea lanes 1884 is an important year because it was then that the Compagnie Generale Trans-atlantique made its first bid for the speed trophy. The bid was a grand gesture—four fine sister ships, *La Champagne*, 6,724 tons; *La Bourgogne*, 7,303 tons; *La Bretagne*, 6,750 tons; *La Gasgogne*, 7,000 tons. All were products of French yards, and the fact that the company operating them has been running ships to American ports ever since testifies to the quality of French builders. The ships' class accommodations are interest-ing. Each carried 390 first-class passengers, only 65 second-class (cabin), and 690 third class. One cannot find their individual speed records, save that *Bourgogne* was the speediest, making 17 knots. All had sails and engines, and only one, *Bourgogne*, seems to have come to a bad end. She rammed a British sailing ship in 1898 in a tragedy that took the lives of 549 people.

There are many men alive today who recall the *City of New York* during her Inman days; many more remember her in her second version as *New York* when she ran in the American Line—a sort of revitalization of the moribund Pennsylvania Railroad–backed American Steamship Company.

The *City of New York* was a vessel of exquisite lines. Al-though following the custom of the day in having both sails and steam, Inman soon discarded the sails. She was one of the last, if not actually the last, passenger liner so built. *City of New York* and her sister ship *City of Paris* made about the same time from Liverpool to New York—5 days and 19 hours. On a subsequent run, the *City of New York* set to work and reduced her own time by more than an hour.

That was more than Sam Cunard could bear, and he decided to beat the *New York's* record. It took quite a while. From 1899 to 1905 the *New York's* record stood. Then the *Etruria,* fresh from a complete overhaul, polished, refurbished, and sleek as a tomcat, came slithering into New York from Queenstown, clipping 3 hours from the *New York's* record.

"Now," Cunard must have commented, *"that* will hold you for a while."

But there came another contender.

Hamburg-American Steamship Company made its bid in 1889 with four fine, though not large, ships—*Normannia, Fürst Bismarck, Columbia,* and *Auguste Victoria.* These were among the earliest three-funnel ships, ranging from 5,000 to 8,000 tons; and each was able to attain a speed of 17 knots. *Columbia* came over from Hamburg in 5 days and 19 hours—a very respectable figure, though it bettered no records.

The North German liner *Lahn* improved upon *Columbia* slightly.

Then *Columbia* improved her own time to 5 days and 16 hours—a top figure. In 1899 the *Deutschland* sped over from Le Havre in 5 days and 18 hours—a record from that port and for that distance. The *Deutschland* was a voracious consumer of fuel. She had fifty-five furnaces to heat her nine boilers; and her triple-expansion engines performed marvelously.

Successive slightly better runs were made by White Star's *Majestic* and *Teutonic.* The *Teutonic* steamed from Queenstown to Sandy Hook in something over 5 days and 16 hours. These ships had cost several million dollars each, carried passengers of all three classes, and both wound up on the scrap heap at about the time World War I began.

Cunard, watching and waiting, launched *Campania* in 1892; *Lucania,* in 1893. And both these proved champions, fighting each other for the crown. They were the first to have large funnels.

These Cunarders' fame was short-lived. For *Kaiser Wilhelm der Grosse,* a big four-stack job of 14,000 tons, built in a German yard in 1897, made a quick trip to America in 5 days and 15 hours. Following close in her track came the *Kronprinz Wilhelm,* which made it in 5 days, 11 hours.

The old century had closed. The turn of the century brought a monster of North German Lloyd, the *Kronprinzessin Cecile.* Her great dimensions were distinctly modern. From the top of her vast funnel to her keel she measured 131 feet. She lacked only 15 feet of being 700 feet long, and was 74 feet in the beam. In 1907 *Cecile* came over from Cherbourg to New York in 5 days and 11 hours.

"She can't top *Etruria's* time!" the Cunard partisans triumphantly roar. But on the next trip she does just that—making it back in 5 days and 8½ hours—thus snatching and holding the prize, and on a westward crossing too! . . .

But in the interim Cunard was nursing ambitious plans for a new ship. A ship that, even in those days of increasingly big liners, would set a mark for other shipbuilders to shoot at enviously. She came out of her builder's yard at Newcastle-on-Tyne in the fall of 1906—760 feet from her cutwater to her stern rail. Four huge funnels marched in a long, stately procession down her top deck.

Four gargantuan propellers sent her skimming through the seas at 26 knots an hour. Around her stem in letters three feet high you could read her name—*Mauretania.*

From another shipyard shortly afterwards came *Mauretania's* sister ship, the *Lusitania* of fragrant and pathetic memory.

Both these mighty Cunarders started at once to make records. *Mauretania* soon achieved 4 days, 17 hours plus on the westward crossing. *Lusitania* made it in 4 days, 11 hours plus. These records were made in 1909 and remained untouched for twenty years.

Then in 1929 a German contender, the *Bremen,* stepped into the leadership, making a new snatch at *Lusitania's* and *Mauretania's* records. *Bremen* was almost 900 feet long and was the first ship to cost as much as $20,000,000. Where, oh where, were the good old days when you could build a pretty good ship for a mere million ?

But the contest went on. Time: July 23, 1929. *Bremen* had a sister ship, *Europa,* born in the yards of Hamburg. Despite a fire which set back her completion and temporarily dampened her owners' hopes, she made a noble appearance—47,000 tons (slightly less than *Bremen*). On her eastward voyage she covered the 3,084 miles to her home port at more than 27 knots an hour—4 days and 17 hours flat.

Consider these ships' size, and remember that they were built a quarter of a century ago. They each had twelve steam turbines equaling 140,000 horsepower.

World War II found the *Bremen* in New York on one of her regular runs. To prevent seizure she made a break for it—her German owners wishing above all things to avoid capture by her enemies. Through the watchful British fleet she went gallantly. Turning her nose far to the north—where few passenger ships dare to venture—she skimmed along the coast of desolate Greenland, skirted the northern shores of Iceland, hugging both coasts as closely as safety permitted. She reached her German home port only to suffer bombing and fire from Allied planes. The Nazis scrapped her.

Europa? Through good luck she survived the war. America seized and used her as a troop ship to bring American soldiers home. The French fell heir to her as part reparation, and out of her created the magnificent *Liberté.* Despite a collision with a former Atlantic liner, *Paris, Liberté* survived, was restored, and you'll often see her today easing into her berth—Pier 88 North River.

In 1932 the Italians entered a racer in the Atlantic ferry—the large and beautiful *Rex,* well subsidized by Mussolini's government. The following year she set out to capture the trophy. From Gibraltar to Ambrose Light, 3,181 miles, she covered the sea leagues in 4 days, 13 hours, averaging 28.93 knots—truly an epic performance. She was a queenly vessel—with accommodations for 2,025 passengers and a crew of 800. Her funnels—she had three of them—reached 51 feet above the hurricane deck. While she was still being built, three Italian steamship companies merged—Lloyd-Sabuado, Cosulich, and the Navagazione Generale Italian Lines; by this consolidation *Rex* fell heir to a sister ship—a running mate—the *Conte di Savoia.* The *Conte* was the smaller of the two. She carried first-class, cabin, and third-class passengers and averaged over 27 knots.

But with such fine racing going on in the ocean ferry, could you expect Cunard to remain long in the background? Far from it! The founder of the line, Honest Sam, had long gone to his reward. But his company continued strong, vigorous, and jealous of its prestige, though today it admits the superior speed quality of our *United States.* By mid-1930's Cunard was building ships with a view to regaining the crown. . . . More of that presently.

Meantime, in the fall of 1932, the Saint-Nazaire shipyards produced a giantess of the French Line—the brave, beautiful, and ill-fated *Normandie.* One thing and another delayed her departure until 1935, and when, early in June of that year, she tied up in New York, she had broken all existing records—making the westward run in 4 days, 3 hours, 14 minutes. It is said that her speed caused such a great vibration that the captain was forced to slow down at night to permit the passengers to sleep. The Frenchmen paid $60,000,000 for her.

In writing of the *Normandie,* you cannot avoid superlatives.

She was the longest (1,029 feet)—the first ship to be longer than 1,000 feet. Her tonnage, 82,000, was far greater than anything at the time. Her masts reached 202 feet above the water line. Her main dining saloon was 380 feet long—1,000 diners could sit down together. She had a garage accommodating 100 cars, a theater seating 300 people, a chapel for religious services.

Remember that Ed Collins's ships had smokestacks (funnels) large enough in diameter for a man to walk through upright. The *Normandie's* huge funnels measured 165 feet in circumference. Elevators darted by the dozens between her decks. Several thousand passengers traveled comfortably aboard her, as did her crew of 1,950.

From 1935 until the United States entered World War II, the *Normandie* maintained her supremacy in the transatlantic ferry, and when the fighting got hot, prior to 1942, laid by safe in American ports. Pearl Harbor found her in New York, and the United States took her for a troop transport and began conditioning her to that end, renaming her *Lafayette*.

I never traveled on the *Normandie*. I wish I had. There was reputedly a grandeur and gesture about her equipment and service, an air of (to use an overworked expression) "gracious living," a Louis-XIV-Sun-King elaborateness which was a pleasure to experience in these modern times. Now, after a pathetically brief but efficient service, *Normandie's* chapter is writ; and her steel fabric—through the junk route—has been molded into other products. Who knows? Perhaps she became airplanes and bombs that returned to France and avenged the betrayal of her attackers, no less than her own defaulting Government within her gates. Let her memory rest.

I beheld her in her final phase on a visit to New York—a vast wallowing hulk lying on her side at a pier in North River in 1942.

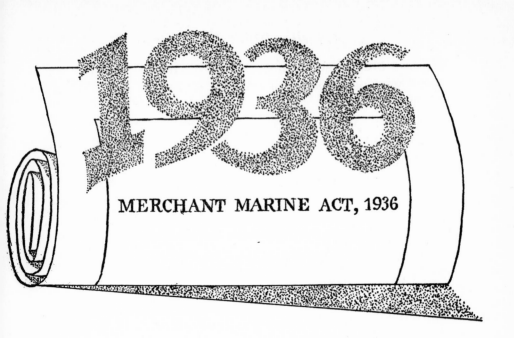

MERCHANT MARINE ACT, 1936

23. *New Lease on Life*

TO American ship men, 1936 stands out as a banner year. Something happened in 1936 that gave our merchant shipping, passenger and freight, the proverbial new lease on life, an undeniable shot in the arm. Congress passed the Merchant Marine Act, which placed a strong foundation under our national maritime industries and charted a sensible future course for them to steer.

It came not a day too soon. In fact, it was long, long overdue. We saw how shipping lines, from the first, encountered competition from foreign ships which they simply could not meet: the foreign companies had strong government subsidies, while our ships had none to speak of. We saw how Congress had indeed granted several more or less temporary subsidies in the form of mail-carrying contracts, and how these had at once stimulated new interest in the shipping business. But we also saw how even these, in time, had been withdrawn. There was nothing of permanence or stability in any of these arrangements.

Even if a concession was in force when a new shipping company started operating, there was no assurance that Congress would not withdraw it at any moment. Hence any company naturally hesitated to expand, to put on additional ships, to improve its services. And if those subsidies *were* withdrawn, pretty soon that line began inevitably to lose business to foreign competitors.

Heads of American shipping enterprises, therefore, found it easier to go into other lines of endeavor, leaving the passenger-carrying business on the ocean ferries to ships of other nations. Since the dawn of the Republic, foreign ships have been seeking our ports because we had our doors wide open and the welcome mat out.

In that period before 1936, what was true of the passenger trade likewise applied to the freight-carrying ships. Cargo vessels of American design, good though they undeniably were, were few in number compared to ships of foreign lands. There was indeed one period in the early 1900's when 90 per cent of all our import-export passenger and freight business moved in foreign ships.

Then World War I broke in 1914 and caught us with our defenses down, clear down. While that war was still confined to Europe, America suddenly and uncomfortably became aware of a vital fact; namely that if we were drawn into the fight, we'd have no merchant ships to move the munitions of war. Right then and there our nation began to plan for a merchant marine.

There was another reason for such planning. European ships of friendly nations, now engaged exclusively in the war effort, had to neglect their regular business. Moreover, German U-boats were sinking them by the score.

These two facts—the threat of impending war and the chance to take over cargoes which foreign ships could no longer carry —induced the building of a number of good ships at American yards as early as 1916. Then, when the guns commenced booming for us, we embarked upon a hurried and none-too-well-thought-out construction program (a "shipbuilding spree," one historian calls it) under the supervision of a new United Shipping Board.

To this day our accomplishment of creating in record time a fleet for the first world war is spoken of, by those who remember it, with deprecation of the methods employed but admiration for the end result. . . . We won't go into detail or the methods. It's part of our national epic, told many times.

The end result, however, was a fleet of about 2,400 ships of all kinds—cargo carriers and passenger vessels, steel, wooden, even a few sailing ships created to help out in the emergency. From the big Hog Island shipyards on the Delaware River, from Newport News, from New York, and from a hundred other yards (many of them emergency plants hastily put up) came almost daily the splashing of great hulls as they slid down the ways to their destined element and, as finished ships, went out to carry the men and cargoes of conflict and loads of food supplies in our united efforts to beat the Hun.

Beat him we did! And the emergency fleet was a prime factor in enabling us to do just that.

When peace came in 1918, the United States thus had a fleet of thousands of ships—cargo carriers and some suitable for passenger use. True, many were "jerry-built," hastily put together out of questionable material to meet the needs of the moment. But hard times came after the end of World War I. There was no shipping business to be had. Hence little demand for ships. Moreover, the Government's policy was shortsighted in the extreme.

Had the Shipping Board gone ahead and placed many of

195

these ships with various private shipping lines at whatever price they could get, the building of additional tonnage no doubt would have been stimulated and a merchant fleet grown up. Instead, the Shipping Board itself decided to operate some of these ships—an arresting illustration of "Government staying in business."

What about the rest of the huge war fleet—all those ships which had performed valiantly in the war or those which had been built too late for service and now were idle? The Shipping Board lashed them together in huge dead convoys, stuck them into coves and inlets of our inland rivers, and left them there to die.

I remember once coming down with an uncle to New York from Chicago on the Twentieth Century Limited. As we were nearing Peekskill, I caught sight of one of the "great still fleets" lying silently against the Hudson's shore and called Uncle's attention to it. He looked at them with eyes full of somber misgiving as we whirled past. (He too had the family love for ships.) He shook his head sadly. "There goes a billion dollars into the mudhole, Addie!" he said with a sigh.

The very speed of our train seemed to accentuate, by contrast, the *deadness* of that once active fleet. . . . There is nothing so pathetic to me as abandoned and lifeless ships.

From the waging of our first world war emerged an increased American interest in Europe—a stepped-up wish to see the countries over which our soldiers had fought. Servicemen wanted to take their wives and families back to revisit old battlefields and haunts they once had known in their initial expedition to save the world for democracy. Businessmen here found many of their commercial ties in Europe. It was then also that the first stirring of an international consciousness—a conviction that this nation no longer could live in isolation but had a stake in world affairs—began to awake here in us at home. Naturally, the net result was a need for more ships, good liners to carry these eager-eyed passengers.

Who met that need? Why, the European shipping companies. In a startlingly short time England, France—even Germany— were once more out of the woods and sending their big liners into American ports and finding plenty of passengers.

Now with such a patent need for ships, with such an evident desire on America's part to visit far lands, and with a big idle fleet on hand, one would think that America would have taken some concrete steps to get the lion's share of business. But no. To illustrate: In 1925, the tonnage that America launched was one-eighth of Great Britain's. Two years more, and the Shipping Board reported that for every ship built in America during the year just ended, the United Kingdom built forty-one ships. America apparently just wasn't interested. There wasn't enough business for American shipyards. The fine old yard of William Cramp & Son—they had built the proud *Indiana* and her sister ships in the 1870's and the beautiful *St. Louis* and *St. Paul* in the 1890's—had to shut down and go out of business for lack of ships to build.

Meanwhile the dead ships in our sequestered rivers and coves continued to rot, rust, and disintegrate. I have heard people speak of them as moth-ball fleets—a misnomer certainly! "Moth-balls" implies adequate preservative measures. The ships left over from World War I had no protection worth mentioning. The science of ship protective coating and dehumidification didn't come into use until after World War II.

"What's the matter with our merchant marine?" someone asked a member of the United States Shipping Board in the mid-1930's.

"The trouble is that we have never had a stable policy of assisting our shipping companies—one that they could depend upon," answered the board member.

The era of hit-or-miss assistance to shippers was at last coming to an end.

> In ocean affairs [commented one historian in 1935] the United States now occupies the position which makes Government planning, intervention and spending, absolutely imperative. As the richest nation, the greatest exporting nation, and—next to Great Britain—the greatest importing nation, the United States simply cannot leave its commerce solely in the hands of other countries: to be restricted or cut off, perhaps, in a new world crisis. However, as one of the two greatest naval powers, the Republic most certainly cannot leave its supply of merchant auxiliaries in time of war, to chance. The first World War taught us both these lessons.
>
> Once upon a time most American citizens shuddered at the word "ship subsidies." Most shipping men frowned at the phrase "Government interference." But that time is now past. Government aid to shipping obviously cannot be withdrawn.

People reading of the postwar shipping comeback being staged by European countries wondered why the United States couldn't do likewise. After her severe war suffering, Great Britain had returned with a flourish by the mid 1930's. In 1936 the huge Peninsular & Oriental Line had 397 ships in service; Cunard had 76. Germany's revitalized Hamburg-American line had 247 vessels, while North German Lloyd had 200.

United States? We had a fleet rotting in the creeks; a small freight and passenger tonnage afloat. In the 1920's the Jones Bill had made some further attempts to help shipping by exempting shipping companies from the excess-profits tax. That helped a little, but not much. Two years later—1928—the Jones-White Bill liberalized the original enactment and granted some mail subsidies, at the same time providing loans to aid in the building of new ships. The bill came at a bad time: world depression was on the way, sweeping in like a grim engulfing tide over the whole world. Merchant shipping, despite the delayed offer of aid, remained largely at a standstill.

New Lease on Life

In 1927-1928, however, the International Mercantile Marine (a group of associated ship companies of various nations, including ours) had built three good-sized liners—*California, Virginia,* and *Pennsylvania*. These entered the intercoastal trade, running via the Panama Canal between New York and San Francisco. Next, the *Washington* and the *Manhattan,* both big passenger ships of 24,000 tons each (largest built in America to that time), entered the North Atlantic trade flying the white-and-blue flag of the United States Lines, inherited from the quiescent American Line. These two were the first American-built ships to run in the North Atlantic trade in thirty-five years. . . .

And that brings me back to the statement made at the start of this chapter—that 1936 was a big year for the American shipping industry. The late President Franklin D. Roosevelt brought with him to the Presidency a deep and abiding love for ships—no less than a firm belief in the sound defense and economical value of a merchant-marine policy.

These beliefs he had inherited from his seafaring ancestors of New York and had bolstered by his personal service as Assistant Secretary of the Navy under Woodrow Wilson.

In the mid-1930's the President stood firmly behind the pending Merchant Marine Act. So did the overwhelmingly Democratic Congress of that time—a Congress that was not averse, you may recall, to appropriating money where it thought money was needed.

The Merchant Marine Act passed in 1936. The Maritime Commission (later the Maritime Administration) came into existence, replacing the Shipping Board; two vice admirals and a number of businessmen have headed it. And for the first time an effective and efficient program of Government assistance to shipping appeared on the statute books. It stipulated:

The Administration would have to approve the service for

199

which you intended your new ships; that service must be a trade route essential to the national advantage.

The Administration would pay the difference between what it cost to build a ship in the United States and what it would have cost in Europe, where prices of labor and material are much lower. This arrangement was called "the construction-differential policy." The subsidy could not exceed half the cost of the ship, but, even so, it provided an enormous boost.

The contract must be let to an American shipyard. The Maritime Administration would approve the letting. All subsidy payments would go to the shipyard, to the engine works, to the various outfitters of the vessel and to their employees. Not a cent of the construction subsidies went directly to the shipowners and operators.

But they received the benefits just the same. Besides providing the cost-differential allowance, the Administration would assume the cost of the ship and let the operator pay off the debt in easy payments stretched over a period of twenty years—the average ship's lifetime—at a very low interest. (This policy of the Maritime Administration assuming the first cost of the ship has been altered somewhat since the Eisenhower Administration came into office in 1953. Under the Republicans the shipowners are expected to do the original financing of the ship. The Government, however, stands back of them in the process: a great advantage to the builder and owner. The construction-differential aspect of the business remains as originally enacted.)

These and some additional provisions enabled American ships to compete *on a par* with foreign ships, although they did not give any big advantage *over* the rivals.

In return for these Government aids, all operators were to keep their books as the Administration told them; to maintain fixed sailing schedules; to make a certain number of voyages each year. And there was, of course, the historic provision that all ships built with Uncle Sam's aid would be so constructed that they could readily be converted to war use should an emergency arise.

The legislation as outlined was enacted in 1936. Though few realized it then, the emergency was fast on the way to us!

Already the iron was being mined in the Mesabi country which, through various mutations, would make the steel for the battle craft, the guns, the tanks, to fight in that emergency. Already young men were in high schools, academies, and colleges who in another four or five years would be in uniform, navigating and manning those ships, those planes, those guns. Yes, by 1936 our second world war was less than five years ahead.

Meanwhile, the beneficial results of the Merchant Marine Act had become apparent. Assured of Government assistance, shipping companies raised their heads once again and began to design ships—passenger liners, cargo ships of various kinds—C1's, C2's and C3's. Shipyards once more took on an alive look and began turning those designs into ships.

Then, just as the full impact of the new maritime policy swung into force, Pearl Harbor called a halt to the normal peacetime program of shipbuilding. War was upon us. But this time we were better prepared for it, ship-wise, than in the previous world conflict.

Now that we were in it, Uncle Sam stepped in and took over everything that floated and had an engine. Among the first passenger ships to enter the military transport service was the fine new *America,* fresh from the ways at Newport News, and flying the house flag of the United States Lines. Ships of the American Export Lines also entered war service, as did, in fact, ships of all other lines, both passenger and freight.

In this war we planned our new merchant fleet with our eyes open. We already had some new shipyards in operation, just as we had some new ships afloat. The demands for still more tonnage became more insistent with each day that passed.

"Give us ships, ships! We must have more ships!" cried the military and naval heads. And our shipyards, working round the clock, responded. A huge building program suddenly became alive, embodying hundreds of new techniques learned since the end of the last war. Seeking short cuts, shipbuilders soon developed an assembly-line construction procedure; ship parts fabricated at one plant were transported to another for assembly and launching.

If you thought the 2,400 ships we built in World War I was an accomplishment, compare it with what we did in World War II. Soon we were building one ship a month, then one ship a week. Before long, one ship was sliding down the ways every twenty-four hours. Our yards designed, built and launched 5,000 ships in that second big fight for world freedom. The record of that accomplishment is still there, and many of the ships built under it are still afloat—tangible evidence of its efficiency.

We won the second world war—something we could not have done in so short a time without the aid of the new merchant ship fleet.

With the coming of peace, the nation found itself once more with a big fleet on its hands. However, the maritime authorities followed a more sensible course. During a period of readjustment for peace following the end of the war, Congress passed another enactment titled the Merchant Ship Sales Act. This retained all the provisions of the 1936 legislation and added something more: Under it American shipping companies were enabled to buy, at a fraction of cost, the best of the thousands of ships left over from Government service.

What was the result? In less than three years an excellent and efficient fleet of first-class cargo ships was plying the seas— each ship flying the American standard. But in this book we are interested mainly in passenger ships, and the plight of passenger ships when the war ended in 1945 was bad.

The Government had taken over 150 American passenger vessels all told—practically all built prior to the new 1936 legislation. Besides those liners in the transoceanic service, coastwise Mallory Line ships, the Old Dominion ships, boats of the Washington-Norfolk Steamboat Company, and various other vessels of all sorts and condition which plied our coastal bays and rivers were all gathered into the Government fold to serve "for the duration." So were the steamers of the Metropolitan and Fall River Line and the Eastern Steamship Company.

These ships had gone out in top condition. They came back soiled, worn, and unsightly from their tour of war duty. Such as could be rehabilitated were reconverted to peacetime passenger use, among them the *America* of the United States Lines, the largest ship ever built in the United States in its day. Soon the wartime fleet had finished its useful life in peacetime service and the new program of building passenger ships (invigorated by the terms of the Merchant Marine Act) got under way. Today there are forty ships composing the United States passenger merchant marine. Practically all those forty were built under the government program. In the North Atlantic trade the *United States,* the *America,* the *Constitution,* and the *Independence* make up the entire all-passenger fleet.

The American fleet of passenger ships is small, compared to the big fleet of American cargo ships—mainly C–2's and C–3's, and some Liberty and Victory types. And there is a new type coming more and more into use, known as the Mariner. It is 13,000 tons instead of 10,000 tons. Many of them service American lines, carrying twelve passengers each, though they are rated as freight ships. Still newer types are now on the drawing boards.

A few weeks ago I talked with Steve Manning of the United States Maritime Administration. He tells me that there is a remarkable reawakening in American shipping now that America has a firm policy of assisting ship operators. Hence we may reasonably expect new passenger liners to help take care of the ever-growing crowds of Americans visiting foreign lands.

24. Steamship Lines
That Flourished and Died

A LISTING OF VANISHED COMPANIES

TIME has taken its toll of steamship companies, even as the sea has taken its toll of ships.

Since the days of Cunard, Collins, Inman, and Guion, many other steamship companies flying the flags of America and other nations have arisen, set their ships bravely afloat, served their allotted period of time, and disappeared—absorbed by larger companies, victims of financial panic or competition too heavy to be met. All, however, are a part of America's ship story.

Let's glance at the casualty list of some of these steamship companies:

First there was the Allan Line, a Glasgow concern which dated back to 1854. Allan began operating with the *Canadian*, a little 1,800-ton vessel plying between Montreal, Glasgow,

Quebec, New York, and Boston. In the fifty-nine years of its existence, the Allan Line built and ran fifty ships. Its last, the *Calgarian* (1913) was 17,500 tons. . . . The great Canadian Pacific Company took over the Allan fleet.

Though I never met any of the Anchor Line officials, I've always had a latent affection for that Scottish company because my first love of all steamships was an Anchor liner—the *Cameronia*. Anchor started out in 1856, only two years after Allan. Appropriately (for a North Atlantic vessel), its first ship was named *Tempest*. She was smaller than many pioneer ships of her day—only 798 tons. From that diminutive start, Anchor ships ran from Glasgow to New York for ninety-one years. A total of fifty-six Anchor liners plied in the service, the largest being the *Caledonia*, 17,000 tons, about 1,000 tons larger than my old friend *Cameronia*. Reason for Anchor's demise? Cunard took over the company—ship, line, and anchor.

The Atlantic Transport Line's ships were designed originally to carry cattle but later each had unusually fine first-class accommodations. Financed in America, it started in 1890 and operated for thirty-four years, running from New York straight to London. Atlantic Transport's ship nomenclature was predominantly American, with a definite Indian influence. There were the *Mohawk, Manitoba, Minnewaska, Menomminee, Manitou, Minnehaha, Minnetonka, Minnekahda*—all combination carriers of good quality. By way of variety, there were also the *Mobile* and the *Michigan,* the *Boadicea* and the *Poland,* to name a few. Atlantic Transport's first ship, *Memphis,* registered only 5,000 tons. Its last, *Minnetonka* (1924) was 21,700 tons. Atlantic Transport was one of the several American steamship companies which early in the twentieth century associated themselves with some foreign lines in the International Mercantile Marine. . . . Atlantic Transport gave up passenger service in 1934.

The year 1900 introduced the Austro-American Company,

with ships plying between Trieste and New York. Its native appellation was Unione-Austriaca. From its beginning to its end it ran twenty-four ships, from the little 3,700-ton *Teresa* to the 13,000-ton *Kaiser Franz-Josef I.* There were also American-named ships in the fleet: *Virginia, Alice, Laura, Atlanta;* the *Georgia,* the *Columbia,* and the *Martha Washington.* But in 1913 Austro-American was absorbed by the Cosulich Line.

Cosulich ran seventeen ships in all, ranging from a small first ship of 4,000 tons to the *Vulcania* of 24,000 tons. Cosulich merged with the Italia Line in 1933.

The German Bernstein Line started ships going between Antwerp, Hamburg, Rotterdam, and New York in 1904. All told, it operated a fleet of five ships, the largest being the *Pennland* (1922), 16,000 tons. . . . The Holland-American Line took it over in 1935.

The post–Civil War needs of our American South—particularly the lower Mississippi Valley and the City of New Orleans —induced an English firm to go after business in that region in 1870. The company called itself the Liverpool & Mississippi Steamship Company, and brought over loads of immigrants and general cargo, taking back cotton. When this company added a line to Quebec and Halifax, it began calling itself the Mississippi & Dominion Line. In time, however, it dropped the New Orleans line and became known as Dominion Line. Its first vessel was the *Crescent City* of forgotten tonnage; in 1900 it built its largest, *Columbus,* 15,000 tons. White Star absorbed Dominion in 1903.

A French company, the Fabre Line, sent its first ship to America in 1874. This began a service between Marseilles, Naples, Palermo, and New York. It continued for more than half a century, and built and operated twenty-four ships, ranging in size from 3,500 tons (the *Brooklyn*) to 12,000 tons (the *Providence*).

Furness-Withy Company, Ltd., of London, mentioned in Chapter 28, made its first impact upon America in 1890. One of its passenger subsidiaries was the Warren Line, which endured for twenty-two years, maintaining a fleet of four ships, none more than 7,500 tons, in the Boston-Liverpool trade.

Greek passenger ships ran between New York and several Hellenic ports, beginning in 1890. The fleet numbered fifteen ships in all, the largest being the *Nea Hellas,* 17,000 tons.

Poland once had a steamship line to America. Do you remember the Gdynia-American Line (Polish Transatlantic Shipping Company, Ltd.)? Its terminal ports were Gdynia, Copenhagen, and New York. Some of its ships were the *Kosciuszko,* the *Sobieski,* and the *Pulsudski;* the largest more than 14,000 tons. This line operated from 1910 to 1939, then expired.

From its founding in 1857, the Hamburg-American Line built and operated more than a hundred ships before it closed shop just before the outbreak of World War II. We are indebted to Hamburg-American, of course, for the *Vaterland,* built in 1914, which became our *Leviathan.* Other big ships of this line were the *Bismarck* and the *Imperator.* Although the war interrupted this valuable line's service, it is now being started again.

Bill Inman's line, though organized in England, was largely financed by American capital. That is most likely why practically all its ships bore American names. In his time Inman ran a fleet of twenty-six ships: the smallest, the Lilliputian *City of Durham* (1865), 607 tons; the largest, *City of Paris* (1889), 11,000 tons. That line became the American Line in 1893, under American registry.

An Italian company, La Veloce Line, started about 1870 and served various Italian ports with ships to New York and to Central and South American ports. It was absorbed by a larger company in 1909, its flagship having been less than 10,000 tons.

The short-lived Lloyd-Italian Line between 1904 and 1908 ran a fleet of six ships between Italian ports and New York. They, too, were little vessels, none being over 8,000 tons. Lloyd Sabaudo Line, running from Genoa to New York, began in 1901 with the big ship (for those days) *Pesaro,* 12,335 tons. This line became part of the Italia Line in 1931, bringing with it, among other ships, the big *Conte di Savoia,* 48,502 tons.

The National Line, established during our Civil War under American capital, had its headquarters in Liverpool, and its ships plied between that port, London, and New York. It lasted for almost three decades, until 1893. Its first ship, the *Louisiana,* was 3,000 tons; its last ship, the *America* of 1884, 5,500 tons.

Generale Italiana, the big line which absorbed La Veloce and Lloyd-Italian and Transoceanic Line, began in 1881. Its first ship was little 2,400-ton *Marco Minghetti* in the New York–Genoa trade. During more than fifty years, forty-five ships of this line plied the sea lanes. Then a merger took place in 1932, and in joining the big Italian combine, it brought along the mighty *Rex* (among other ships) of 51,000 tons—one of the greatest liners lost in World War II.

When we come to the North German Lloyd Line, we encounter the company which built and operated more ships than any other ever to serve American shores. . . .

The name *Lloyd* in connection with steamship lines has a curious connotation, an equally interesting history. Back in the reign of King James II, a modest Welshman named Lloyd had a coffeehouse in London, not far from the wharves. There, in midafternoons, would foregather groups of British insurance men interested in underwriting "ventures" (cargoes) sailing for foreign ports.

One group—the most important of these insurance-minded men—became unofficially known as "Lloyd's Insurance Committee," and in time became a recognized authoritative body. When the Lloyd's Committee put its seal of approval upon a ship by underwriting it, you could be certain that the ship was strong of timber, sturdy of mast, and operated under a competent master and crew.

After a while the Lloyd's Committee became a great insurance company. Meantime, the very name *Lloyd's* (because of its association) was appropriated and adopted by steamship lines as a connotation of dependability and service. Hence we have the North German Lloyd Line (the largest); Lloyd-Italian Line, Lloyd Sabaudo Line, and so on.

I don't know whether these various companies in thus appropriating the Lloyd name and reputation, paid Mr. Lloyd's descendants and successors for the use of his name. They certainly should have done so. In any case, the companies believed, and the public apparently also believed, the name had an authenticating quality that made it synonymous with dependable steamship operation.

Nearly 250 ships have sailed under North German Lloyd's house flag in the 100 years of its existence. It was just a century ago (1856) that its pioneer craft—the small *Bremen*, 2,500 tons —nosed into New York, bringing cargo and immigrants from Central Europe.

Like all foreign steamship companies, N.G.L. intersprinkled some American names among the ships it ran in the North Atlantic. You'll find *Hudson, New York, American, Union* in the earlier fleet of this line. After 1881, however, the owners seemed to become doubly conscious of their national homogeneity, and from that year until World War II, when service was discontinued, there were nothing but German names in the North German Lloyd fleet.

Outstanding among its ships have been the *Kronprinzessin Cecile* of 1906 (fast and high-stepping lady!), 20,000 tons, and, in later years (1929–1935), the *Bremen* and *Europa*. Two others, *Scharnhorst* and *Gneisenau* (intended as transatlantic liners but destined to be bêtes noires of the Allied navies in the great struggle), were converted into pocket battleships. . . .

The Red Star Line, of Belgian origin, was another of the companies making up the International Mercantile Marine. Its terminal ports were Antwerp, Southampton, New York. Its ship names smack of their Low Country origin: *Zeeland* (the first in 1865, 2,600 tons); *Waseland, Pennland, Neder-land,* etc. Largest of the fleet, the big *Belgenland,* 27,000 tons, was built in 1917. The Bernstein Line took over Red Star in 1935.

Spain, the land of Isabella—the good Queen who helped one of the most famous of navigators, Christopher Columbus, to discover our own continent—organized and started its own line of ships from Barcelona to New York, South and Central American ports in 1866. It was called Compania Transatlantica, but Americans soon shortened it to the "Spanish Line." The little *Christobal Colón* of 2,800 tons led off, followed by the slightly larger *San Ignacio Loyola.* Though none of its ships exceeded 11,000 tons register (*Reina Victoria Eugeinia* and *Infanta Isabella* were 10,000 tons each), the Spanish Line continued until 1928.

The State Line, another Glasgow company in which many American dollars were invested, put in its bid for Atlantic passenger patronage in 1873. Each of its ships bore the name of an American state, hence the company name. *State of Louisiana* headed the fleet in 1873, a small vessel of 1,869 tons, advertising a fast and comfortable service, Glasgow to New York. The line survived eighteen years, and during that period built and ran nine ships—the largest, *State of Florida,* being 4,000 tons. It became part of the Allan Line.

Although the great White Star Line has disappeared as an entity from the list of companies serving America, ships of its fleet now form a part of the massive Cunard organization and still have their distinguishing nomenclature, although sailing under the red-and-gold lion rampant.

From the date of its organization in 1871, White Star sailed sixty ships in the North Atlantic ferry. Many of their names still ring nostalgically in the minds of those who loved and traveled aboard them.

The first White Star ship, as we have read, was the huge (as size was then reckoned) *Oceanic* (1870) 3,800 tons. Then followed a long roll call of *ic*-named vessels—from the *Atlantic,* built the same year as the *Oceanic,* to the first 10,000-ton *Georgic,* the 1914 *Homeric* (32,000 tons) and the mighty *Majestic* (56,000 tons)—until White Star was absorbed by the Cunard organization in 1933.

Probably the best known among the White Star ships is the one whose name brings to mind the sea's greatest peacetime tragedy. As of course you know, *Titanic* went down off the Grand Banks in an iceberg collision of 1912 while endeavoring to establish a record on her maiden trip. But though *Titanic* carried down with her 1,500 victims, she did not die in vain.

Successive safety measures evolved from that catastrophe and the investigation following it which have made such horrors as her sinking well-nigh impossible: more life boats; stronger ship materials; more rigid inspection; more watertight compartments; better trained crews; ice patrols; no more racing to establish records, save under close supervision. These and the improved quality of modern ships have made sea travel the delight that I find it today, as do millions of other people.

Some time during the 1920's, while Mother and I were in Europe, we made a side trip to the North Cape on a forgotten liner named *Arcadian.* One of the fellow passengers with whom we made friends was a gentleman who had gained some firsthand knowledge of the *Titanic* tragedy. He told us about it. On that fateful night in 1912 he was on duty as a night operator at a lonely wireless station on Long Island shore.

There were not many wireless stations anywhere then—Marconi's invention being still in its experimental stage—and few ships had wireless equipment.

Over his crude, sputtering, flashing apparatus—out of that ice-cold Arctic fog—came the intelligence which brought the young operator up sharp with horror. The great White Star ship on her maiden trip to America had met with tragedy, was sinking, and other liners were hastening to her aid as fast as they could make it. Through that one station this young operator relayed to all America the dire intelligence long before a ship could come in bringing survivors and detailed information from those who had seen it.

From that night on, wireless became an essential factor in our modern civilization; and the young man—as time proved—became an indispensable figure in the wireless world. He is General David Sarnoff, now head of the Radio Corporation of America.

My old friend the *Olympic* was about the same tonnage as the *Titanic* and equally beautiful. The vast *Majestic,* built in 1921, tipped the scales at 56,000 and is recalled today with regret by many who loved her in her luxury-liner days.

I am glad to report, however, that she lived out an honorable old age. She became H.M.S. *Caledonia* in 1936, a training ship of the King's Navy. Fire destroyed her in 1939.

These, then, are the principal transoceanic steamship companies whose vessels served America during the last century and a half but which no longer exist (as separate companies) as part of the world merchant marine. They had fleets of many kinds of ships: small, large; safe, unsafe; graceful, ungraceful; comfortable and uncomfortable. Ships whose identities have long since been forgotten. Ships which are spoken of today because of some recorded or remembered characteristic such as beauty or speed.

Once they were ocean liners—ferryboats in the ocean ferry. Once the companies which operated them waxed rich and powerful. Now all are gone. But each and every company, each and every ship of the vast still fleets, contributed its meed to the total knowledge of ship construction, of ship operation. From their experiences—ships and companies—we have learned something that enables us today to create finer, stronger, and faster ships than ever before.

25. *The United States Lines Company and the Man Who Heads It*

AROUND the turn of the century, that giant of finance, J. Pierpont Morgan the elder, decided to go into the steamship business—the financial end, not the operating end. And of course he entered it in a big way. Gathering about him a number of other financiers versed in the art of large-scale steel mergers, Mr. Morgan, it was said, proceeded to "(M)organize the ocean, after the manner of king-size railway combination deals."

Out of this arrangement there emerged in 1902 the International Mercantile Marine (commonly known among shipping men as I.M.M.)—a giant holding company which began to buy up steamship lines here and overseas. The first and largest acquisition was the British White Star Line. Shortly thereafter, the Atlantic Transport Line, referred to earlier, came in. Then the American Line, Leyland Line, and Red Star Line also became members.

But Morgan's plans did not stop there. They also included acquisition of (no less!) the Cunard Line, the Hamburg-American Line, the North German Lloyd Line. However, the British and German governments respectively had something to say about that: they turned thumbs down on the idea. Then, to insure the continued ownership and operation by their own nationals, these governments granted even larger subsidies to the lines.

I.M.M.—probably the mightiest steamship organization that ever existed—continued to operate for nearly thirty years. Among its real contributions from the American viewpoint, were the building, in 1928, of three large turbo-electric ships— the *California, Virginia,* and *Pennsylvania*—and operating them between New York and the Pacific Coast via the Panama Canal.

One of its later components which survived when I.M.M. went out of business was the United States Lines. Today this company operates the largest two American ships in the North Atlantic trade—the *United States* and the *America*.

General John M. Franklin, who served in the Army Transportation Corps during World War II, heads the United States Lines Company, bringing to it a shrewd ability in the shipping business and a forthright integrity. During the war General Franklin was Assistant Chief of Transportation and Director of Water Transportation, Army Service Forces—one of the first steamship executives to be called from civilian life when the guns started booming, to aid in the gigantic logistics job. In meeting the various transportation problems, ocean ships played a most conspicuous part. In recognition of his achievements, Franklin was awarded the Distinguished Service Medal in 1945 for "contributing in a conspicuous degree to the success of the Transportation Corps and of the entire supply mission of the Army."

At the peak of operation, Franklin had under his supervision about 2,000 vessels—the largest fleet, surely, ever under the direction of a merchant mariner! A little later, while he was on a flight around the world, Franklin called at the headquarters of General Dwight D. Eisenhower and the President-to-be pinned upon his lapel the Bronze Star medal for meritorious service in military operations against an enemy.

John Franklin is the son of the late P. A. S. Franklin, an international figure in steamshipping and one-time head of the I.M.M. A remarkably reticent and modest man, he avoids publicity, and his unwillingness to talk about himself is proverbial, both among newsmen and his shipping associates. Those who know him, however, piece out the pattern of his life for the inquirer. They claim he is the outstanding figure in American shipping today. That his ability to direct a great line of passenger and cargo ships, and provide the kind of service shippers and the traveling public want, stems from his abiding and deep interest in shipping plus considerably more than a quarter-century's solid experience.

Graduating from Harvard in time to take part in World War I, Franklin served as a captain in the United States Army Tank Corps overseas and participated in fourteen engagements. He commanded his battalion in the Battle of Mormal Forest. The British gave him the Military Cross for meritorious service to the Allied cause.

After the Armistice he returned to civilian life and jumped at once into the shipping industry.

His first service was with the old Argonaut Line, freight carriers; he was made general manager. Then the Roosevelt

Steamship Company took him on as vice-president. In 1931 the Roosevelt Line merged with I.M.M., of which the elder Franklin was then head. Franklin, junior, soon became its operating vice-president. During the same year the I.M.M. acquired the United States Lines. In 1943 the I.M.M. of New Jersey and the United States Lines Company of Nevada merged. The resulting organization became the United States Lines Company of New Jersey, with General Franklin as the line's president. That ended the I.M.M. company.

At once John Franklin began an intensive study of the company, its business, real and potential, its ships, and the trade routes they plied. In this he worked closely with the Maritime Commission (later the Maritime Administration) to further cooperative arrangements in aid of American shipping and equally valuable to the Government.

In 1932 the company built for the European trade the two largest passenger vessels ever constructed in the United States up to that time. They were the *Manhattan* and *Washington*. They introduced for the first time a top passenger accommodation known as "cabin class" instead of the usual "first class." *Manhattan* and *Washington* ran between New York and the Channel ports, touching at Hamburg, upholding the traditional honor of the United States on the shipping lanes. "They recaptured," it is said, "American patronage lost to foreign-flag ships."

Today the United States Lines Company operates a fleet of fifty cargo vessels in addition to its two large passenger ships —the superliner *United States,* described elsewhere, and the beloved *America.*

It was not until the United States Lines—following World War I— took over the *Vaterland* as part of our reparations from Germany and renamed her the *Leviathan,* that its fame became world-wide. The *Vaterland* was a huge liner of almost 60,000 tons, built in German yards and slated for the New York–

Hamburg trade. Frank Braynard, author of *Lives of the Liners* [1] explains how we fell heir to this giant of the sea ferry:

> Germany has built five superliners. Three of these ships were the *Vaterland, Imperator* and *Bismarck,* all taken over by the Allies at the war's end (1918). *Vaterland,* making only two voyages as a German liner, became the *Leviathan,* largest ship ever to fly the American flag. The *Imperator,* after less than two years of service under the German colors, became the British *Berengaria* [which raced the *Olympic* unsuccessfully, as I have told in another chapter]. Not quite completed in 1914, the *Bismarck* never sailed under the red-white-and-black, being turned over to England and renamed the *Majestic* of the White Star Line. [1]

Legend gathers around *Leviathan's* prow. Statistically she was mighty and impressive, 59,000 tons, 907 feet long, 100 feet in the beam. She had three fat funnels—the day of the four-funnel ship having waned. Under Commodore Herbert Hartley of the United States Lines, she entered the lists and became a prime favorite of travelers of all nationalities after peace had once again come to the world.

It was a time that demanded a dramatic American flagship. When President Wilson learned of the dimensions of the liner to which we had fallen heir and which was to run in the United States fleet, he exclaimed, "She's a veritable leviathan—monster of the deep, as the Bible says." And *Leviathan* she became.

Over in Germany, I imagine, there is many an aging lover of ships who recalls the *Vaterland* with nostalgic wistfulness and regret that she served her homeland for so short a period. But to Americans who love the seas, she is the *Leviathan*—whether our last recollection of her is as a giant rising and falling majestically over the Atlantic swells, or as a fallen Goliath rusting away against the piers at Hoboken pitifully neglected after a long service.

[1] New York, Cornell Maritime Press, 1947.

Such was my last—indeed, my only—sight of her.

Herbert Hartley, who was captain of the American Line's *St. Louis* during World War I, had earlier and more poignant recollections of the great ship. Hartley, retiring from American Line service after the *St. Louis* ceased operation, determined to go to his comfortable home (he was about to be married to a charming Alabama lady) down South. He was war weary, half sick with gastric ulcers due to the worry of taking his ship back and forth, zigzagging through mine fields; of embarking and delivering load after load of American soldiers in France and bringing them home again. But just at that moment the United States Lines (working with the officials of the U.S. Shipping Board) offered Hartley command of the great *Leviathan*. She was then being reconditioned under famous Iron-Hat Gibbs, naval architect.

Vaterland had originally cost Germany $25,000,000. Gibbs was at work on her (even while Hartley was standing in the company's office at 45 Broadway, receiving his commodore's stripes), reconditioning her to the tune of $9,000,000 more. She was in a fearfully dilapidated condition after her war service. Hartley, from the *St. Louis,* had seen *Leviathan* before, early in the summer of 1914. He records his impressions as follows:

> We were steaming up the English Channel. The *St. Louis* had pointed her bow towards Southampton. Capt. John Clark Jamison was her master. I was mate. Far ahead, off our starboard bow, a streak of smoke showed over the horizon. I raised my binoculars. What I saw was enough to take the wind out of any sailor's canvas. There she stood out to sea, her three funnels towering proudly above her upper deck. She was the biggest ship that had ever sailed the seas.
>
> "She's the *Vaterland,* Mr. Hartley," Capt. Jamison said.
>
> I knew who she was. Except for the ill-fated *Titanic* that had gone down two years earlier, the *Vaterland* was the main topic of conversation wherever seagoing men gathered.

She was larger and faster than the *Titanic,* 15,000 tons heavier, 67 feet longer and she could do five knots more than the highly publicized English luxury liner. The *Titanic* has cost England $10,000,000. The *Vaterland* was Germany's bid for ocean supremacy at a cost of twenty-five millions. There she was on her maiden voyage bound for New York. . . .

"Sir," I said to Captain Jamison, "the Captain of that ship must indeed be a proud man." Jamison switched his grubby little pipe . . . twitched at his goatee . . . spat to leeward and grunted.

"Let him try to get her up the English Channel some dirty night when he doesn't know where he is and he won't feel so damn proud." [2]

While Gibbs was putting the finishing touches on the *Leviathan's* reconditioning at Newport News, Hartley spent most of his time at the yard studying the great ship: her complicated machinery, her hull design and deck arrangements, her general equipment. She was now once again ready for peacetime service. Next Hartley took the *Leviathan* up the coast to South Boston dry docks, where her mammoth hull was given a final coat of paint. Fifty thousand people came down to the dock for a sightseeing tour of the new American queen of the seas. She must have been to the Boston of 1923 what the *Britannia* had been to the Boston of 1840.

When speaking of a great ship, comparisons are not necessarily odious. The *Leviathan* was so large that her bridge stood ninety feet above the water level—approximately the height of an eight-story building. Under water she ran down the equivalent of three stories. She had forty-eight boilers, fired from both ends. Her propellers were eighteen feet in diameter. On each round trip she burned up 1,462,300 gallons of oil.

The loss of the *Titanic* ten years earlier had resulted in new

[2] *Home is the Sailor* by Herbert Hartley, as told to Clint Bonner. Birmingham, Ala, Vulcan Press, 1955.

safety laws that required every ship to carry enough lifeboats to accommodate both passengers and crew in an emergency. The *Leviathan* therefore had seventy-eight huge lifeboats.

For passenger comfort and pleasure, Gibbs had built into the *Leviathan* a swimming pool 38 by 20 feet; two libraries of 5,000 volumes; and a 34-bed hospital.

It would have taken the output of a large dairy and truck farm to supply the needs of the great ship. For one round trip her list included: 95 tons of meat; more than 12,000 quarts of milk; 7,000 dozen eggs; 36 tons of dressed chickens; 28 tons of fish.

Those being Prohibition days in America and the *Leviathan* having become an American ship, she had no bar and served no liquor, though there was no ruling against passengers bringing along whatever they wanted to drink.

On the *Leviathan*'s trial run, Hartley had aboard his old skipper, Captain Jamison, now well advanced in years, though recovered from a recent illness, and sharing the bridge as a guest with the new commodore. And when the ship achieved 25 knots, 27 knots, 28 knots plus, and held that speed for an hour, thereby beating the *Mauretania,* Jamison's pride knew no bounds, for an American-flag ship had once more seized the speed crown of the Atlantic ferry.

Subsequently she held the 28-knot speed for six hours.

Leviathan ran for several years in the United States Lines. Though she held the speed crown and won a huge following which loved her for her great spaciousness no less than for the impeccable service offered, she was not a money-maker. She never sailed with a full passenger list. The very expense of operating her (even with a full house) was well-nigh prohibitive. Some say that if she had had a well-stocked bar, she might have made money. I wouldn't know about that. It seems to me a bar is only one factor in a very long list of imponderables when it comes to running a superliner.

The United States Lines Company

The company's experience with the *Leviathan*—distinguished though it was—very likely started the trend toward smaller ships, although a number of even larger "queens" were even then scheduled for the future.

The United States Lines's next ship was the *President Harding*, a 13,000-ton steamer the same size as her sister *President Roosevelt*.

Then came the *Manhattan*, 24,000 tons, as mentioned already. She was one of America's most famous passenger ships. From the date of her first trip she became a great favorite. With her red, white, and blue funnels, her clean, sweeping lines, her comfortable and homelike service, she served as a passenger ship for only nine years.

Each of these two ships, *Manhattan* and *Washington,* had cost $10,500,000 to build. Their service verified the wisdom of the company in building them.

In 1940 the Newport News Shipbuilding and Dry Dock Company had on its ways the largest ship yet built in the United States, and for the United States Lines. She was the *America,* nearly 30,000 tons, 660 feet long. Her keel had been laid down in 1938. She was launched in 1939. Before she had time to go into regular passenger service, however, she had to shoulder her duties as a troopship under the name of *West Point,* and performed her stint satisfactorily. She carried almost half a million troops during her period of service. Not until late fall, 1946, did she enter her regular North Atlantic trade as the largest American passenger carrier. She made a very good crossing from Ambrose Light to Daunt's Lightship in 4 days, 22 hours, averaging 24.5 knots.

As one who has crossed twice on the *America,* I can testify to her satisfying accommodations and, more particularly, to an air of friendly and homelike luxury which pervades the entire passenger section of the ship. She is one more evidence in support of the just claim that the American merchant marine, given half a chance to compete with foreign ships on an equal basis, can hold its own on the world sea lanes.

Though her fame is eclipsed by her younger and much larger sister, *United States,* she has nevertheless her own following who would think of crossing on no other ship if they can get passage on the *America.*

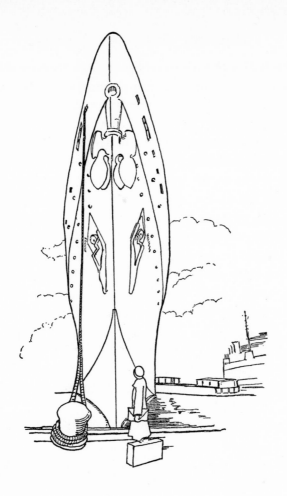

26. I Meet a Great Lady

I BECAME acquainted with the *United States* very shortly after her launching; in common with millions of other Americans, I felt, upon seeing her, a swelling of pride within my heart that the shipbuilding genius of our country has created and is maintaining her. Our country has a big stake in this huge vessel. Although much of the inner details of her mechanical and structural aspects is top secret, we do know this: the United States is built so that with a minimum of delay and mechanical effort she can be converted to some war use for which she has been specifically designed. Equipped as she is with all the latest radar and electronic devices, she offers one of our greatest threats to aggressive attack.

On an early morning three years ago, the day before sailing on the *United States* for England, I went over to her berth on the North River to see what she looked like close up. I had never before given any ship on which I was to travel such a careful "sneak preview." But about this, the largest American ship ever built, the fastest ship on the seas, I felt an irresistible desire to behold her objectively, so to speak, from shore.

When you are on board a ship, with the boundless sea stretching away on all sides of you, your ship—big and safe though she may be—is bound to seem rather small in comparison. (Nature, untamed, dwarfs the creations of man's hands!) You've nothing save this "gray unrest" by which to measure and judge her lineaments. It's when you compare a ship with familiar things on land that she assumes the vast proportions which are actually hers.

In describing the *United States,* dry statistics fail utterly to convey any idea of the impressiveness, the distinctiveness, the individual personality of the ship. Oh yes, I can tell you that she's 990 feet long. That 2,200 units of her enormous mechanism and equipment were preassembled (many of them singly weighing a lot more than some early ocean ships complete) before being included in her great innards. That her towering elliptical funnels are each 55 feet high. That she cost something over $70,000,000. That the mere temporary lumber used in shoring her up and for supporting frames during her building would—laid board-end to board-end—reach 200 miles. That there are 1,500 miles of plate welding in the extensive sheet of her steel skin. That materials from all 48 states were assembled to bring her to completion—1,500 carloads of them from 800 different production plants. That more than a million separate blueprints guided her builders.

I Meet a Great Lady

All these facts I find interesting, and so may you. But they convey nothing of the ship's individuality, her "personal" qualities. I might go on to explain that she is safer from fire, the sea's greatest hazard, than any ship that ever floated: she has not a yard of wood in her make-up. Absolutely nothing on board, save the piano, and the butcher's block in the galleys, is made of wood. She's a steel, chromium, aluminum giantess, clad in a colorful dress of fire-proof paint. Quarters for passengers, officers, and crew are air-conditioned. You could, after a manner of speaking, prowl around her engine room in your clean nylon summer suit without getting it soiled.

One need not stop there. One could point to a whole shipload of luxury facilities throughout her many acres of deck; 14 public rooms—lounges, ballrooms, cocktail rooms, chapels, theaters, libraries; refrigerator space for the almost 100,000 pounds of fresh meat which passengers and crew consume on an average crossing and for the 50,000 pounds of poultry; the essential 87,000 sheets and pillow cases; the 8,000 champagne glasses, the 3,000 pieces of galley equipment, the table facilities for serving 9,000 meals each day on any voyage.

All these are true. All these, added together, do not give you an adequate picture of the ship and convey a complete idea of her personality, her uniqueness as a liner.

It was to see if I could lay hold of those elements of difference, those individualizing qualities of the great ship, that I went out to her pier that spring morning three years ago.

There she lay, lashed to her dock with her huge prow not more than thirty feet from where I stood on shore. The lettered scale on her hull showed that she was drawing only about thirty feet, but by the time embarkation was completed and her hold filled with the "express" type of freight she carries each trip, the water line would, I knew, take her higher in the waist.

Great hawsers ran from the mooring posts close at my feet straight up to her main deck. Other lines, I could see by looking down the seemingly endless length of her hull, joined her tightly to the pier. Somewhere, far away and high up, a canopied gangplank that looked like a covered Venetian bridge joined ship to pier.

From the point where the water line met her prow, her stem curved and slanted straight up and over until it completely bridged the intervening space. Looking above, I could see just above my head the tip of her prow and forward railing.

There is a ponderous quality about the *United States*—a solidity and sense of enduringness which made me feel almost as though she were veritably part of the shore. Just as though, each time she casts loose from her mooring and sails away, America were sending overseas a slice of the continent itself.

Yet that solidity and heaviness (Good Lord, she is more than 54,000 tons!) is contradicted by the sloping, cutaway bow, swelling gradually from her stem out in front, back to the body of the ship. There is speed and strength in every line of her! I know what Grandfather would say could he stand here with me and see her. That rakish prow, that shapely cut-in bow— Granddad would have whistled and exclaimed, " 'Y God, Addie! slap a bowsprit on her and she'd be a clipper ship—a steel, steam-powered clipper! And Lord, what a whopper!"

To me, the *United States* is a very great lady of the sea. A tailored lady—a trifle severe in her appointments, but with a rich severity which marks her as one of the aristocracy.

27. *More American-Flag Lines*

AMERICAN EXPORT LINES

As THE Christmas season of 1954 approached, I made my plans—not very happily—to spend the holidays at home in Chicago. Having no family, I was very lonely. But early in December came an invitation from an old friend in Naples, the Duchesse de Presenzano, to spend Christmas with her. It fitted in exactly with my mood! More too, Olaf, that Norse ancestor of mine, had been at work again, and I'd commenced to think of the pleasure I'd have in making an ocean trip.

And there was yet another reason. I'd never yet made a trip on an American Export Lines ship, though I had been hearing more and more about them. And here was a chance to make it and have a festive time in Naples, to boot.

So I hopped to the telephone and called a transportation friend in New York.

"There's just one stateroom to be had on the *Independence,*" he said, "sailing a week from today."

"Nab it for me!" I told him. Then I cabled to Naples: "SAILING TUESDAY ON INDEPENDENCE. ARRIVE NAPLES 23RD. WHAT HO AND A HAPPY HOLIDAY."

So, had you been loafing casually around the Battery gazing out over the water on December 13, you would have seen the great ship *Independence* slipping smoothly and easily down toward the sea with me up near the bow, open-eyed as always when I start another ocean voyage.

As I walked about the deck, the winter sunlight waging a fairly successful fight with the winter wind for supremacy, I wished, as I always do, that my Grandfather—dear old man!—could be with me. I feel that way especially when I board a ship for the first time. What fun we'd both have had exploring the *Independence,* comparing her features, her personality, her qualities with those of the ships he had known in the past and those I know at present.

The *Independence* is a twin of the *Constitution,* the two being the prize sister vessels of the American Export's fleet. Hence what I say about one applies equally to the other. The *Independence* is about 30,000 tons; nearly 700 feet long; 90 feet in the beam; top speed, about 26 knots. Thus we can cover the 4,192 miles to Naples in 9 days. She has accommodations for about 1,000 passengers in three classes—first, cabin, and tourist. All, I found, were just about jammed full for this Christmas cruise.

With these qualifications, we can place *Independence* in the medium-liner class. That way, she does not rate with the *United States,* the Cunard *Queens,* the French Line *Isle de France* and other liners of more than 50,000 tons. For luxury, convenience, and service, however, she's right up there in the front line with the best; and on that nine-day trip to Naples I enjoyed myself as much as I ever did on any trip that I can think of.

One reason was that we were following the milder sea tracks to the Mediterranean. Also, we had good weather. But the facilities of the ship, its roomy comfort, and a nice air of hominess which did not—thank heaven!—obliterate the fact that we were on shipboard, no less than the company I met aboard, had a lot to do with making the trip an event to remember with pleasure. . . .

American Export stands as a living, breathing refutation of the sometimes heard statement that overseas air travel has superseded travel by ship. Look at this company's record! It came into being just after World War I as a freighting concern with several slow Hog Island cargo ships, leased and later purchased from the Government when the guns ceased booming. Later, *just when the airplane was beginning to become an important factor* in foreign travel, American Export suddenly testified to its faith in ocean travel by going deeply into the passenger business.

This happened just after World War II, when the company launched and put into service a fleet of four combination passenger-freight ships. These replaced four similar ships bearing the same names which had served during the war and had been sunk. Like the former ships, the new fleet all have the *ex* nomenclature, to jibe with the company's name. They are the *Excalibur, Exochorda, Exeter,* and *Excambion;* the company calls them its "four aces."

These liners are quite unique among the fleets on the ocean today. They are not large as liners go, being 10,000 tons each. But they were the first to be completely air-conditioned. Each has accommodations for 124 first-class passengers. The Maritime Commission rates them as combination ships. As in the case of all cargo-carrying vessels, they ride as easily and smoothly as a rocking chair. American Export takes great pride in maintaining its fine passenger service: roomy, airy staterooms; pleasant and elaborate lounges; a cuisine with which nobody could quarrel. Its ships ply between New York and the Mediterranean and Near East ports. Every other Friday one of these "four aces" sails on a forty-five-day cruise.

However, with the addition in 1951 of the heavenly twins of the Mediterranean, *Constitution* and *Independence,* the company entered the luxury-liner trade. Though on the seas for less than six years, the twins have developed a long list of loyal partisans—and I'm one of them.

First under the leadership of William H. Coverdale, a well-known transportation expert and industrialist; later headed by Joe Thomas, now chairman of the board; and at present under the presidency of John Slater, American Export runs its thirty U.S.-flag vessels the year round, from New York to certain North Atlantic ports, to Mediterranean ports, to the Adriatic, the Black Sea, the Red Sea, to India, Pakistan, Ceylon, and Burma.

The company has never given up its freighting activities and still operates a big fleet of express-cargo ships.

AMERICAN PRESIDENT LINES

Remember the old Pacific Mail Company which as we have seen, picked up mail on the west side of the Panama Isthmus and carried it up to San Francisco and the settlements in Oregon? That line was the ancestor of the big American President Lines of today. The gold rush gave Pacific Mail its start. By 1867 it had extended its service across the Pacific in a lucrative China, Japan, and Philippine trade. . . .

The modern phase of this great company began just after the turn of the century.

Pacific Mail had by then virtually been "legislated out of existence" by the withdrawal of subsidies. But along came a lanky Scotch-Canadian lumberman with ship ideas, named Robert Dollar. He began to buy and build his own ships to serve his world lumber markets, including those formerly served by Pacific Mail—mainly China; and before long Dollar was operating ships to the Far East, under a restored mail-subsidy contract, formerly held by Pacific Mail.

The Dollar Line continued to grow and prosper, and in January, 1924, it sent its first "president" liner—*President Har-*

rison—steaming out the Golden Gate to inaugurate what was to become a well-liked round-the-world service.

But because of financial difficulties in the depression, Dollar had to relinquish the company. The Government took it over and reorganized it under the name American President Lines. It was Government-controlled until October, 1952, when American President Line Associates, Inc., purchased the controlling interest at public auction. Then George Killion, who had become president of American President Lines in August, 1947, and was retained by the new private ownership as its operating head, entered the picture. His job was to rehabilitate and re-establish. He has done a fine job, and today he is rated high among the top shipping executives in the country.

American President Lines operates approximately thirty ships in the three major trade routes—Trans-Pacific, Round the World, Atlantic Straits. The pride of the fleet is the flagship *President Cleveland* and her sister ship *President Wilson,* each 23,500 tons, each costing $22,000,000. Both were commissioned in 1948.

These ships run regularly every three weeks, between San Francisco, Los Angeles, and the Orient via Honolulu, Yokohama, Hong Kong, and Manila.

President Polk and *President Monroe* run in the Round-the-World service, calling at widely separated ports.

A.P.L. is known as "the longest steamship line on earth"— and, geographically speaking, it is most certainly that.

When Killion took over the job at the American President Lines, a competitor exclaimed, "No man ever walked into a worse shipping mess!"

Well, Killion changed all that. That line of fine presidential liners is no longer a mess. The ships won definite fame and respect during World War II when they performed nobly in carrying troops and cargo. Now back at their old runs, they fill an essential role on the Pacific lanes.

Not many years ago, I rode the *President Polk* out to the

Orient. She's an easy-riding ship of only a little more than 10,000 tons; but I don't think there is a vessel in our merchant marine which has more beautiful shear and hull lines.

FARRELL LINES

Following the sea is hereditary with the Farrell brothers, John and James, chairman and president respectively of the Farrell Lines. This is America's only direct passenger service to the Dark Continent. An earlier John Farrell commanded one of the later clippers, in the 1870's, and died at sea. The captain left a widow and six children. One of the sons, John A., began life as a wire-factory laborer in Fair Haven, Connecticut, and wound up as president of the United States Steel Corporation—a fairly successful accomplishment, one would say off-hand.

But the inherited love of ships cropped out in steelman Farrell's later life. In 1915 he organized the Isthmian Steamship Company as a carrying unit for his steel firm. Later he induced his two sons John (III) and James to buy the line in order to continue and maintain a ship line direct to South Africa. The Dark Continent, the elder Farrell believed, had a great future. That belief he imparted to young John and James.

"Father was right," John Farrell, present chairman of Farrell Lines, said not long ago. "We began with cargo ships exclusively. Today we consider our passenger business equal if not more important than our freight-carrying activities."

The Farrell brothers established their passenger service in 1928 when they received a mail contract that made it worth their while to build ships designed primarily for passengers, but with ample holds for cargo. They called their original line to Africa the American–South African Line. Their first ship bore an honored name—*City of New York*. Soon they had acquired two other smaller lines, and by the time World War

234

II had ended—a conflict in which they lost most of their ships—they commenced to rebuild their fleet along modern lines. Though the Farrells run sixteen ships in the South Africa Service, their passenger line consists mainly of the *African Enterprise* and *African Endeavor*—both, though not large, being luxury liners in the matter of equipment and ability to get over the water.

And just to make certain that the family sea traditions continue, two young Farrells of the fourth generation, William H., II, and Ralph, greatgrandsons of the clipper skipper, Captain John Guy Farrell, have entered the offices of the Farrell Lines at 26 Beaver Street, New York, to learn the business from the ground up—or rather from the water up.

Someday I must ride these Farrell liners!

MATSON LINES

Matson Lines's story began in May, 1882, when the little 300-ton three-masted schooner from San Francisco, *Emma Claudina,* dropped anchor for the first time in the Hawaiian Islands, at Hilo. She was owned by her captain, William Matson, and a group of his friends, and was the first of a proud line of ships to play a vital role in the building of Hawaii. Before three years had passed, *Emma Claudina* was not able to care for the trade. Demands for cargo space mounted. So, Captain Matson replaced her by the *Lurline I* in 1887.

Next, Matson took his first step toward acquiring a fleet. In 1891 he bought the wooden brig *Harvester.* She carried ten passengers, a crew of thirteen. In a very short time he added the steel bark *Santiago,* followed by the *Rhoderick Dhu* in the run to the islands. The *Rhoderick Dhu* was a wonder ship of her day—the first *sailing* ship afloat, it is said, to have a cold storage plant and electric lights.

Other ships appeared—ships of varying rig and size. All had one characteristic in common—they were fast.

235

Matson was a true American in one respect, if for no other: he believed in sail, and it is surprising to discover that he clung to canvas until 1901. By then steel ships and steam propulsion had been firmly established on the Pacific. In that year he added his first steamship, the *Enterprise.* She was the first off-shore ship in the Pacific to burn oil for fuel. Next came the *Hyades, Rosecrans,* and *Hilonian*—all converted from coal to oil burners. Another first for Matson (in the Pacific): *Hilonian* was the first Pacific steamship to have radio communication equipment at sea.

Up until 1903 Matson passenger facilities were only a few passenger cabins on freighters. But in that year *Lurline II* came along, having space for fifty-one passengers in good accommodations. Then, just before World War I, Matson added yet another ship, with de-luxe accommodations for 146 passengers.

The Government, of course, requisitioned all Matson ships for war service. Each hopped in and achieved distinction in transporting troops and munitions.

Next came the 21-knot passenger ship *Malolo,* a real luxury vessel, shortly after renamed the *Matsonia.* She soon had running mates comparable in speed and luxury—*Mariposa, Monterey,* and *Lurline III*—each fast, with accommodations for 728 passengers. The *Lurline* and *Matsonia* ran in the San Francisco–Hawaiian trade exclusively. *Mariposa* and *Monterey* went to Australia by way of Hawaii, Samoa, Fiji, and New Zealand.

World War II came and once again all Matson vessels (cargo, as well as passenger) took up Government work. Equipped as hospitals, some of them were used to bring home wounded soldiers and prisoners of war.

It took $20,000,000 to reconvert the *Lurline* for modern passenger service after the war. She now runs steadily in the Pacific ferry. She is 632 feet long and about 29,000 tons. She has 25,000 horsepower steam engines. She carries about 900 passengers and 444 in crew. In addition, the line has a fleet of eighteen fast freighters which carry twelve passengers each.

William Matson had that well-known Scandinavian love of the sea flowing in his veins. He was born in Sweden in 1849. Orphaned at an early age, he ran away to sea, shipped as a handy boy, and at the age of fourteen stepped off the ship *Aurora* which brought him to New York. A clipper took him to California in the gold rush days; but he stuck to ships instead of losing his head over gold, and after many different sea jobs was made a master mariner at twenty-one. He was in his early thirties when he started his line with the *Emma Claudina.*

28. Ships in the Neighborly Trades

DELTA LINE

THE late Theodore Brent, traffic expert and waterways authority, brought into being the present Mississippi Shipping Company, commonly known as the Delta Line. They say in southern Maritime circles that Brent raised the company by hand.

Delta opened the pioneer trade route from New Orleans to South America just after World War I. Moreover, it provided the first two-way passenger service from the Crescent City to Brazil.

Like many another passenger company, Delta began as a cargo line—primarily to carry in coffee from Brazilian ports and take back general products from the American South and Midwest. Prior to that time Americans had been depending largely on British and German ships. Now they found Delta a convenient medium for both imports and exports.

Within two years the company began to run additional ships to Uruguay and the Argentine. Planters down there needed American agricultural implements and other products. Delta's service fitted in with their scheme very well indeed. But South America likewise was beginning to draw more and more tourists and visitors. To meet that need Delta began its passenger service with two reconditioned ships—*Del Norte* and *Del Sud*. Each had accommodations for twenty-eight passengers. Their first run was in 1931 and were followed by two ships, *Del Mundo* and *Del Valle,* each with accommodations for thirty-six passengers. Three more ships—*Del Brazil, Del Orleans* and *Del Argentine*—were commissioned in 1940. They took the water just in time to serve as war transports before going into their regular peacetime service.

Delta lost three of its ships to German guns and submarines. In 1944 it launched a new construction program: three cargo ships of the C3 type obtained from the Maritime Commission. These they built into combination passenger-freight ships which served very well until the new *Del Norte* went into service, followed by the new *Del Sud,* and, a year later, by the *Del Mar.*

Feeling that there was business to be had in the North African service, Delta began running four motor ships to the dark continent.

Thus the fine old Crescent City has something it should never be without—a weekly passenger service to foreign ports.

GRACE LINE

A young Irish lad in the mid-1850's took a job in a ship-chandlery business in Callao, Peru. He was an industrious youngster and possessed a keen idea on how to run his own business that many people (if he told them of it—most likely he did not) thought outlandish. And such indeed (in a very literal sense, at least) it proved to be. But profitable!

The trouble was too much competition in supplying the ships that put into Callao in search of supplies. A ship chandler can't make money unless many ships needing supplies come to his port.

Day after day this young Irishman talked with captains of

ships which touched at Callao, and from them he got a share of the business, true; but not the bulk needed to ring up those profits that point to wealth.

Day after day he saw great ships arrive and depart, or sail snootily past, far out at sea—mighty clippers with sky-raking masts, bound to or from New York and New England around the Horn. There *was* business to be had. Those ships needed supplies. How could he get to them ahead of the others? It was something to think about.

And so this Irish boy—his name was William Russell Grace —thought about it. Then one day, he acted. He filled up a big barge with ship chandlery items; set up his living quarters aboard; had himself towed out to the Chincha Islands, a hundred miles off the coast. Most ships touched there first for guano, a well-known fertilizer; and thus he was able to serve them before they reached Callao. His business began to thrive.

When his stock of supplies ran out, he had his barge towed into town for another load. It was pretty grueling business, but he kept it up for several years.

He became friends, it is said, with the captains of hundreds of American ships. Meeting the daughter of one of them, he decided someday he'd marry her: and I can imagine she was a charming and demure New England lass!

It meant leaving his business temporarily in the hands of his brothers (whom he had brought over from Ireland) for some months. But that he was willing to do while he made the voyage up to New England, wooed, won, and brought back his bride. Then once more he took over his now prospering business.

"Look," his doctors told him. "You can't keep this up. You'll knock out that heart of yours in no time! Take it easy, man! And get out of this climate."

Grace "took it easy" by moving bag and baggage to New York in 1867. By now he was wealthy, having invested in a moderate way in South American enterprises of many kinds.

Moreover, he had further designs upon the shipping business: he would run his own ships.

Our bloody States' War was over in America. North and South were beginning once again to think along business lines when Grace opened his New York office on Wall Street. He had some more ideas to express about clipper ships.

"Yes, they are fast; but they don't carry enough cargo to be profitable over a long period!" he said, echoing an historic appraisal.

And with that he chartered and operated ships with larger cargo space, trying where possible to retain also the speed essentials. But if he could not, he sacrificed some speed to the need of pay load. Grace had won friends and gratitude among South Americans because he had invested money in commercial and industrial enterprises there: they furnished a nucleus for a good business for his own ships. He began a "triangle trade" between New York, Peru, and the Pacific Coast of the United States with chartered ships.

Meanwhile he invested money in various New York enterprises. There his name had become well and favorably known in business circles. To prove that statement, New York City elected him mayor in 1880. And a very good mayor he made!

In 1890 he started replacing his chartered sailing ships with new steamers; and he kept on replacing until his fleet serving New York and South America had become world famous—each ship with the *Santa* prefix in its nomenclature.

If you look at a map of the Western Hemisphere, you will see that a plumb line dropped southward from our East Coast falls *not* on the *east* coast but on the *west* coast of South America—by way of Panama—that section where Grace had built up his enterprises. It is that section of South America (in the main) that the great line of Grace ships serve today.

When William R. Grace died in 1904, he left a thriving sea business to his son Joseph P. Grace; and Joseph is the man who transformed the Grace Line into the fine fleet which we know today.

Federal Shipyard & Dry Dock Company, Kearney, N. J., built a number of the best known—the first four *Santas* for example, *Santa Lucia, Santa Elena, Santa Rosa, Santa Paula*. After establishing a profitable South American service, these and the rest of the *Santa* fleet served their country during World War II. *Santa Elena* and *Santa Lucia* were lost; these were luxury liners, about 15,000 tons, with accommodations for 225 passengers in each.

Now, in these piping days of peace, Grace has other fine new passenger ships (in addition to the *Santa Rosa* and *Santa Paula*): *Santa Clara, Santa Monica, Santa Sofia, Santa Cecilia, Santa Marguerita, Santa Isabel, Santa Maria, Santa Luisa,* and *Santa Barbara*. Each carries fifty-two passengers and a big cargo load.

Add to these a big fleet of freighters, built on the type hulls that have long proved seaworthy by Maritime Administration standards, and you have a picture of the largest American fleet today serving the Caribbean ports and west coast of South America: The region to which, long ago, came William Russell Grace to enter the ship chandlery business, serve New York as mayor, and leave an honored name and commercial empire.

MOORE-McCORMACK

Take a total capital of $5,000, two enthusiastic young men with a yearning for ships and the sea, and some good business ideas; two desks and one small office at 29 Broadway. Now mix them up. In forty years you'll have a flourishing passenger and freight steamship business connecting the United States with various South American and Scandinavian ports.

That at least was what happened in the case of Albert V. Moore, of Hackensack, New Jersey, and Emmet J. McCormack, of Brooklyn, founders in 1913 of the great Moore-Mc-

Cormack Lines. You'll hear it spoken of today as Mooremack. A dark *M* on a white disc marks the funnels of this company's sister ships, *Argentina* and *Brazil,* each 20,000 tons. These are the largest ships in the "neighborly trade"—luxury liners that would stack up well against ships in the transatlantic trade. They were built at Newport News, and each is nearly 600 feet long, carrying 356 first-class passengers and 180 cabin class.

The founders of Mooremack reopened a dormant trade. Back in 1882 America had a direct regular steamship from New York to Rio de Janeiro, Congress was at that time in an appropriating mood, and laid out $150,000 annually to this line for carrying the mail. But times changed, the ships—so it was claimed—were too slow, and far from satisfactory carriers. Hence subsidies were withdrawn. Regular steamer connection from Brazil to New York ceased.

When Moore and McCormack joined up in 1913, they already had their eyes on the possibility of reopening the trade. The importance of South America to the commerce of the United States was already becoming apparent—though no one then dreamed it would assume the importance it has since the adoption of our Good Neighbor Policy. It took several years for Mooremack to get their first ship into the trade. Meanwhile, they did coal bunkering for ships in New York harbor, keeping their eyes peeled for a suitable vessel for the new enterprise. They found her—the *Montara.* She was an ancient craft—built in 1881 of charcoal iron, less than 900 tons—old but sturdy.

When she sailed on her first trip to Brazil, she was re-establishing a service on which no ship flying the Stars and Stripes had sailed for twenty-six years. That was before our country had an ambassador in Brazil. But we did have a minister in Rio. And when the first Mooremack ship nosed into Rio, the whole American ministry crowded down to the piers to welcome her. She carried on this first trip a full cargo of dynamite from Wilmington. This lethal commodity, however, seemed not to dampen the ardor of the welcomers, who with camera and flag celebrated her coming.

"Well," commented Moore, "on that trip we had a fifty-fifty proposition. She'd deliver the cargo or she'd blow up."

She didn't blow up. The new intercontinental trade was resumed. In the wake of the *Montara* came the wooden Mooremack *Barnstaple,* whose master, Captain Moon, had shipwreck experience of the Robert Louis Stevenson variety; the *James E. Spaulding;* the *Saga*—formerly a Swedish ship. The *Saga* inaugurated the Mooremack passenger service.

It is a long voyage down to Brazil from New York. Look at the map and you'll see it's much farther than from New York to Liverpool. By 1919, however, Mooremack was making eighteen round trips a year with its three ships—*Anglia, Malm,* and *Calabria*—calling at Pernambuco and Bahia as well as at Brazil. Later Santos (the great coffee port) was added to the Mooremack calling list.

In time Mooremack extended its freight service (with specially designed ships) to European and other world ports. But its passenger service remains a big link between the United States and South America's east coast. That service had had quite a history.

Back in 1936—the same year, you recall, that the Merchant Marine Act passed—President Roosevelt was diligently pushing his Good Neighbor Policy. Visiting Buenos Aires that year, the President was deeply disturbed to see so many fine, sleek new ships flying flags of just about all nations—except the U.S.—crowding the Argentinian port. His broad program to solidify the American republics envisioned a fleet of American ships moving constantly between the two continents. These fleets would be an indispensable part of the Good Neighbor program.

"Put at the top of the list of ship projects a first-class passenger-cargo service joining our East Coast with Brazil,

Uruguay, and Argentina," F.D.R. notified the Maritime Commission.

Meanwhile a number of things in the shipping industry had been happening to speed up the President's plan. Munson Steamship Line, which had a South American service, folded. The Panama-Pacific Line, which had been running three passenger-cargo ships (*Virginia, Pennsylvania,* and *California*), as we saw, in the intercoastal trade, discontinued its service. Whereupon the Maritime Commission purchased the three Panama-Pacific ships and created a new American Republic Lines. Then it proceeded to rebuild these three vessels at a cost of about $1,000,000, making them modern to the last welding— with swimming pools, air-conditioning, modern stateroom accommodations for 500 passengers each. As a gesture of good will, the ships were given names of the three neighboring countries they would serve—*Brazil, Uruguay,* and *Argentina*.

In mid-1938 Moore-McCormack put in a bid to operate the ships under the Maritime Commission agreement. Their offer was accepted, and with the new passenger liners the company took over likewise an additional fleet of eight cargo vessels.

Like those of other patriotic steamship companies, Mooremack vessels served valiantly in the two wars. Not until 1948 did the *S.S. Argentina* re-enter her trade: that marked the resumption of the Mooremack service to our neighbor ports. Today the company retains both *Brazil* and *Argentina* in a trade that grows with our growing mutuality of interest with the friendly countries to the south.

BERMUDA FERRY

Though not an American Company, the Furness-Bermuda line provides the only regular ship service between New York and those "friendly isles" lying 700 miles off our Carolina coasts, which have become an irresistible lodestone for American vacationists. We feel we have a special claim to the "colony." Hence, I include Furness-Withy Company in my list of American lines.

I had crossed the ocean a score of times on as many ships before I decided to visit Bermuda. And I have regretted ever since that I delayed so long in going. Furness-Withy Company, British operated, maintains a regular two-ship Bermuda service out of New York, with the *Queen of Bermuda* and the smaller but more modern *Queen Monarch* alternating.

Formerly a place of relaxation in wintertime, Bermuda of late has become a year-round resort. Throughout the year ships enter and leave Hamilton and St. George harbor; and for three seasons of the year—spring, fall, winter—they seem to arrive and depart with cabins full.

A trip to Bermuda, for me at least, is next best to a cross-ocean trip. In fact, if you take one of those weekly cruises on either the *Queen* or the *Monarch* which allows you several days on the island, the other five on the mild southern sea lanes, you come back with a feeling you have indeed been abroad.

Bermuda is a strange and deliciously contradictory place. It is closer to the United States than to any other large country. More Americans visit Bermuda than people of any other nationality. American money is good there, yet the colony has its own local currency, too. It is foreign in government, in allegiance, in population—most being English descended from British settlers who came there about the time Jamestown, in Virginia, was settled. There's also a large Negro and mixed-blood population, and all—black, white, and intermediate—speak with definitely broad English accents.

I am sure that nowhere else in the world are there so many store "clarks" who, in their Bermuda shorts and Highland hose, resemble the Duke of Edinburgh, Lord Mountbatten, and Anthony Eden. Yes, I had great fun shopping in Bermuda!

When my father and mother visited Bermuda just after their marriage, they went by ship, of course. That was the only way to go then. Getting there was quite a chore, too. You had your choice from among one ship weekly! And that ship was a single-stack tub with one propellor. She used to make several trips a month, weather permitting. Old-time Bermudians still talk of the excitement in Hamilton and St. George on "steamer day"—the day on which the ship from New York came in and docked.

Getting back to the Furness ships. The *Queen* is a well-constructed, well-furnished, and pleasantly equipped lady, some 650 feet long. She tips the scale at 24,000 tons; has three impressive black-and-red smokestacks; and boasts only one class of accommodations—somewhat better than cabin class on the big liners but not so elaborate as their first class.

I've yet to hear any complaints about her cuisine and service. I certainly could find no fault with it, save this:

Like all Furness ships, the *Queen* is manned and officered by Britishers; and they cannot, apparently, impart the strength and flavor to their coffee which we Americans demand. Let me make a suggestion. Cunard has pretty well mastered the trick of making good strong coffee. Why can't Furness-Bermuda? The coffee, however, is only a very small fly in an otherwise fine ointment.

The *Queen* has had a colorful career. Frank Braynard, who has at his fingertips the life stories of more famous ships than any one man has a right to know, says he was returning on board the coaster *Robert E. Lee* from Newport News, Virginia,[1] to New York one day in 1940 when he met the *Queen* coming down the harbor. She seemed to have aged and grown gray overnight—so changed was she in her new drab coat of wartime dull gray, with her guns mounted on deck—ready not only to transport, but to fight as well if the need arose.

"She was the first ship to give up her peacetime role for war service," Braynard told me. "The sight of her—once so gay and ornate in her rich coats of paint and varnish, with passengers

[1] He was coming home from the launching of the United States Lines's *America*.

crowding her sides, and now sadly changed—pounded home in my consciousness the fact that war was coming very close to our ships and our shores. (I've always thought of the *Queen of Bermuda* as being American. She spends more time in American ports than in British.)"

"That was the very beginning of her war work. From the first it took her right through the main danger zone. Her skipper had not yet learned the technique of zigzagging. She dashed straight across the Atlantic, following, by the Grace of God, a lane that avoided lurking German U-boats!"

The Furness *Queen* was built in 1933 and intended specifically for the 700-mile passenger run between New York and Bermuda. This easily classed her as a luxury ship. But when the British Admiralty put her to work in the war effort, she took on a variety of strange and outlandish jobs:

> She helped maintain the blockade of German ports.
> She served as a troop- and supply-ship escort.
> She patrolled lame ducks.
> She sought down enemy raiders in debatable waters.
> Once she made a safety expedition to the Antarctic.

And more than once, her ancient six-inch and three-inch guns boomed defiance to the Axis powers through the chill Atlantic mists.

To add buoyancy to her and thus make her suitable to carry larger loads of men and material, her crew stored thousands of empty barrels down in her hold. Hence she rode high and handsome through the big fight; and as soon as the guns ceased booming, back she went! Refurnished and refurbished, gay, plump, and comfortable, she sailed into her old route once more, making her weekly trip to the colony.

The *Queen's* sister, *Ocean Monarch,* runs alternately in the same trade. She's snappier and probably more in accord with one's present ideas of what a modern ocean liner should be.

She's about 14,000 tons and does more in the way of cruising than her older and more sedate sister. To me, however, the *Queen* has a quality that makes for affectionate remembrance.

Furness has been part of the American shipping picture for sixty-five years.

The United States figured in the plans of sturdy young Christopher Furness of 'Artlepool, England, when he began running steamships. Though he was by trade a wholesale groceryman, and a very young member of the House of Commons, Furness had long dreamed of a line of ships to the United States. That was just at the time when Collis P. Huntington in America was building a big shipyard at Newport News, Virginia, and bringing the Chesapeake & Ohio Railway from Cincinnati down to Tidewater. Huntington's plan was to make the little town of Newport News *the* great port of the Atlantic seaboard. Furness, seeking more business from inland America, entered into arrangements with Huntington. Thus, before long, there was a C & O line of steamships operated by Furness as an extension to Huntington's railroad, which had its terminus right there on Hampton Roads.

These were all cargo ships of course. The service continued for many years, with successively larger ships carrying bigger cargoes. Although, so far as I have heard, Mr. Huntington's dream of making Newport News the Nation's number one East Coast port has not yet materialized, that town has most definitely become the country's largest shipping point for bituminous coal and location of our largest shipyard. Together Huntington railroads and Furness steamships made that possible. . . .

Not until 1919 did Furness commence his passenger-ship operation to Bermuda. The small vessels with which the service began have given place to larger and still larger ships through the years as Bermuda has become more and more known as a favorite recreation place.

PANAMA CANAL COMPANY

We wrote of the little Panama Railroad across the Isthmus of Panama. In 1856 this little company, working in conjunction with Law and the Aspinwall on the West and East Coasts of the Isthmus, began to operate the Central American Steamship Line with two ships, *Columbus* and *Guatemala,* running from Panama down the West Coast to Costa Rica, Salvador, and Guatemala.

In 1861 the company also had sailing vessels plying regularly between Liverpool and the Port of Panama (Aspinwall). By 1880, however, all its operations had ended. In 1893 a new service began between New York and Cristobal. That happened when contracts between the Old Panama Railroad Company and the old Pacific Mail Steamship Company (between New York and the Isthmus, and from Panama to Central America, Mexico, and California) expired. At first the Panama Company chartered its ships. Later it purchased fourteen ships outright.

Some of those old steamers were still in service when the United States began the construction of the Panama Canal. The *Finance* was sunk in New York harbor in November, 1908 (in a collision with the old White Star *Georgic*), but the other two, *Alliance* and *Advance,* continued in service for about a year longer—until they were sold in 1923. They "done their bit" in World War I, carrying supplies (coal from Hampton Roads).

Then the company took over four small German vessels interned at Cristobal since the outbreak of the war (1917) and renamed them, appropriately, for men whose names are honored in Panama—*General G. W. Goethals, General W. C. Gorgas, General O. H. Ernest,* and *General H. E. Hodges.*

In 1918 some of the company's vessels carried coal, cargoes, and troops.

Three new 10,000-ton liners—*Panama, Ancon, Cristobal*—

were launched in 1939, at a total cost of more than $12,000,000. These ships are high-type ocean-going vessels and maintain a weekly sailing schedule between New York and Cristobal, via Port-au-Prince, Haiti.

UNITED FRUIT COMPANY

On almost any day at the crowded docks of one or more of America's biggest seaports you will see trim white ships topped by red funnels marked with white diamonds.

Are you familiar with funnel markings and house flags? If not, you'd probably exclaim, "What lovely private yachts!"

More than one first-time observer has said this. Actually, these are the trig little ships of the United Fruit Company. There's a reason for the company's label "The Great White Fleet" seen in magazine display ads.

And there's also a reason for one of the larger ships being named *Fra Berlanga,* since that sixteenth-century cleric who bore the name conferred a boon upon posterity. For the Fra introduced to the Western Hemisphere the much loved *musa,* which we know today as the banana.

America today consumes millions of stems of bananas each year; and the largest purveyor and transporter of bananas is the United Fruit Company. Many of the thirty-odd ships in its fleet carry, not only cargoes of the green-and-golden fruit, but passengers too.

None of the United Fruit ships tops the 8,000-ton mark. But each of the passenger ships is designed for its particular job in its special trade—namely, transporting people and bananas between Central America, the Caribbean islands, and the ports of the United States.

United Fruit has gone to great lengths to keep its passenger service from being overshadowed by its cargo business. The ships are one class only—and that first-class. Each vessel boasts the means of making its passengers have a good time aboard which transoceanic liners possess.

United Fruit has a fine war record. When the second world war started, company officials went to Washington.

"Here's our fleet," they said simply to the War Department. "Here are our crews. We're ready."

Counting their own ships and those additional vessels they were called upon to man, United Fruit crews operated 174 ships in war service. Of these, thirty-six went down fighting with their antiaircraft guns going; six other were badly damaged.

United Fruit ships were sunk in the North Atlantic, in the English Channel, in the Caribbean, in the Gulf of Mexico. But peace and Maritime Administration co-operation brought another fleet into being; United Fruit today operates its ships in the same thriving banana-passenger trade. And possibly the spirit of old Fra Berlanga himself presides benignly over the sailings and arrivals of each load of the green and gold cargoes.

I have yet to travel on a United Fruit Company ship. Olaf will be taking me aboard one of these days. Meanwhile, I consume a favorite dish each morning—a dry cereal topped with a sliced-up *musa* and covered with half and half. With each mouthful I thank the old Fra for introducing this fruit to our shores.

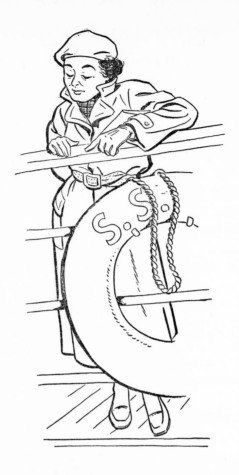

29. Conclusion

WHICH ship do you like best?" someone asked me recently. That is really difficult to answer. Individual ships have individual qualities, both tangible and intangible, just as homes have; just as people have. However, I do retain memories of certain characteristics which I instinctively associate with some particular ship, when its name is mentioned.

Let me elaborate on that a little. For speed and sheer up-to-the-minute modernity, I think I would place the *United States* at the top. She has many attributes that make her the last word

253

in shipbuilding art. In another chapter I have given my impression of her in detail.

For grandeur in the impressive historic English manner, the two *Queens*—*Elizabeth* and *Mary*—stand out distinctly.

For informal fun and friendliness among the passengers (such as I imagine marked travel on old-time Mississippi steamboats) I'd nominate the one-cabin *Parthia*.

For highly individual food that has a tangy tastiness, give me the French Line's *Ile de France*.

For just the proper mixture of informality and dignity, the *Independence* of the American Export Lines has no peer.

And so I could go on and recall every trip I have made and the ship on which I made it. Each vessel would evoke some pleasurable experience, some startling, humorous, or happy circumstance which has made that particular ship live in my consciousness.

It may be the recollection of a hilarious New Year's Eve party which enlivened one voyage and is connected in my memory with a certain ship's grand ballroom. It may be some people I met on board—interesting men and women whom I found good companions and whose names and personalities are inevitably entwined in my mind with that ship. Or it may be the manner in which one ship takes the big seas with easy grace—lifting and sinking over great watery hills in a manner that pays tribute to the men who designed and created her.

Again, it may be the artistic slope and slant of a ship's hull lines, such as the *President Polk's;* or the shear of her decks; or the rake of her funnels and masts—the very appearance of dash and flourish which marks her.

Or, possibly, it may be the way she breathes. . . . Didn't you know a steamship breathes? Often, when you are located on the boat deck, A deck, or the promenade deck of a ship, you're not conscious of the pulsations from the almost noiseless throbbing of her vast unseen machinery far below. But it's there, nevertheless—the throbbing, the breathing. Often I have awakened at night and, because of the stillness, have heard and felt the rhythmic throbbings, as sure and steady and relentless as Destiny itself, while my ship moved toward her port. You hear it especially when your ear is down against the pillow. The larger the ship, the deeper her respiration. . . .

And now I approach the end of this informal story of America's passenger merchant marine, based on my love for the ships I have known and my inherited love of the sea. Our nation's passenger fleet today is still small in comparison to those of some other nations. But now that we have a well-functioning, sensible Government-assistance program implemented by the Maritime Administration, indications are this fleet will increase. Already new passenger ships are in the drawing-board stage. Some are even now taking shape in American shipyards. With Government assistance available, ship men are more ready than formerly to expand, to build and launch new tonnage, to go after more business.

Men may never again build ships as large as the *United States,* the *Normandie, Leviathan, Queen Mary,* or *Queen Elizabeth.* In the opinion of some top-flight ship designers and architects, the day of the huge superliner is passing. That may be true; I wouldn't know. Certainly I have never noticed any remarkable lack of patronage when I've been aboard these big ships to indicate their popularity is on the wane.

The leaning these days, however, seems to be toward the medium-sized liner—from 20,000 to 40,000 tons. Single-class ships, or ships with one class (first or cabin) and tourist accommodations seem to be the greater favorites.

As I near the final pages of this yarn, I feel an uncontrollable desire to go down to the sea again. Olaf has been after me for months, so my bags are packed. I'm starting on a long cruise. I turn the key in my home here on the shores of Lake Michigan. Tomorrow I shall be in New York, where ship reservations await me.

America Rides the Liners

HERE I GO AGAIN

My taxi driver heads west out Forty-second Street.

"Go straight out to Twelfth Avenue," I tell him, "and turn uptown."

"Gosh, lady! Traffic's awful over there! Be quicker to let me turn up Eighth Avenue and—"

"No!" I interrupt, "straight out Forty-second and up Twelfth. I'm in no hurry. And drive slowly! I want to see things as I go along. I'll make it worth your while."

He shrugs off the responsibility and we roll out past the huge green McGraw-Hill Building and the lesser structures that diminish in size as you approach the docks. A fog hangs over the river, though the May sun is shining behind us. And now, as we near Manhattan's western watery girdle, the smell I had been waiting for these last landlocked months in Chicago strikes me full in the face. A blending, as it were, of tar and hemp with the united fragrances of the multifarious cargoes which the ships of all the years have left on these sprawling, ungainly docks. And the whole seems to be sprinkled over and seasoned with the salt water of many seas. With deep content I breathe it in!

Not, of course, that the smell of the dingy trash-cluttered water washing the pier pilings of North River is like that of the sea. Far from it! But the *suggestion* of the sea is in it nonetheless. Some of the other contributory smells—of refuse, bilge water, oil, even garbage—seem to me to impart an intriguing if not an altogether pleasant aroma. And I welcome it now as the convincing evidence that I'm actually ocean-bound once again.

The taxi rolls on. Soon we are working our way slowly up Twelfth Avenue between files of heavy trucks and truck trailers, loaded and unloaded. My driver, morosely intent upon his job, edges and blares his way carefully along. Life roars noisily by us. Overhead, the elevated expressway bears New York's unending stream of hurry-up autos.

Conclusion

Though I have seen it dozens of times, this waterfront panorama never fails to allure me. Mile after mile, greater pier fronts stretch along the river, with occasional open spaces between them. Look! There, through that opening not fifty feet from this noisy street where my taxi pauses a moment—there's a ship! A mighty French liner, comfortably at rest. Ponderous, impressive, a prisoner in lines and hawsers, she leans quiet and docile against her berth. . . . Just as though she had not, within the last few days, left the distant shores of France and, only twenty-four hours ago, had been breasting the vast swells of the plunging Atlantic, her bows bubbly with foam!

Another opening between the piers, and I behold my ship. The ship I've been waiting to see—that is to be my home for weeks to come. Her sky-raking masts and huge funnels overtop the pier shed.

How assiduously I had studied the literature sent me by the travel agent! Months ago, back in Chicago, while the winter wind whipped Lake Michigan into choppy whitecaps, I'd sat in my window, only a few hundred yards from the lake shore, and conned the garish travel folders. Pictures of the ship in all her shapely length, and shots of her ornate interior.

With what care I had selected my stateroom, made my reservations—just as though I had never done it before! Every hour of every day from that time to this, I had looked forward impatiently to this moment when I should first catch sight of her among the other ships of New York's waterfront. That thrill would be surpassed only by the joy of actually sailing aboard her. . . .

"Here y'are, lady. Here's your pier!"

I climb out of the taxi. A porter takes my bag and leads the way. Embarkation is already going ahead—people pressing in eager, good-natured crowds to get aboard, each claiming his luggage as it comes up the escalator. I join the crowds. My papers are approved. I go through the customary tedium of essential detail: claim my space; arrange for a seat in the dining saloon; for a deck chair. Within an hour I am settled, my luggage properly stowed. And while embarkation continues, I begin to explore the ship, to drink in the details of her design and arrangement. Forty thousand tons of her! From cutwater to stern rail, she's shapely, well proportioned and with a lot of sex appeal, so to speak. Allure, that is, which makes you want to get better acquainted with her.

There is a symmetrical shear to her decks. They dip daintily from fore and aft to a low point amidships. There are lounges; smoking rooms; bars; libraries; ballrooms; a theatre; a chapel. Yes, my grandfather would have loved this ship too.

After my tour of inspection I flop down in my deck chair and close my eyes happily.

She's ready to sail! I've been sitting an hour here in my deck chair and must have dozed. But I'll miss no part of the thrill of leaving if I can help it. So I push forward against the rail to hear the shouted good-bys; to see the paper streamers joining the ship to the dock with filmy tentacles! My friends call me a globe trotter. But they'd think differently if they could see me now—eager and agape as any first-time crosser, watching what goes on as though I had never seen it before. I can't help it. If I lived to be 150 and made a crossing each year, I'd never outgrow this inside exhilaration of starting on a voyage.

The lines are cast off, the gangplank drawn in, the tugboats busy down below us. But, as always, I'm never quite aware of the exact moment when we begin moving. One minute I'm watching a snorting tugboat down below, and the next, I glance up and see that the pier shed is slipping away from us. The gay little paper streamers have snapped, severing us completely from the shore. The shouting rises to a crescendo. *Ave atque vale!* Out into the wide river channel the ship is towed, as though incapable of managing her own affairs.

But wait! Before long the tugs have cast off. The big ship

herself takes over. From far down in some hidden recesses of her gigantic hold the gentle, hardly discernible pulsings of her own engines now come up to us faintly. Her sharp nose, keen as a greyhound's, points down the harbor. And she begins her steady movement down the great river.

What's that stanza from Coleridge's "Rime of the Ancient Mariner"?

> "The ship was cheered, the harbour cleared,
>   Merrily we did drop
> Below the kirk, below the hill,
>   Below the lighthouse top."

But it will be quite a while before we clear *this* harbor! New York harbor is a mighty area of rivers, bays, the Narrows, and other channels. Miles of these we shall traverse ere we drop our pilot at Quarantine and head out across the Atlantic.

Meanwhile, here on the port side, I sit and watch the city slide by. The towers of the great metropolis make an impressive backdrop before which our greatest seaport displays her shipping might as evidence of her many tentacled foreign trade. Pier after pier, an impressive panorama of world geography set forth in the very ship names and the national flags fluttering at the taffrail staffs. Ships berthed stern on or bow on. Ships coming into their berths; ships sliding from their berths. Ships loaded and light; passenger ships; cargo ships; combination cargo-passenger ships.

A high-riding freighter, innocent of cargo, moves by to an oil dock up at Seventy-second Street for fueling, her propeller blades showing. A low-riding commerce carrier with probably a cargo of supplies for hungry nations overseas slips down the soundless tide. We catch up with her. Pass her. Her crew cheers us. We respond. North River gives way to the Upper Bay. Upper Bay to the Narrows. The Narrows to Lower Bay. There! Far off, Ambrose Light Ship! And yonder comes the pilot boat. We are to sever our last connection with home. The undeniable smell of the Atlantic, now in full force, blows over the ship's deck from the big rollers cresting ahead of us, and a peace of mind and body (such as I find nowhere save on a ship at sea) settles down over me.

All right, Olaf! Be quiet. Here I come!

Bibliography

Albion, Robert Greenhalgh, *The Rise of New York Port*. New York, Charles Scribner's Sons, 1939.

────── *Square Riggers on Schedule*. Princeton, New Jersey, Princeton University Press, 1938.

Babcock, F. Lawrence, *Spanning the Atlantic*. New York, Alfred A. Knopf, Inc., 1931.

Bowen, Frank Charles, *Conquest of the Seas*. New York, Robert M. McBride & Co., 1940.

Bradlee, Francis B., *Blockade Running During the Civil War*. Salem, Massachusetts, Essex Institute, 1925.

Braynard, Frank O., *Lives of the Liners*. New York, Cornell Maritime Press, 1947.

Brewington, M. V., *Chesapeake Bay*. New York, Cornell Maritime Press, 1953.

Brown, Franck C., *A Century of Atlantic Travel—1830–1930*. Boston, Little, Brown & Co., 1930.

Clark, Arthur H., *The Clipper Ship Era, 1843–1869*. New York, G. P. Putnam's Sons, 1910.

Cropley Papers. Washington, D. C., Smithsonian Institution, 1939.

Cutler, Carl C., *Greyhounds of the Sea*. New York, G. P. Putnam's Sons, 1930.

Bibliography

Denison, Archibald Campbell, *America's Maritime History*. New York, G. P. Putnam's Sons, 1944.

Down, George Francis, *Sailing Ships of New England*. Salem, Massachusetts, Marine Research Society, 1928.

Eskew, Garnett Laidlaw, *Pageant of the Packets*. New York, Henry Holt & Co., 1929.

Fletcher, R. A., *Steam Ships and Their Story*. London, Sedgwick-Jackson, Ltd., 1910.

Flexner, James Thomas, *Steamboats Come True*. New York, Viking Press, Inc., 1944.

Gibbs, Commander, C. R. Vernon, R.N. (Ret.), *Passenger Lines of the Western Ocean*. London, Staples Press, 1952.

Hartley, Herbert, as told to Clint Bonner, *Home is the Sailor*. Birmingham, Alabama, Vulcan Press, 1955.

McKay, Richard C., *South Street: A Maritime History of New York*. New York, G. P. Putnam's Sons, 1934.

Maginnis, Arthur J., *The Atlantic Ferry*. London, J. Whitaker & Sons, Ltd., 1892.

Marvin, Winthrop L., *American Merchant Marine: Its History and Romance, 1620 to 1902*. New York, Charles Scribner's Sons, 1916.

Morris, E. P., *The Fore and Aft Rig in America*. New Haven, Connecticut, Yale University Press, 1927.

Morrison, John H., *History of New York Shipyards*. New York, William F. Sametz & Co., 1947.

Nevins, Allan, *Sail On*. New York, privately printed, 1946.

Pinckney, Pauline A., *American Figureheads and Their Carvers*. New York, W. W. Norton & Co., Inc., 1940.

Reisenberg, Felix, *Vignettes of the Sea*. New York, Harcourt, Brace & Co., Inc., 1926.

Bibliography

Shoemaker, Elisabeth, *Ship Figureheads of Old Cape Cod*. Privately printed, 1936.

Smith, Eugene W., *Trans-Atlantic Passenger Ships, Past and Present*. New York, George H. Dean & Co., 1947.

Taylor, Donald Budlong, *Steam Conquers the Atlantic*. New York, D. Appleton-Century Co., 1939.

U. S. Department of Defense, *Your Navy*. Washington, D. C., Government Printing Office, 1946.

Index

Index

267

Index

Index

Index